Italy at the Polls, 1983

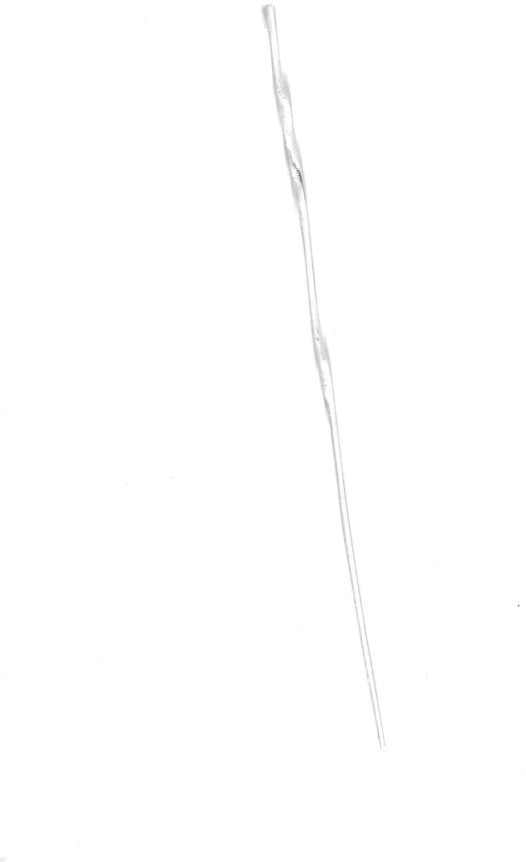

Italy at the Polls, 1983

A Study of the National Elections

EDITED BY HOWARD R. PENNIMAN

An American Enterprise Institute Book

Published by Duke University Press

1987

© 1987 AEI (American Enterprise Institute
for Public Policy Research)
All rights reserved
Printed in the United States of America
on acid free paper ∞

Library of Congress Cataloging in Publication
Data appear at the end of this book.

Contents

Tables and Figures

FIGURES

Preface

──────*Italy at the Polls, 1983: A Study of the National Elections* is the third volume on Italy in the At-the-Polls series produced by the American Enterprise Institute for Public Policy Research (AEI). The series began with descriptions of two general elections in the United Kingdom, the general elections in Canada, the election of the president of France, and the election of members of the House of Councillors in Japan, all in 1974. These four volumes have been followed by twenty-two more books describing thirty-five national elections in democracies around the world.

The series also includes two comparative studies. *Democracy at the Polls: A Comparative Study of Competitive National Elections* discusses similarities and differences in the conduct of elections in twenty-eight countries. *Competitive Elections in Developing Countries* examines problems associated with the evolution of democracy in nine countries whose citizens have had little experience with or understanding of representative institutions.

Recent Italian Elections

Voter turnout for most Italian national elections since World War II has been quite high. Contributors to the At-the-Polls volume on the 1976 elections commented on the large vote and the fact that nearly three-fourths of the vote was cast for the nation's two largest parties—the Christian Democrats (DC) and the Italian Communist party (PCI).

Douglas A. Wertman in his chapter on the 1976 elections stated that a study of voting in France, Germany, Great Britain, Italy, and the United States shows that "Italy has the highest level of voter participation. In the seven Italian Chamber of Deputies elections between 1948 and 1976, turnout ranged from between 92.2 and 93.8 percent of the eligible voters. In 1976 93.2 percent of the eligible electors voted." Using figures on the electorate in Giacomo Sani's chapter 2 in this book, we find that even after subtracting the number of blank and spoiled ballots from the turnout figures, the effective vote in 1976 was still 90.9 percent of the eligible citizens.

In his chapter on the Italian electors in 1979 and 1983 Sani notes a significant decline in the number of eligible voters going to the polls and an increase in the number of voters casting spoiled or blank ballots. Eligible voters who cast valid ballots for the Chamber of Deputies fell to 86.7 percent in 1979 and to 84.0 percent in 1983. In the latter year, Sani writes, the " 'party of non-voters' became the third largest bloc of electors." If the 1979 vote was the beginning of a trend, then 1976 may have been the last year to witness the traditionally large vote. At the current turnout rate of 80 to 85 percent, Italy's voter participation will continue to rank high among democratic countries of the world.

Since 1976 more than the traditional number of voters changed, at least temporarily, their party preference. In 1976 the DC won 38.8 percent of the votes. In 1979 the DC's vote fell to 38.4 percent. Four years later, contrary to the projections of most opinion polls, the DC vote plunged to 32.9 percent of the valid ballots.

Voter support for the Communist party has also declined. In 1976 the PCI vote reached an all-time high of 34.4 percent. In 1979 it fell sharply to 30.4 percent, and in 1983 dropped by 0.5 percentage points. Marcello Fedele, in chapter 4 on the PCI in this volume, argues that "this statistic, however, takes on quite a different light if we consider that in 1983 the PCI combined its ballot with the Democratic Party of Proletarian Unity (PDUP), a small, extreme left-wing party that garnered 1.5 percent of the votes in 1979." Further, Fedele points out that the preference vote was considerably larger for the PDUP candidates than for the Communist candidates on the same ballot. He concludes therefore that in 1983 "the Communists lost at least 1.9 percentage points" from their 1979 vote, bringing the PCI's seven-year decline to 5.9 percentage points—exactly the same loss as that suffered by the Christian Democrats during the period.

In all postwar Italian national elections the DC has finished first and the PCI second. In 1976 the combined DC/PCI vote reached a two-party high of 73.2 percent. In chapter 6 on small parties in this volume, Robert Leonardi recalls that after the 1976 elections, "political commentators were predicting that the minor parties would quickly disappear [and] a standard two-party system" would develop. In fact, the two-party vote declined to 68.8 percent in 1979 and 62.8 percent in 1983. If we subtract Fedele's estimate of the PDUP vote credited to the PCI in the latter election, the DC/PCI vote would have slipped to 60.9 percent. In any case, support for the two largest parties clearly has fallen far below the level predicted only seven years earlier.

Undeterred by their erroneous 1976 predictions about the demise of the small parties, after the 1983 elections commentators forecast the drastic decline of the Christian Democrats. Sample headlines noted by Sani read "Collapse of the DC," "Historic Turning Point," and "Surprise and Trauma." Sani argues that the elections resulted in an "ambiguous verdict" that opened the way to many interpretations. He suggests that in spite of the shift of a few seats from one party to another, one could correctly say that "the strength of the five-party coalition which has ruled the country in recent years has hardly changed." The vote for the five parties together declined by only 0.3 percentage points, from 56.7 to 56.4 percent of the total vote.

Joseph LaPalombara makes a similar point in the concluding chapter of this book. He says that "except for a few essentially cosmetic changes, today's [1983] coalitions look arrestingly like those that held the seats of power in the 1950s."

The small parties gained seats that catch the eye because the base from which the gains were made was so small. Nonetheless, Leonardi correctly states that "in 1983 the major gains were made by the minor parties of the center—the Republicans (PRI), the Social Democrats (PSDI), and the Liberals (PLI) that are squarely in the thick of the battle." The Republicans gained 2.1 percentage points between 1979 and 1981 to raise their share of the total vote to 5.1 percent. Neither of the other two parties gained as much as 1.0 percentage point.

Recent Governments

June 1981 witnessed a major event in Italian politics. Giovanni Spadolini, secretary of the PRI and a member of the national Senate, was asked to form a new government. He did so and the parliament approved his proposal. In Spadolini's words, it was the "first secular government in the history of the republic." He also stated that his government was an "historic event because it established for the first time the practice of rotation of the prime ministership between the secular and the Catholic forces in the country." [1]

When his government fell in the summer of 1982 Spadolini was again named prime minister–designate and again his government was approved. This time, however, it lasted only a few months.

The Spadolini government was replaced by a coalition headed by Amintore Fanfani. His government fell in April 1983 when Bettino Craxi, secretary of the PSI, announced on behalf of his party that "in our opinion, the Government has exhausted the important function it was called upon to carry out, and we have exhausted our parliamentary support for it." [2] Without the support of the PSI, no proposed government could gain parliamentary approval. The parliament, therefore, was dissolved on May 4, 1983, and elections were set for June 26–27.

In chapter 5 on the PSI, K. Robert Nilsson reports that the party sent a memorandum to all PSI candidates "suggesting that they emphasize *not* coalition prospects . . . but *program*." This report, which had been prepared for distribution early in the campaign, covered a wide range of economic, social, and foreign policies. It made a case for reforms that would be acceptable to an audience that included the center and the center-left. Support for the PSI moved from 9.8 percent in 1979 to 11.4 in 1983—hardly a massive gain but the best Socialist vote in twenty years. It was enough for the president of Italy to ask Craxi to form a new government. Craxi had failed to gain approval of his first proposed government in 1981, but this time his government was accepted, and he became prime minister in August 1983. Sani suggests that one could "say that Craxi won the election because he became prime minister rather than the other way around."

Contributors

Nine longtime students of Italian politics have contributed chapters to this volume. They include Carol A. Mershon, instructor of political science, Washington University, St. Louis; Marcello Fedele, professor of sociology, University of Rome; Norman Kogan, professor of history, University of Connecticut; Joseph LaPalombara, Wolfers Professor of Political Science, Yale University; Robert Leonardi, associate professor of political science, DePaul University; K. Robert Nilsson, professor of political science and director of international studies, Dickinson College; William Porter, professor of journalism, University of Michigan; Giacomo Sani, professor of political science, The Ohio State University; Richard M. Scammon, director of the Elections Research Center, Washington, D.C.; and Douglas A. Wertman, United States Information Agency, Milan, Italy, and USIA Office of Research.

I wish to thank Dr. Douglas A. Wertman for providing appendix A, which describes the formation of governments in Italy, and for providing sample ballots shown in appendix B. I also wish to thank Randa Murphy for her great help in preparing the manuscript for publication.

Howard Penniman, General Editor
At the Polls Series
February 1987

Notes

1   Quoted in *Facts-on-File*, July 3, 1981, p. 460.
2   Quoted in Keesing's *Contemporary Archives: Record on World Events*, Robert Fraser, ed., XXIX, no. 9 (London: Longman, 1983), p. 32376.

1 Background

NORMAN KOGAN

──────The Constitution of the Italian Republic requires parliamentary elections at least every five years.[1] From the first parliamentary election of 1948 to the election of 1968, each parliament lasted the five-year term. Since 1968, however, no parliament has survived a full term, an indication of the continuing crisis in Italian political life.

The First Elections of the Postwar Period

The first national election of the postwar period did not choose members of parliament; it chose delegates to a constituent assembly to draft a new constitution for the Italian state. Held on June 2, 1946, the election included a referendum on the monarchy. For the first time in Italian history women were allowed to vote. The Italian people voted by a margin of 54 percent to 46 percent to eliminate the monarchy and to institute a republic. On this question the country was divided by region: The South voted for a monarchy, while the North and center gave substantial majorities to a republic. The monarchist vote was less an expression of legitimist sentiment than a mark of southern resentment toward the other parts of the country and a vote against poverty, despair, and disorder.

The vote for the constituent assembly gave the first formal evidence of the distribution of party strengths and established a pattern that, with a few exceptions, has lasted throughout the postwar period. The vote revealed the leading position of the three major parties—Christian Democratic (DC), Communist (PCI), and Socialist (PSI)—and the numerical weaknesses of the minor ones. These results are shown in table 1-1.

In 1947 the Socialists split, and the smaller of the two factions formed the new Social Democratic party (PSDI). After the Socialist split the Communists became and have remained the leading party of Marxist inspiration, in part

Table 1-1 Percent of Popular Votes by Party in All Postwar National Elections

Party	1946	1948	1953	1958
Christian Democratic (DC)	35.2	48.5	40.1	42.4
Communist (PCI)	19.0 ⎱	31.0	22.6	22.7
Socialist (PSI)	20.7 ⎰		12.8	14.2
Social Democratic (PSDI)	—	7.1	4.5	4.5
Unified Socialist (PSU)	—	—	—	—
Socialist Party of Proletarian Unity (PSIUP)	—	—	—	—
Liberal (PLI)	6.8	3.8	3.0	3.5
Republican (PRI)	4.4	2.5	1.6	1.4
Radical (PR)	—	—	—	—
Neo-Fascist (MSI)	—	—	5.8	4.8
Uomo Qualunque (UO)	5.3	2.0	—	—
Monarchist (PM-PNM)	2.8	2.8	6.9	4.8
Other	5.8	2.3	2.7	1.7
	100.0	100.0	100.0	100.0

Notes: The figures are for the vote for the Chamber of Deputies in all parliamentary elections except for 1946. The 1946 figures represent the vote for delegates to the Constituent Assembly. Not all parties entered candidates in every election.

because the Social Democrats rejected the idea of continued cooperation between Socialists and Communists. Originally this cooperation had been formalized in the Pact of Unity of Action negotiated in 1934 by the two parties in exile. Although the agreement was broken in 1939 at the time of the Nazi-Soviet Non-Aggression Pact, it was renewed in 1941 after the Nazi invasion of the USSR. It endured throughout World War II and well into the postwar period.

The Constitution of the Italian Republic produced by the constituent assembly took effect on January 1, 1948.[2] The election of the first republican parliament, set for April 18, 1948, was held in an atmosphere of full-blown cold war. Tension was high throughout Western Europe: civil war was raging in Greece; in February 1948 the coup d'etat in Czechoslovakia ended with the defenestration of Jan Masaryk and the Communist takeover of the Czech government; soon after the Italian election the Soviets blockaded Berlin, necessitating the Allied airlift to supply the beleaguered city. In this political context the Italian Communists and Socialists agreed to present a joint slate at the April election. The preelection campaign became hysterical: the political propagandists of the Christian Democrats employed the psychology of Rome versus Moscow, Christ against the anti-Christ, the Huns at the gates. A frightened population responded and gave the DC the largest vote in its history

1963	1968	1972	1976	1979	1983
38.3	39.1	38.7	38.7	38.3	32.9
25.3	26.9	27.1	34.4	30.4	29.9
13.8	—	9.6	9.6	9.8	11.4
6.1	—	5.1	3.4	3.8	4.1
—	14.5	—	—	—	—
—	4.5	1.9	—	—	—
7.0	5.8	3.9	1.3	1.9	2.9
1.4	2.0	2.9	3.1	3.0	5.1
—	—	—	1.1	3.4	2.2
5.1	4.4	8.7	6.1	5.3	6.8
—	—	—	—	—	—
1.7	1.3	—	—	—	—
1.3	1.5	2.1	2.3	4.1	4.7
100.0	100.0	100.0	100.0	100.0	100.0

Sources: Italy, Istituto Centrale di Statistica, *Annuario Statistico*, 1944–1948, 152–53; 1958, 143; 1968, 124; 1979, 93. The 1983 figures are unofficial, taken from *Il Popolo*, June 29, 1983.

(see table 1–1) and the only absolute majority of parliamentary seats it has ever received, 305 out of 574 in the Chamber.

Though the DC could have governed by itself, Prime Minister Alcide de Gasperi preferred to bring some of the small lay parties into his cabinet. The Social Democratic, Liberal (PLI), and Republican (PRI) parties accepted the invitation to participate in the government. In one form or another, the four-party Centrist Coalition they created ran the country for the next decade. Though cabinets fell an average of once every ten months, each one was replaced by another version of the coalition. The DC dominated its allies, controlling the prime ministership and most of the ministries. It colonized the bureaucracy, the state and parastate agencies, and government corporations, leaving only patronage crumbs to its allies.

The Centrist cabinets made the major choices that determined most of Italy's policies in the postwar period. They brought Italy decisively into the Western camp, making the country a participant in the Marshall Plan and a member of the Western European Union, the North Atlantic Treaty Organization (NATO), the European Coal and Steel Community, and the European Economic Community. Domestically the Centrist governments opened up the economy, reduced the controls remaining from the Fascist period, and stimulated the country's second industrial revolution. In the 1950s and 1960s the economic boom transformed Italian society, providing Italy with one of the highest rates of real economic growth in the Western world. Vast population shifts occurred: from the country to the city, from the South to the center and North, from agriculture to industry to the service occupations, and from Italy to northern and western European nations and overseas. In a relatively short period the country was electrified, motorized, and blanketed by television. The educational system was expanded to encompass the vast mass of young people at elementary and secondary levels. The universities were opened to much larger numbers of students than before the war.

The changes stimulated public expectations and aspirations, however, that outran the pace of change. The parties and the political system had to adjust and found it difficult to keep up. It was apparent that the comfortable majorities that had sustained the cabinets for five years were not likely to be repeated. In local and provincial elections held in 1952 the parties of the Centrist Coalition experienced substantial reductions in votes. In the consequent anticipation of a difficult parliamentary election, the governing coalition changed the rules, adopting a new electoral law that awarded two-thirds of the seats in the Chamber to the alliance of parties that obtained one vote more than 50 percent of the total. The Communists and Socialists baptized the revised election rules the "Swindle Law." (It resembled the Acerbo Law of 1923, which, by granting two-thirds of the seats in the Chamber to the party winning 25 percent of the vote, had enabled Benito Mussolini to gain a Fascist majority in the Chamber in the 1924 election.) Such was the political climate in 1953 when the term of office of the first parliament ended.

For the 1953 election each of the two major opposition parties ran its own slate. The three small allies of the DC reluctantly supported the changed rules, but a number of their members and sympathizers deserted them. Indeed, on election day the four alliance parties received only 49.2 percent of the votes. The defectors had cost the Centrist Coalition its prize (see table 1–1).

Socialist Challenge Nevertheless, the Centrist Coalition retained a small majority of seats in the Chamber. Its continued survival as the governing coalition was challenged in 1953, however, by the first proposal for a political realignment. Pietro Nenni, the Socialist leader, suggested that his party was available for an "opening to the left," that is, a coalition extending from the Christian Democrats to the Socialists. The proposal was a major issue for the next decade. It implied the termination of the Unity of Action agreement between Socialists and Communists, and it meant making room for a major force for political action within the governing establishment. The Socialists' negative judgment of Italian foreign and domestic policies would have to change, but at the same time the establishment would have to accept Socialist demands for economic and social reform. The political rationalization for the opening was that Socialist participation in the majority would help consolidate parliamentary democracy, while economic and social reform would attract workers and peasants away from the Communists to the PSI and to the political system.

Opponents of the opening argued that bringing the Socialists into the majority meant providing the antisystem parties with the opportunity to erode parliamentary democracy from within, but factions within both the DC and the PSDI were attracted to the possibility of expanding the non-Communist left. In 1954 when Amintore Fanfani became secretary general of the Christian Democratic party, he gradually began shifting his own party to the left. In 1956 the shift was hastened by events outside the country. Nikita Khrushchev's exposure of the crimes of the Stalin era in the spring of 1956 and the Soviet suppression of the Hungarian revolt in the fall exacerbated relations between the PSI and PCI. The PCI, lamely defending Soviet behavior, at the same time moved further away from the Soviet model and proclaimed that the Italian way of socialism was the democratic way. Later that year Nenni met with Giuseppe Saragat, leader of the Social Democrats, to discuss reunification of the two parties. Although the discussion was premature, in 1958 the PSI finally terminated the Unity of Action pact; however, it continued to collaborate with the Communists in local governments, in the cooperative movement, and in the Italian General Confederation of Labor (CGIL).

Coalition Governments the Norm   In this era of transition the 1958 parliamentary election was held in a much calmer atmosphere than previous elections. The results rewarded the strategies of Fanfani and Nenni and strengthened the possibilities for the opening to the left. Opponents of this course inside the DC, the Vatican, and the business community rebelled; at the end of 1958 Fanfani was pulled down by his enemies in his own camp. Aldo Moro succeeded him as secretary general of the DC. Because the center coalition was no longer manageable, however, a succession of unstable and minority cabinets governed the country. Finally, in the spring of 1960, when Fernando Tambroni headed a DC cabinet that depended on neo-Fascist support in parliament, anti-Fascist riots forced the government to resign, making it possible for Fanfani and Moro to convince an alarmed Vatican and business community that no alternative to an arrangement with the Socialists remained.[3]

Christian Democrats and Socialists work together   It took time and careful maneuvering before the agreement between the Socialists and the Christian Democrats could be consummated; not until 1962 did Moro's party endorse the strategy of collaboration with the left. Also in 1962, to help Nenni convince reluctant Socialists that Christian Democrats were serious about reform, the government nationalized the private electric power industry. Another election was necessary, however, before the opening could be effected.

The election campaign took place in a strange atmosphere: the country was prosperous as never before, but the parties of the right nevertheless denounced the DC as traitors to country, morality, religion, and Western civilization; on the left the Communists denounced a perfidious Socialist party for betraying the workers to the class enemy. Two weeks before the election, however, Pope John XXIII published the encyclical *Pacem in terris* (Peace on Earth), in which, among other things, he noted the propriety of collaboration for peace and social justice between people who differed ideologically. In Italy this was interpreted as an endorsement of the opening to the left.

Center-left coalition controls cabinet in 1963   In the 1963 election the opponents of the prospective coalition on the right (Liberals) and on the left (Communists) made important gains. The proponents, especially the Christian Democrats, suffered the losses (see table 1–1). Nevertheless, a center-left coalition was the only feasible government, and the negotiations took months to conclude. Not until December 1963 was a four-party center-left cabinet of Christian Democrats, Social Democrats, Republicans, and Socialists installed. A minority of the Socialist parliamentarians refused to vote for it, though, and the following month they broke away to organize yet a third Socialist party, the Italian Socialist Party of Proletarian Unity (PSIUP), committed to collaboration with the PCI.

The participation of the PSI in the cabinets of the next years changed the label of the coalition from centrist to center-left. What else changed is more difficult to determine. The PSI claimed and received a share of the patronage and other spoils of government. The government developed a series of five-year programs (the word "plan" was avoided), but there is little evidence that the programs were taken seriously, either by the government or the voters, or that they had any real effects on the economy. The major agricultural reform was a law of 1964 that gradually eliminated sharecropping (*la mezzadria*). The government, through its principal holding corporations, the Institute for Industrial Reconstruction (IRI) and the National Hydrocarbons Agency (ENI), expanded investments in southern industry. Government commitment to subsidize higher costs made the agreements possible; the agreement did not persuade the government. The government persuaded the employers. (Many of these investments ran into serious trouble in the 1970s when the economic climate changed.)

Socialist factions reunite   In 1966 the PSI and PSDI joined to form the Unified Socialist party (PSU), a Socialist reunification that had been discussed since 1956. Saragat, the PSDI leader, became president of the republic, and Nenni, of the PSI, became the secretary general of the new party. The PSU underwent its first test in the 1968 election and failed: it suffered substantial losses in both popular vote and parliamentary seats compared to the 1963 election results for its two component parties (see table 1–1). The consequent strains caused a split in the party in July 1969, and the PSI and PSDI reemerged as separate entities. Many Socialist leaders interpreted this electoral failure as their constituents' negative verdict on the center-left strategy, their rejection of five years of collaboration with Christian Democrats and Social Democrats.

A Turbulent Italy in the Late 1960s and Early 1970s

Youth Revolt The year 1968 ushered in a new period in postwar Italian history. A student movement for education reform developed and erupted into violence that closed the universities for months. Demands for the reform of the educational structure soon grew into condemnations of the political, economic, and social system. The youth organizations of the parties lost control over the student generation. Bedazzled by third-world revolutions and revolutionaries and stimulated by a mixture of Catholic and Marxist utopianisms, the movement produced a bewildering variety of ideas and schemes and groups that fluctuated in membership and lacked organization and discipline. Eventually the student revolt weakened and disappeared, having achieved only a few reforms of the educational system.[4]

Turmoil in the Industrial World In the fall of 1969, when major trade union contracts came up for renewal, an aroused and pugnacious labor force, stimulated by a younger generation of workers and urged on by student agitators, erupted in a series of violent strikes. The traditional trade union organizations, associated with the political parties, temporarily lost control over the rank and file. The "Hot Autumn" of 1969 produced new collective-bargaining agreements favorable to the workers, and the government committed itself to subsidizing the ensuing higher operating costs of the firms. A strengthened labor movement regained control of the organized labor force. Other consequences of the violence were parliament's passage of a new and expanded code of labor legislation, the establishment of regional governments for the fifteen regular regions of Italy,[5] and the emergence of the terrorist movements that plague the country to this day. In addition, 1970 marked the end of two uninterrupted decades of economic growth. The economic miracle that transformed the nation into an advanced industrialized and urbanized country (though with remaining pockets of underdevelopment, especially in the South) sputtered into the stop-and-go economy of the 1970s and 1980s.

Continuing Political Upheaval Since 1968 no parliament has survived a full five-year term. For example, the parliament elected in 1976 lasted three years, and the subsequent one was dissolved in 1983 after four years. The radicalization of the atmosphere since 1968, of which terrorism is the most extreme manifestation, is a persistent source of crisis. Another source has been the instability of the coalitions supporting the government, in particular the ambivalence of the Socialist party. The indecision of the party's factions about their alliances, with whom and under what terms, has been the critical factor in precipitating new elections. The PSI has straddled this problem by collaborating with the DC at the national level and with the PCI at regional and local levels.

After 1968 the center-left coalition was again the only political alliance that could support a national government; the question was whether the four parties would participate in a cabinet as they had in 1963 or permit a minority DC government to function with the direct or indirect parliamentary support of the other three. As it turned out, in 1969 and 1970 both forms of cabinet government were used. Then in June 1970 the first election of the fifteen new regional governments was held. The parties on the left led in the Red Belt regions of Emilia-Romagna, Tuscany, and Umbria; the PSI joined with the PCI in coalitions in those regions while participating in a center-left cabinet at the national level. Socialist-Communist alliances at the local level, which were common during the Unity of Action period, declined substantially during the center-left period of the 1960s. In 1970, however, they obtained a new lease on life.

The turbulence, violence, and terrorism of these years stimulated a law-and-order response. Even the PCI became an outspoken proponent of order as it pursued a strategy of deradicalizing its programs, gradually abandoning its hostility to Italian membership in NATO and reinforcing its commitment to parliamentary procedures. The Communists were well aware that they were the favored enemy of the extreme left, accused by the extremists of having abandoned both revolutionary principles and the working masses.

In the hostilities between the DC and PSI over the Socialist attempt to legalize divorce, the PCI proposed compromise solutions rejected by the Catholics. In 1970, however, parliament passed a divorce bill over DC opposition; but by 1972 Catholic organizations had collected enough signatures supporting repeal of the divorce law to force a referendum. Growing strains among the government parties and a desire to stave off the referendum forced the early dissolution of parliament in the spring of 1972. In anticipation of the election, the remnants of the Monarchist party merged with the neo-Fascists.

Election Results since 1972

Compared to 1968, in 1972 the Christian Democrat and Socialist votes remained relatively stable, the Communists continued their slow growth, and the neo-Fascists, successfully exploiting the law-and-order issue, made substantial gains (see table 1-1). The PSIUP, suffering extensive losses, dissolved shortly after the election, and most of its leaders joined the PCI. The years from 1968 to 1972 were among the most tumultuous in postwar Italian history, yet the ferment appeared to have little effect on the voting behavior of the electorate. The DC again demonstrated its critical role in the political spectrum, operating as a force for stability and continuity.

The summer of 1970 began a period of variable and fluctuating economic growth. The rate of increase in the real gross national product slowed down. Then in 1973 prices began to spurt upward. Since then Italy has been living with one of the highest rates of inflation among the industrialized countries of the West. The worldwide price increases in raw materials and foodstuffs, especially the fourfold increase in petroleum prices imposed by OPEC after 1973, hurt the Italian economy severely. In 1975 Italy suffered its first postwar recession. Unemployment grew and the young were particularly vulnerable. Nevertheless, it is fair to say that official government statistics exaggerated the economic setbacks, for throughout the 1970s the submerged or underground economy was expanding. Productivity and employment in this sector, however, could only be estimated.

Communists and Catholics Attempt a Compromise   Economic problems exacerbated a political atmosphere already tense with rumors of potential military coups and growing terrorist activities. The outcome of the 1972 election aggravated the continuous debate within the PSI over the center-left strategy. Supporters argued that Socialist participation in the government gave the party more influence on policy than would a return to the opposition and prevented the DC from making a further conservative shift. Opponents argued that only by allowing the PCI to participate in policy making could the government tackle the country's problems successfully. PCI participation could be accomplished by extending the center-left to incorporate the Communists, or by creating a left alternative composed of Socialists, Communists, and selected extraparliamentary groups.

The Communist leadership preferred an accommodation with the Christian Democrats to a showdown between left and center. In the fall of 1973 PCI secretary general Enrico Berlinguer proposed a "historic compromise" between the Marxist and Catholic camps (between the PCI and the DC as a whole, including its conservative factions); the left alternative was thus rejected by the largest party of the left. Such a compromise between Communists and Christian Democrats might have excluded a future role for the Socialists, although Berlinguer seemed to welcome Socialist participation in the enterprise. His historic offer of compromise stimulated much discussion and analysis but little political action. The official Catholic world rejected the suggestion in principle, although individual Catholics, lay and cleric, were attracted by the idea.

Several important political developments took place in 1974. Parliament established public financing for political parties. It also reduced the minimum age from twenty-one to eighteen for voting in elections for the Chamber of Deputies. The PCI announced publicly that it accepted Italy's membership in NATO. Most important from an emotional point of view was the settlement of the divorce issue. The petition to repeal the divorce law by national referendum could no longer be ignored. The DC and the Catholic church threw themselves into the antidivorce campaign, while the lay parties, conservative and radical, continued to oppose repeal. The referendum resulted in a victory—59 percent to 41 percent—for those who opposed repeal of the law allowing divorce. The vote showed more than the state of public opinion on divorce. It was a political defeat for the DC, an expression of the growing secularization of society, and an indication of the weakening social and cultural controls of the predominant church and party.

In the fall of 1974 Berlinguer offered Communist participation in the parliamentary majority supporting the cabinet without demanding membership in the government. The Socialists, who had been in and out of the cabinet for the previous two years, endorsed the Communist offer. The DC rejected the Communist proposal (although its leader, Aldo Moro, consulted with PCI leaders behind the scenes), and the cabinet fell in October 1974. The PSI would not participate in a government again until 1980. Nevertheless, the Socialists continued to support the subsequent minority cabinets in parliament.

The regional and local elections of June 1975 were the first in which the new young electorate, five million strong, voted. Economically, 1975 was the worst year in postwar Italian history. The PCI gained the most ground in the elections, the PSI made lesser gains, the DC lost the most. As a result, leftist coalitions took control of additional regional and provincial governments. In most of the major cities from Naples northward Communist or Socialist mayors headed leftist-coalition municipal governments. At the national level the PSI concluded that the election results endorsed its leftward swing. By the end of 1975 a majority of the Socialist party leadership was ready to withdraw its support of the minority cabinet, and in January 1976 the government resigned. The power of the center-left, progressively shakier since 1969, had come to a temporary end. A minority DC cabinet, dependent on PSI abstentions, struggled through the spring but broke down when the Socialists shifted from abstention to opposition in the dispute over the abortion issue. Parliament was dissolved, and in June the country went to the polls.

1976 Election Leads to One-Party Minority DC Government   In 1976 the DC recouped its losses from the previous year's regional election, the PCI consolidated and advanced on its gains, and the PSI suffered a setback (see table 1-1). Disappointed Socialists revolted successfully against their senior leaders, and a new generation of forty-year-olds, led by Bettino Craxi, took over the party's direction. They were in no mood to consider a return to the center-left, nor were the smaller Republican and Social Democratic parties. The previous election results had severely restricted the DC options as well; a centrist or center-right coalition was numerically impossible. At the opposite end of the political spectrum a left alternative was theoretically feasible, but the Communists rejected it out of hand. What remained was a choice between a renewed center-left or a government of national emergency.

The DC preferred a renewed center-left; the Communists pushed for their own inclusion in a government of national emergency. Both the United States and West German governments publicly opposed PCI participation in the cabinet. Socialists, Social Democrats, and Liberals, however, rejected a renovated center-left. The impasse was finally resolved by the creation of a one-party minority DC government, surviving on a formula of "non-no confidence." Liberals, Republicans, Social Democrats, Socialists, and Communists all abstained, but the PCI abstention was the one that installed the DC government. If it had voted with the remaining opposition, composed of neo-Fascists, Proletarian Democrats, and Radicals, the cabinet could not have survived. For the first time since 1947 the Communists were not in opposition. Although not in the cabinet, they held key posts in parliament—the presidency of the Chamber of Deputies as well as some committee chairmanships and deputy chairmanships in the Chamber and the Senate. In addition, Communists were cut into a share of the patronage and spoils of the public economic sector. Such indirect PCI support of the DC cabinet, however, enraged the extreme left.

The coalition of national emergency had been created to wrestle with a serious economic recession. The economy did revive in 1976, although improvement could be ascribed more to developments on the international economic scene than to specific governmental policies, for Italy's economy is heavily involved in international trade. Communist leaders endorsed policies of wage restraint and austerity in the provision of public services but soon found that the labor unions, the workers, and the public were in no mood for sacrifices. In the spring of 1977 public order was shaken by a new wave of student uprisings more violent than the student revolts of 1968–69, for the prospect of joblessness or underemployment reinforced ideological hatred.

These actions did not destroy the coalition, however. In July 1977 the parties endorsing the government issued a domestic-policy statement that reaffirmed the restrictive economic program and approved further expansion of the powers of the regional governments. On December 1 a foreign affairs declaration, drafted with PCI participation, reasserted the coalition's support for NATO and the European Economic Community as the cornerstones of Italian foreign policy. At the end of 1977 Berlinguer demanded the formation of a coalition cabinet to include the Communists.

Berlinguer's demand caused a political crisis that lasted more than two months. Opposition inside the DC to admitting the PCI into the government was strong and was reinforced by both Vatican and American objections. At the time, the issue was primarily symbolic. All major policy decisions already required consultation with and clearance by the leaders of the abstaining parties. Inclusion in the cabinet, however, would mean the final legitimization of the PCI in the political system. With resistance hardening, Berlinguer hinted that Communist presence in the government was not absolutely essential. The hint gave Moro, president of the DC, the opening he needed, and he effected a compromise whereby the cabinet would remain a minority DC government, and the abstaining parties would vote for it and become part of the parliamentary majority. The Liberals opposed admitting the PCI to the majority and returned to the opposition, but they were too small to change the result. On March 16, 1978, the day of the scheduled vote of confidence for the new cabinet, Red Brigades terrorists kidnapped Moro. Fifty-four days later they executed him.

This was a terrible period for the Italian political system and for the population as a whole, which rallied in support of the state. A month after Moro's death, the political system was put to another test. On June 15 the new president of Italy, Giovanni Leone, resigned from office under accusations of earlier tax fraud and financial corruption. On July 9 parliament elected as president the eighty-two-year-old Socialist, Sandro Pertini. The political system had survived. The coalition of national emergency, originally constructed to deal with an economic crisis, had steered the country through dangers of a different order.

The fall of 1978 saw relations among the parties of the majority deteriorate. Christian Democrats, Socialists, and Communists were bickering. Mutual suspicions and disputes over economic policy aggravated tensions. The Communist leadership was aware that its rank and file had little enthusiasm for the strategy of moderation, and disillusionment among the young was eroding an important sector of its electorate. By the end of 1978 the PCI was giving clear evidence that it wanted to return to the much more comfortable opposition. In January 1979 the party demanded direct participation in the government, knowing that its demand would be rejected. On January 31 the PCI withdrew from the parliamentary majority.

The Communist withdrawal brought down the cabinet but not the parliament. The Socialists' unwillingness to collaborate with the DC in another center-left government made the June 1979 election necessary. The Socialists expected an increase in voter support that would improve their bargaining position in a new round of cabinet negotiations, and Craxi was ambitious to become prime minister.

1979 Election Produces Three-Party Minority Government   In the 1979 election a clear drop in voter turnout was noticeable. Whereas the average turnout in previous elections had been 93 to 94 percent, in 1979 for the first time fewer than 90 percent of the electorate voted. At the same time the number of spoiled and blank ballots increased. These were all signs of growing voter disaffection.[6] Although DC votes dropped marginally, the big loser was the PCI, whose share of electoral support dropped for the first time in postwar parliamentary elections. Socialist gains were negligible (see table 1–1). The most impressive advance was made by the small Radical party, which was contesting its second parliamentary election. Its support came mainly from young voters.

Forming a new government took most of the summer of 1979. The PCI reiterated its earlier refusal to support any cabinet of which it was not a member. The other alternatives were a revival of the center-left coalitions of the 1960s, which would bring the Socialists back into the cabinet along with the smaller parties, or a minority government dependent on Socialist support or abstention. Craxi, then secretary general of the PSI, demanded the prime ministership as the Socialist price for its participation in a cabinet. While some Christian Democratic leaders were willing to pay this price, the majority refused. The DC was four times larger than the PSI in parliament. It had held the premiership uninterruptedly since 1945. After lengthy negotiations a truce cabinet was created under the DC leader Francesco Cossiga. It was a minority government of Christian Democrats, Social Democrats, and Liberals. The Socialists and Republicans abstained. If the PSI had been willing to accept this solution in the spring, the 1979 election could have been avoided.

The economy falters   The Cossiga government faced disconcerting economic problems. The economy had revived in 1978 and 1979, but in the first half of 1979 the rate of inflation sped up. OPEC had imposed a major increase in petroleum prices in the summer of 1979, and in September the Italian government raised prices on gasoline, heating and diesel fuel, and electricity. Such increases took effect throughout the economy, and by the end of 1979 the consumer price index had risen 19 percent over the previous year. Reacting to increases in food prices, in September the Italian government attacked the European Community's Common Agricultural Policy. The agriculture minister claimed that during the previous year his country spent 1,200 billion lire more in food imports from the EC than it would have if it had purchased the same products from outside the Common Market. The treasury minister complained that Italy's portion of the EC budget was too big. Because the United Kingdom shared these complaints, the two countries agreed to cooperate in an attempt to change EC policies, but by 1983 that agreement fell apart.

Disputes over U.S. missile installations   In October 1979 the government made an important foreign-policy decision concerning defense strategy, accepting the U.S. proposal to upgrade medium-range nuclear missile installations in Italy. Italy had resisted Leonid Brezhnev's threats and blandishments, agreeing with the Social Democratic–Free Democratic government of West Germany that there was time to negotiate with the Soviet Union about nuclear parity in Europe before the installation of the missiles in 1983. All the parties supporting the Cossiga government endorsed the decision, although Craxi had to overcome some resistance within the Socialist party. The Italian Communists opposed the acceptance, taking a stand equidistant from the Soviet Union and the United States; they called for immediate U.S.-Soviet negotiations before deciding whether to accept the new missiles. They also called on the Soviet Union to stop its installation of new missiles in the interim. The Communists' position was similar to that of the Dutch government and the left wing of the German Social Democratic party.

Once more in opposition, the Communists distanced themselves from the government in both domestic and foreign policy; their efforts to attract the Socialists to the same position failed, however. Under Craxi's leadership the PSI gradually but consistently moved away from the left alternative toward the center. In the spring of 1980 the Socialists entered the cabinet. Their participation made possible the first center-left government and the first majority government since 1975. For half a decade the country had been governed (more or less) by minority, truce, or caretaker cabinets.

In the fall of 1980 the miniboom of the late 1970s faded and the economy experienced three years of slow or negative growth. Hard times did not deflect the Socialist pursuit of moderation. The PSI negotiated an agreement with the PSDI to consult, collaborate, and establish joint positions on policy issues. The two parties affirmed their adherence to "Western Socialism." By the spring of 1981 Craxi consolidated his control over his own party, renamed his faction the Reformist faction to emphasize moderation, and at the same time redefined the Socialist program as one of Liberal Socialism, a euphemism for Social Democracy. The PSI's strategy was to penetrate the growing middle class, which Craxi perceived as the critical population group in the Italian electorate. He had to compete with the DC, the PCI, and the smaller lay and centrist parties, however, for the bourgeois vote.

Electoral bastions of the major parties shaken in 1981   The Catholic culture and the DC received a severe blow in May when, in a national referendum, over two-thirds of the electorate voted to uphold a liberal abortion law. Though the DC had not made the abortion referendum a party issue, its position was shaken. Subsequently, when Arnaldo Forlani, the Christian Democrat who was then prime minister, mishandled a new scandal that involved a secret Masonic lodge, Propaganda 2, the Socialists pulled down the cabinet. Craxi's ambition to become prime minister was thwarted once more, however, when Giovanni Spadolini, secretary general of the small Republican party, became the leader of another center-left cabinet and the first head of the government since 1945 who was not a Christian Democrat. The larger parties looked upon the arrangement as temporary. Spadolini, however, proved quite skillful at keeping his allies at bay. Although he faced difficult economic problems, he managed to gain considerable public approval for his vigorous leadership. Twice in 1982 the Socialists forced the government's resignation but failed each time to get government leadership. The first time, Spadolini returned to office with the same cabinet; the second time, in December, Christian Democrat Amintore Fanfani came back to head a new cabinet, leaving the Republicans outside in disgust.

At the end of the year, when martial law was imposed in Poland, PCI leaders reacted against the Soviet Union, which they held responsible for the military takeover in Warsaw, and issued a devastating critique of the entire Soviet–East European system. Berlinguer concluded that the international workers movement based on the October Revolution had "exhausted its propulsive capacity and is historically finished."[7] The Soviet Union responded with a slashing attack on the PCI, an attack that stopped just short of excommunicating the Italians from the international communist movement.[8] Two traditional sources of authority had been challenged.

In the spring of 1983 the political atmosphere presaged new parliamentary elections. In March Berlinguer called on the Socialists to abandon the center-left and to join the Communists in an electoral alliance. By the next month the government appeared to be tottering. The reason given officially was disagreement between the PSI and the DC over tax policy. The real reason was the Socialist fear that, after three years of improvement in public opinion polls, its party's popularity was waning. In the third week of April Craxi brought Fanfani's cabinet down, parliament was dissolved, and June 26 was set as the election date.[9]

Summary

This brief background survey emphasized two themes: the party choices of the voters as expressed through parliamentary elections, and the various coalitions or alliances of the political parties that have made governments possible and enabled the political system to survive. The overall stability of party strength was the result of a clearly defined electorate, sometimes categorized into three political subcultures—a Catholic, a Marxist, and a bourgeois-secularist culture. Though the Marxist and the bourgeois-secularist camps include more than one party, shifts among them are minor. In fact there has always been more voter movement than the election returns revealed, but to a considerable degree the shifts offset each other. The biggest source of change in voting patterns came from new voters entering the electorate and old voters passing from the scene.

In the 1970s the political subcultures began to erode under the cumulative effect of extensive secularization and modernization. Voters, particularly the younger ones, loosened their ties to the political parties. Many youth have become hostile to the parties and to the political system.[10] Nevertheless, on the whole they continue to vote for the parties that support the system, to which they give little verbal allegiance. Antisystem parties have not made much headway. The reduced effectiveness of traditional identifications increases the salience to the voters of issues and personalities. Corruption is one such current issue. Although corruption has existed throughout Italian history, it did not affect electoral behavior in the past as it apparently does today.

Two major coalition systems have dominated the republican period, and the DC is at the core of both. In the 1950s the centrist coalitions, in the 1960s and into the early 1970s the center-left, and in the 1980s again the center-left prevailed. In the years of transition between major coalition systems, minority governments, truce governments, and caretaker governments ruled. The minority cabinets from August 1976 to January 1979, backed by the indirect and then direct support of all the parties from the Liberals on the right to the Communists on the left, were not much different from other transitional governments despite their label of governments of national emergency. The center-left coalition renewed in the fall of 1979 could just as well have been labeled a centrist coalition, since the Socialist party of the 1980s has moved substantially toward social democracy. Although the election of 1983 resulted in the selection of a Socialist prime minister for the first time in Italian history, it did not transform the party system, the political system, or the country.

Notes

1   The constitution originally provided for a six-year term for the Senate and a five-year term for the Chamber of Deputies. It was amended to reduce the Senate's term to five years. In practice, both houses have always been dissolved simultaneously.

2   An English translation of the constitution was published by the United States government. U.S. Department of State, *Documents and State Papers* 1, no. 1 (April 1948): 46–63.

3   K. Robert Nilsson, "Italy's 'Opening to the Right': The Tambroni Experiment of 1960" (Ph.D. dissertation, Columbia University, 1964).

4   Gianni Statera, *Death of a Utopia: The Development and Decline of Student Movements in Europe* (New York: Oxford University Press, 1975); Lucio Colletti, "Le ideologie," *Dal '68 a oggi, come siamo e come eravamo* (Rome-Bari: Editori Laterza, 1979), 103–66.

5   The 1948 constitution provided for the establishment of regional governments throughout the country. Prior to 1970, however, only five special governments had been created: on the northern periphery of Italy where ethnic and linguistic minorities lived, and on the islands of Sicily and Sardinia, where separatist movements had emerged since World War II.

6   See Howard R. Penniman, ed., *Italy at the Polls, 1979* (Washington, D.C.: American Enterprise Institute, 1981).

7   *L'Unità*, December 18, 1981.

8   Excerpts from the *Pravda* attack appeared in the *New York Times*, January 25, 1982. A full Italian translation appeared in *L'Unità*, January 25, 1982.

9   For an extensive review of the postwar period, see Norman Kogan, *A Political History of Italy: The Postwar Years* (New York: Praeger, 1983).

10   Robert D. Putnam, Robert Leonardi, and Raffaella Y. Nanetti, "Polarization and Depolarization in Italian Politics, 1968–1981" (Paper read at the 1981 Annual Meeting of the American Political Science Association, New York City, September 1981, mimeographed).

2 The Electorate: An Ambiguous Verdict

GIACOMO SANI

Election results can be examined from a number of viewpoints: The focus can be on the changes in the balance of forces among the contending groups, on the consequences of these changes for coalition alignments and for rotation of incumbents in power, or on the extent and the direction of change in voter behavior and on the reasons behind different choices. Results can be examined for the contrast between the expectations and the actual outcome. Finally, the focus can involve the interesting task of looking beyond immediate consequences to the long-term trends, treating returns not as an isolated episode but as an installment of the continuing story.

Since every election has multiple dimensions, a variety of meanings can be extracted from its outcome. Interpretations appropriate for one of these dimensions may spill over and contaminate the interpretations pertinent to other aspects. When the returns are ambiguous, as is often the case, the risk of transferring meaning from one domain to another is compounded.

The Italian election of 1983 is a good case in point. Many observers greeted the results as proof of a dramatic change, a significant turn that had inaugurated a new phase in Italian politics. "Collapse of the DC," "Historic Turning Point," and "Surprise and Trauma" were common headlines in the aftermath of election.[1] There were certainly good grounds for this interpretation. The size of the loss suffered by the Christian Democrats (DC) was unprecedented: the party had fallen to the lowest level of support ever obtained in postwar history. Its status as the largest political force of the country was threatened, and its difference in strength with the Communist party (PCI) had shrunk to three meager percentage points. More important, as PCI secretary

The author is grateful to Giuliano Urbani and Maria Weber for making available to him the data from a survey of the Italian electorate conducted by the Doxa Institute for the Milan daily *Sole-24-Ore*.

Enrico Berlinguer hastened to point out, the losses suffered by the DC meant that the Christian Democrats were no longer an essential component of future government coalitions. Others could legitimately point out that the election was significant because the major parties had *both* declined, and the bloc of intermediate political groups, the so-called *polo laico* or intermediate pole, had managed to attract almost a fourth of the valid votes. The shrinking of the two major poles, it could be argued, represented in and of itself a major development, one which, if the trend were to continue in the future, would change the landscape of Italian politics. Moreover, since the head-on confrontation between the DC and the Italian Socialist party (PSI) turned out in favor of the latter, the Socialists received the boost they needed to claim the post of prime minister for the first time—a significant development and a first in Italian history as well.

Yet the returns were ambiguous enough to justify the claim that the changes brought about by the 1983 election were, all things considered, not dramatic. In support of this thesis, the mean gain or loss incurred by a party in 1983 was a modest 1.6 percent, not much higher than the corresponding value for 1979 and practically the same as in 1976. The "victory" of the PSI, moreover, was not grounded in significant gains in votes or seats but was rather a psychological victory.

Similarly, the increase of votes for the neo-Fascists, however upsetting from an ideological point of view, was hardly a cause for concern. Although the gains of the three centrist parties were certainly not irrelevant, they remained small, if significant, components of the party system. As for the PCI's support base, erosion had not reached the proportions that some had hoped (and others had feared), and the Communists remained the dominant force of the left. Finally, the overall balance of forces in the traditional grouping of Italian parties had basically remained unchanged (see table 2–1). The left dropped from 45.8 to 45.0 percent of the vote; the center from 47 to 45 percent; the center-left from 54.9 to 53.5 percent. The strength of the five-party coalition that has ruled in recent years hardly changed (from 56.7 to 56.4 percent).

As one can see, both arguments are reasonably plausible, and it is hard to come to a definite conclusion as to the true meaning of the 1983 election. Very possibly the exercise is not important. In Italy, the real meaning of an election depends less on the numbers and more on how the major protagonists choose to interpret the figures and act on their interpretations. In the end, the inauguration of Bettino Craxi as prime minister, with the somewhat reluctant consent of the DC, clearly overshadowed the Socialists' gains, which were modest and had fallen short of the party's expectations. One might say that Craxi "won the election" *because* he became prime minister rather than the other way around.

Table 2-1 Percent of the Vote by Party,
Chamber of Deputies Elections, 1972–1983

Party	1972	1976	1979	1983
Minor leftist groups	3.0	1.5	2.2	1.5
PCI	27.2	34.4	30.4	29.9
PR	—	1.1	3.4	2.2
PSI	9.6	9.6	9.8	11.4
Total left	39.8	46.6	45.8	45.0
PSDI	5.2	3.4	3.8	4.1
PRI	2.9	3.1	3.0	5.1
DC	38.7	38.7	38.3	32.9
PLI	3.9	1.3	1.9	2.9
Total center	50.7	46.5	47.0	45.0
Monarchists and MSI	8.7	6.1	5.9	6.8
Other	0.8	0.8	1.3	3.2

Source: Compiled by the author from official statistics.

Voters, Parties, and the Campaign

Since the preceding parliamentary election in June 1979, the Italian electorate had increased from 42.2 to 43.9 million registered voters, or by approximately 4 percent. The net-growth figure (1.7 million voters) does not, however, tell the full story. Between the two elections, 3.7 million new voters had been added to the electoral registry, and the names of about 2.0 million electors had been deleted because of death and other causes. The true extent of change in the composition of the electorate was therefore greater than might appear on the surface. While it is impossible to estimate exactly the impact of these two flows of voters in and out of the electorate, it is not unreasonable to suppose that the electoral turnover affected, to some degree, the outcome of the election. This point will be elaborated later.

In 1983 there were few changes in the parties contesting the election nationwide. The major protagonists and the symbols with which they were identified on the paper ballot remained the same. The major novelty was perhaps the decision of the Radical party (PR), after a heated internal debate, to present lists of candidates and to contest the election but, at the same time, to encourage voters to express their feelings of dissatisfaction with the system. Voters could do this either by depositing in the urns a blank ballot or by spoiling the vote with statements written on the ballots. After the election Radical party leader Marco Pannella revealed that he had done exactly that: he had written on his ballot, "Long live the Republic, long live democracy."[2]

Another change was the decision by a minor communist group, the Democratic Party of Proletarian Unity (PDUP), to present joint lists of candidates with the PCI, in the understanding that the PDUP would receive in exchange six parliamentary seats. Another small leftist group with the label Proletarian Democracy (DP) was the only party challenging the PCI from the left.

More interesting, if not necessarily more significant, was the emergence among the 1983 contestants of parties representing special social groups or regional minorities. Most noteworthy of the social groups was the list of candidates presented in twenty-two of the thirty-two districts by the *Partito Nazionale Pensionati* (National Party of Retired People). Regional parties sprang up in several districts. The most significant ones were the *Liga Veneta* (Veneto League), present in the districts of the Veneto area, and the Sardinia Action party, a revitalized group active in the island of Sardinia. A *Lista per Trieste* (List for Trieste), though local in nature, was present in twenty-six of the thirty-two electoral districts. The most important regional party remained the *Sudtyroler Volkspartei* (South Tyrolean People's party), the group that has traditionally represented the German-speaking people residing in the province of Bolzano. As a result of this proliferation of options, in 1983 Italian ballots were as crowded as ever, and the voters had a wide variety of choices, some traditional and some new.

There were also quite a few novelties among independent candidates. In the early part of the postwar period, the most prominent candidates were either well-known professional politicians or well-known public figures from outside the world of politics. The latter, however, were so closely connected to a specific party, or a specific political tendency, that they could hardly pass for independents. In the past decade or so, partly because of the greater role played by the mass media during the campaign, things have changed. Parties have made more determined efforts to sponsor outside candidates known for their endeavors in the arts, the professions, academia, and other walks of life. In 1983 the drive to attract independent candidates was particularly pronounced; a number of well-known figures were included in the list of candidates presented by the various political groups. These special candidacies included established writers, such as Natalia Ginzburg, Paolo Volponi, Alberto Abrasino, and Carlo Cassola, and well-known social scientists, such as Gianfranco Pasquino, Laura Balbo, and Gianna Schelotto. Other distinguished figures included movie director Franco Zeffirelli, historian Gaetano Arfe, architect Bruno Zevi, and cardiovascular surgeon Gaetano Azzolina. The world of sport was represented by Gianni Brera, a popular commentator, as well as by Ferruccio Valcareggi, former head coach of the Italian national soccer team.

A name that attracted particular attention among the independent candidates was that of Guido Carli, prestigious economist and a former head of the Bank of Italy and of the Association of Manufacturers (*Confindustria*), who accepted a candidacy for the Christian Democratic party. Carli's move came as a surprise since he had been expected to seek a parliamentary seat as a candidate of the Republican party (PRI). Another choice, one that provoked controversy, was the PR's inclusion on its lists of Antonio Negri, a well-known intellectual and professor at the University of Padua, who was indicted and jailed in 1979 for his alleged role in a number of episodes of terrorism. If elected, Negri would be freed, according to a law granting immunity to members of parliament; at a later stage, a parliamentary committee would decide whether there were grounds for his indictment and incarceration. The decision by PR leader Marco Pannella to co-opt Negri was widely publicized as a protest against the excessive length of preventive incarceration. The Radical party made its point, but the move proved embarrassing later. Negri was elected and took his seat in parliament; but when it became clear that the parliamentary committee in charge would return him to jail, the newly elected PR representative fled abroad and refused to return in spite of Pannella's proddings.

As in previous elections, the central focus of the 1983 campaign was on future governmental alliances. Media headlines and speeches by political leaders gave priority to coalition-related issues over substantive policy questions. To be sure, the themes of the campaign debates included economic policies, international tensions, the deployment in Sicily of the cruise missile, and prospects for reform of governmental institutions. But most of the discussions and speculations of observers revolved around the question whether the "new DC" forged by party secretary Ciriaco De Mita would succeed in halting the ambitious bid by the Socialist party to carve for itself a larger role in the political system. It was the head-on confrontation between De Mita and Socialist leader Bettino Craxi that spiced up the campaign. The PCI occupied a less central position in the debate in 1983 than in previous elections. This marginal position of the PCI makes sense, given the logic of a campaign oriented largely toward future coalitions. Since the Socialists had already excluded, at least in the short run, an alliance with the PCI, the "left-alternative" strategy forged by PCI leadership remained for the moment a purely theoretical scenario devoid of immediate practical applications. PCI efforts to make the deployment of cruise missiles a major theme did not fully succeed, nor did other planks of the party's elaborate platform attract much attention. Moreover, the widely shared view that the PCI was experiencing difficulties gave the impression that the party was no longer as dangerous and formidable a threat as it had been. Anticommunism, though not entirely absent, was not a major theme of the campaign. The PCI could not be entirely ignored by its adversaries, but neither Craxi nor De Mita chose to attack the PCI overtly.

Another theme that was deemphasized in 1983 was the appeal to religious values. Traditionally important, especially in the early postwar period, messages by the Catholic hierarchy urging the voters to support the DC have become less explicit over the years. In 1983 the Conference of Italian Bishops (CEI) issued a mild statement that went largely unnoticed and did not refer to the "unity of Catholics"—the traditional formula through which the church had sought to assist the DC in the past.[3] As Douglas Wertman points out in chapter 3 of this book, the pope's non-Italian background accounts, in part, for the diminished role of the church in those aspects of Italian life not directly related to matters of faith. The softer approach of the bishops could also reflect their realization that in a progressively more secular society, where practicing Catholics are a minority, a hardline approach is not likely to be very fruitful, indeed could possibly be counterproductive. Whatever the reasons, the CEI statement in 1983 emphasized more the duty of Catholics to vote than the direction in which they should vote.

The bishops were not alone in urging the citizens to exercise their right on election day. Similar appeals were made by spokesmen of other organizations. Naturally, all parties (with the already noted exception of the Radicals) were on the forefront of this aspect of the campaign. The concern with turnout levels was reinforced by the well-publicized findings of opinion polls, suggesting that the turnout rate, which had already declined in 1979, was likely to be even lower in 1983. While projections from various polling agencies varied somewhat, most polls estimated that abstentions and nonvalid ballots might reach and perhaps even exceed the 20 percent mark.[4]

Uncertainty as to what the voters would do was heightened when sizable proportions of the people polled preferred not to disclose their voting intentions or the name of the party toward which they were leaning. Many of these voters were registered by the pollsters as likely to abstain or to cast blank ballots. The same problem plagued the experts as they attempted to come up with reliable estimates of the electoral outcome.[5]

Reflecting upon these expectations, intellectuals and observers pointed out that turnout levels, traditionally very high in Italy, had gradually declined over time to the point where the "party of the nonvoters" constituted the third largest bloc of electors. Commentators tended to interpret this trend as a sign of growing disaffection toward political institutions and especially toward the parties.[6] This point of view was fully supported by the findings of survey research.

Two months before the election, a national sample of voters were queried about their feelings toward political leaders, political parties, and other politically relevant social actors. Neither politicians nor parties fared very well. The mean evaluations of parties and leaders on a "feeling thermometer scale" ranging from zero to ten were uniformly below the neutral point. PCI and PRI secretaries Enrico Berlinguer and Giovanni Spadolini fared slightly better than other party secretaries, but they too fell far below the high point set in the popular evaluations of President Sandro Pertini.[7] Feelings toward parties were hardly more positive. In fact, parties received a more negative evaluation than other social "objects," such as the two police corps (*polizia* and *carabinieri*),

Table 2-2 Feelings Expressed by Party Supporters
for Their Party Leaders (percent)

Feelings	Party Leader				
	Berlinguer	Spadolini	Craxi	De Mita	Longo
Very positive	48.3	34.9	21.9	18.7	12.5
Positive	22.3	36.0	24.4	15.9	19.6
Neutral	14.2	14.0	17.6	30.6	19.6
Negative	9.2	9.3	22.5	21.3	32.1
Very negative	6.0	5.8	13.6	13.5	16.2
Number surveyed	(435)	(86)	(279)	(422)	(56)

Source: Computed by the author using data from a Doxa survey conducted in April 1983.

Table 2-3 Trust of Italian Voters in Different Political Systems (percent)

Degree of Trust	Political System							
	West Germany	Sweden	United States	France	Great Britain	Italy	USSR	Poland
A lot	15.8	14.3	13.9	5.1	9.9	5.4	4.9	1.8
Some	52.9	45.9	45.8	47.3	42.6	31.9	17.4	11.9
Little	20.7	24.6	29.1	38.7	35.8	51.6	32.2	36.6
None	10.6	15.2	11.2	8.9	11.7	11.2	45.6	49.7

Source: Computed by the author using data from a Doxa survey conducted in April 1983.

big and small business, and the clergy.[8] These overall scores could have resulted in part from a combination of positive and negative feelings toward the
various parties, reflecting an underlying partisan antagonism. In 1983, however, sympathy for parties appeared low, even among groups of voters inclined
to vote for them.

As the figures of table 2–2 clearly demonstrate, many supporters held
a less than enthusiastic view of their respective party leaders. In particular,
voters leaning toward the DC and the PSDI had very mixed feelings about De
Mita and Pietro Longo. Craxi did only slightly better among likely PSI voters.
Of the leaders of the ruling coalition, only Spadolini was given widespread
approval from PRI supporters. Clearly, the overall negative evaluations discussed earlier were more than just a simple reflection of partisan antagonism.
Certainly there was antagonism, but it involved mostly degrees of negative
feelings.

Another item from the same survey provides additional evidence in favor
of the dissatisfaction thesis. Voters interviewed were asked "how much they
trusted" different political systems. The pattern of answers shows that the
Italian system was ranked last among six Western democracies and barely

ahead of the Soviet and Polish political systems (see table 2–3). Since a number of the people interviewed were unable to rate some of these foreign systems, the findings must be interpreted with a great deal of care. They dovetail quite well, however, with other studies that have documented widespread feelings of unhappiness among the Italian population with various aspects of Italian life.[9]

In brief, as the election approached, the mood of the electorate reflected a mixture of unhappiness and frustration, and in some quarters a considerable amount of indifference. This might very well be another way in which voters distance themselves from a political system about which they do not particularly care. Reported interest in political affairs was lower in Italy in spring 1983 than in practically all other countries of the European community.[10]

The Returns

Fear that Italian voters might desert the polls in large numbers proved to be exaggerated. The anticipated decline in turnout and in percentage of valid votes *did* materialize, but the phenomenon was less pronounced than had been feared. Of 43.9 million registered voters, 89 percent went to the polls, and the overwhelming majority of those cast valid votes. As table 2–4 shows, however, the rate of abstentions, blank ballots, and nonvalid votes over 1979 did increase. Noting that 16 percent of registered electors, or some 8 million people, had failed for one reason or another to cast valid ballots, some observers stressed again that this was the third largest "bloc" of voters after those of the DC and the PCI.[11] It is doubtful, however, that these "no show" voters can be

Table 2-4 Abstentions, Blank Ballots, and Nonvalid Votes, Chamber of Deputies Elections, 1946–1983 (percent of registered voters)

Year	Abstentions	Blank Ballots and Nonvalid Votes	Total
1946	10.9	6.9	17.8
1948	8.7	2.0	10.7
1953	6.1	4.4	10.5
1958	6.3	2.6	8.9
1963	7.1	3.0	10.1
1968	7.3	3.5	10.8
1972	6.8	3.0	9.8
1976	6.7	2.4	9.1
1979	10.0	3.3	13.3
1983	11.0	5.0	16.0

Source: Compiled by the author from official statistics.

Table 2-5 Correlation between 1979 and 1983 Votes
for Various Parties at the Provincial Level

Party	Correlation Coefficient	Party	Correlation Coefficient
PCI	.99	PR	.84
PLI	.95	PSI	.82
PRI	.84	MSI	.96
DC	.97	PSDI	.86

Note: Figures are linear correlation coefficients computed by the author from provincial-level returns published in the press.

called a political bloc. Many of those who failed to show up live in one part of the country and maintain legal residence and registered-voter status in another. Other electors were affected by age, disability, work commitments, and the like. Moreover, in 1983 the election was held at the end of June, after the beginning of the summer vacation; a number of vacationing voters may have failed to return home to cast a ballot.

Nevertheless, political reasons may lie behind the lower rate of participation. A number of voters probably heeded the advice of the PR leader Pannella and chose to invalidate their ballots to express their dissatisfaction. But all of the invalid votes were unlikely to be rooted in dissatisfaction. Nonvoting can also indicate indifference to the game of politics and to the election outcome. The election may not have appeared to some segments of the electorate to be a pivotal one. Whatever the reasons, the gradual downward trend in rates of electoral participation is a phenomenon to reckon with. If the trend continues, turnout rates are likely to become a factor in the future elections.

Detailed examinations of the returns for the different parties are presented in separate chapters of this book together with interpretations as to why certain groups did well and others did poorly. Only some general observations on the results are presented here. Analysis of returns at the provincial level show that changes in party strength in 1983 have not significantly altered the preexisting pattern of vote distribution over the national territory. The correlation between the 1979 and 1983 votes for the various parties over the ninety-four provinces remained as high as it had been in the past (see table 2–5). Thus, at least in terms of electoral geography, no earthquake occurred in 1983. After the election the parties remained strong where they had already enjoyed widespread support and weak where their support had traditionally been limited.

Examination of the patterns of gains and losses for the various parties at the provincial level confirms what is already apparent from the variations in the distribution of the national vote. In most of the provinces too, the major beneficiaries of the losses suffered by the DC were the Italian Social Movement

(MSI) and two of the three small parties of the center, the PRI and the Italian Liberal party (PLI). In the Veneto and Sardinia regions, the Christian Democrats also lost votes in favor of regional parties. In particular, the newly emerged *Liga Veneta* cut heavily into DC support in this region that has traditionally been a DC stronghold. Support for the *Liga* apparently came mostly from disgruntled DC voters, especially in the rural areas.[12] According to some observers, the PSI also gained directly from the decline of the DC.[13] Analysis of the variations in the returns at the provincial level does not, however, support the thesis that a number of former DC voters shifted to the PSI. With the exception of a few southern provinces in which the Socialists apparently did benefit from the erosion of DC support, the gains of the PSI appear to be unrelated to the decline of the DC. Aggregate returns do not, however, provide a good basis for estimating flows of voters to and from the various parties. Moreover, rates of voter turnout or turnover were not built into these estimates, though they must be taken into account since all losses suffered by the DC can hardly be explained by defections of former DC voters.

Between 1979 and 1983, approximately 2 million voters were excluded from the electoral registry because of death or other causes. Assuming that the level of DC support in these cohorts was the same the party enjoyed in the rest of the electorate (38.3 percent in 1979), DC losses due to these cancellations would amount to about 770,000 votes. Analysis of the sociodemographic characteristics of the DC electorate suggests, however, that Christian Democrats were actually overrepresented among the older cohorts, and thus their losses were probably larger, perhaps as high as 1 million votes.

The same data suggest that the DC might have attracted less than its share of the people who had become eligible to vote since 1979, a considerable bloc of 3.7 million potential voters. The distribution of partisan leaning in the various cohorts indicates that the DC might have had difficulties in securing enough of these young people to compensate for attrition among the older cohorts.[14] In this case precise estimates are difficult because the data on the partisan preference of Italian voters leave much to be desired, but available evidence suggests that the problem of replacing voters was a fairly important component of DC losses.

Finally, one cannot ignore the impact of the increased number of abstentions and blank ballots. Some observers have argued that the DC was penalized more than other parties in this respect. That might very well have been the case. Even if the Christian Democrats had only their fair share of abstentions and blank ballots, their losses would still have amounted to some 600,000 votes (or 38.3 percent of the 1.5 million additional nonvalid votes). In summary, two sets of estimates of the causes of DC losses are presented in table 2-6. Estimate A gives more weight to defections of former DC voters to other parties. Estimate B stresses the effects of the turnover factor. Naturally, these

Table 2-6 Two Estimates of the Causes of DC Losses in 1983 (millions of votes)

DC Vote	Estimate A	Estimate B
Electoral base in 1979	14,046	14,046
Vote losses		
Cancellations of voters from the registry	−766	−1,000
Abstentions and nonvalid votes, increased rate of 2.9 percent of surviving DC voters	−385	−378
Vote gains		
Newly eligible voters (38.3 percent of 3.1 million)	+1,190	+777
Shifts to other parties	−1,939	−1,299
Total 1983 vote	12,146	12,146

Source: Estimates compiled by the author from official statistics.

are only conjectures; they do, however, provide some indication of the *range* of votes that the DC could have lost through different channels. Clearly, shifts of voters away from the DC remain an important component of this party's losses, though they were not the only type of loss.

A Changed Electorate?

In the past ten years or so, it has become commonplace for students of Italian politics to state that the foundations of electoral behavior in Italy have changed and that voter choices can no longer be explained by the factors that were important in the early postwar period.[15] Economic development has transformed the country and has directly or indirectly affected many aspects of life. Social modernization has gradually eroded many of the barriers that had earlier insulated voters within their own political subcultures. Increases in education levels and the diffusion of political messages through the media have given the public greater access to the political world and a more direct view of political elites. Secularization has diminished the effect of institutionalized religion and of religious feelings in mass politics. The Communist party has changed in several important respects, and appeals based on visceral anticommunism are no longer automatically successful. The political arena is less polarized than it once was, and the sharp tones of past polemics among elites have been replaced by more urbane political discourse. Given all of this, it could be maintained that with the passing of time voters become progressively less constrained in their choices and more open to the parties' contending appeals. This would eventually increase the proportion of floating voters, of people whose electoral decisions would depend more and more on the political circumstances surrounding an election than on long-term party loyalty, habit, long-standing fear, or visceral preclusions toward certain groups. It could also be argued that this new electoral logic could reduce the significance of traditional divisions and eventually lessen the role of left and right as the central axis of electoral competition.

The surge of the PCI and its partial decline in 1979, the growth of the "intermediate pole," and the emergence of the Radical party have often been cited as evidence to favor this thesis. Until 1983, however, the proponents of this point of view had to contend with the fact that since the election of 1963 the level of support for the DC had remained basically unchanged. How could the argument about change in voter behavior hold in the face of the overall stability of the major Italian party? The decline of the DC in 1983, however, can be invoked as fresh evidence that some basic changes in the nature of electoral choice have occurred. And thus one should ask: to what extent are these claims justified? What does the 1983 election say about voters and the logic of their choices? These are difficult questions, especially given the paucity of data that bear directly on the issue. My impression, based on the available evidence, is that the changes, while real, are not as far-reaching as has been claimed.

To begin with, only modest changes seem to have occurred in the social bases of the various political groups. Although economic and social changes have been profound, their effects on the distribution of party preferences are not greatly evident. By and large, in the early 1980s the characteristics of the various groups of partisans do not differ much from what they were a decade ago or even earlier. A comparison of socioeconomic traits of the electorate and of the various partisan groups, reported in table 2-7, confirms the persistence of long-standing trends.[16]

Similarly, it appears that there have been only slight changes in the distri-

Table 2-7 Socioeconomic Characteristics of Italian Partisans, 1983 (percent)

Characteristic	Party Preference					Total Sample
	PCI	PSI	PSDI-PRI-PLI	DC	MSI	
Male	52.2	52.3	59.5	42.7	66.1	49.3
Residence in communities of fewer than 20,000 inhabitants	38.6	39.4	29.2	50.5	30.7	42.0
Elementary education	61.6	52.4	33.1	60.2	30.6	54.7
Housewife	23.0	20.1	14.7	27.0	8.1	22.6
Retiree	19.5	24.7	24.7	26.8	24.2	21.9
Lower class	53.2	38.4	27.5	46.4	42.0	43.8
Age under 35	38.4	26.1	26.9	26.3	32.3	31.1
Age over 65	11.7	15.4	16.3	21.8	21.0	16.2

Source: Computed by the author using data from a Doxa survey conducted in April 1983.

Table 2-8 Party Choices Considered Acceptable or
Unacceptable by Voter Sample, 1983 (percent)

	Voter Preferences	
Party	"Would Never Vote For"	"Might Consider Voting For"
PDUP-DP	70.1	13.9
PR	71.4	13.5
PCI	43.3	45.0
PSI	34.5	51.4
PSDI	47.7	36.4
PRI	50.1	34.6
DC	36.3	50.9
PLI	59.3	24.5
MSI	75.3	12.0

Source: Computed by the author using data from a Doxa survey conducted in April 1983.

bution of Italian electors on the left-right continuum. When asked to place themselves on a ten-point left-right scale, the sympathizers for the different parties did so in a manner only marginally different from the distribution of the past. Comparison of 1983 data with earlier surveys shows that the mean left-right location of PCI and PSI sympathizers has moved somewhat to the right.[17] While this reduces to some extent the distance between supporters of left-wing and center parties, the change is hardly major. Moreover, left-right self-locations continue as in the past to be a good predictor of feelings of sympathy (or hostility) toward parties and politicians, of evaluations of foreign political systems, and of the voters' positions on various issues. Furthermore, it can be shown that left-right scores differentiate within, as well as across, partisan groups. In short, it seems premature to celebrate the demise of the left-right dimension as the major axis of attitude structure among Italian voters.[18]

The major novelty of the last few years appears to be a lessening of psychological constraints on voter choice. The "political market" in Italy has been recognized for most of the postwar period as a segmented market made up of smaller submarkets within which only some of the parties could compete with a chance of success. Many observers have stressed that in the past voting shifts took place mostly within blocs, with exchanges occurring primarily with parties adjacent to one another on the left-right continuum.[19] Although this is by and large still the case, some recent evidence indicates that the boundaries between blocs might have become more permeable and that, indeed, the blocs might be losing their identity. Two months before the 1983 election, a sample of Italian voters was asked to list the parties for which "they might consider voting" and those for which "they would never vote." The answers to these questions provide some useful indications about the logic of the voters' choices.

Clearly, the market is still considerably segmented. On the average, the voters interviewed ruled out six parties as unacceptable choices, reducing their alternatives to three. A comparison of the figures in the two columns of table 2–8 indicates both the potential reach and limitations of the appeals of the various political groups. On the one hand, the MSI continues to remain anathema to a very large majority of electors, and the market for the smaller groups of the left (PDUP-DP, PR) is also quite limited. On the other hand, the PCI, while still unpalatable to four voters out of ten, is included in the set of viable choices by 45 percent of the electorate. The DC and PSI fared even better, with approximately equal shares of rejections (35 percent) and acceptance (50 percent) rates. As for the smaller centrist parties, even though they are ruled out by half of the electorate, they seem to be more popular than their actual strength would warrant. Clearly, these parties, and the PSI as well, represent for many voters a very popular "second choice."

Analysis of these data confirms that the segmentation of the political market continues to be along the usual left-right continuum. The inclusion or exclusion of parties from the range of acceptable alternatives parallels the voters' self-locations on the political spectrum (see table 2–9). The pattern of answers, in effect, limits the range of segments of the spectrum in which competition is likely to be rewarding for the different parties. The left-right continuum therefore remains the fundamental axis of competition between or

Table 2-9 Range of Acceptable and Unacceptable
Voting Choices on the Left-Right Continuum, 1983

Party	Left 1	2	3	4	5	6	7	8	9	Right 10
PCI	+91	+84	+74	+24	−20	−44	−52	−53	−61	−77
PSI	−11	+33	+56	+64	+17	+11	+ 4	−21	−39	−42
PSDI	− 5	−34	−20	+ 6	+11	+ 6	+11	−22	− 9	−20
PRI	−67	−39	−14	− 1	− 2	− 5	+ 4	− 7	−15	−63
DC	−80	−64	−32	+ 1	+50	+74	+52	+43	+56	+26
PLI	−85	−81	−63	−45	−23	− 8	+ 8	−18	− 3	−26
MSI	−89	−90	−92	−85	−72	−55	−41	− 9	+ 5	+40

Note: Figures indicate the percentage of voters who "might consider" minus the percentage who "rule out" voting for a given party (within each left-right group). Boxed figures outline the areas of the spectrum in which competition is more likely to be rewarding for the various parties.
Source: Computed by the author using data from a Doxa survey conducted in April 1983.

Table 2-10 Size and Direction of Potential Shifts in Voting Choice, 1983

Main Party Preference	Party Shifted to, if Shift Were to Occur						
	Minor Leftist Groups	PCI	PSI	Laici	DC	Other	Total
PCI	24	—	32	30	11	3	100
PSI	13	20	—	43	20	3	100
PRI, PSDI, PLI	11	15	31	—	35	8	100
DC	7	8	20	59	—	6	100

Note: Figures are estimates of direction of shifts based on second-choice party mentioned by the people interviewed. The figures do *not* say anything about the probability of shifting.
Source: Computed by the author using data from a Doxa survey conducted in April 1983.

among parties. In fairly large segments of the continuum, however, several parties can compete with more than a token chance to attract voters, particularly in the heavily populated center-left portion of the spectrum (boxes 3, 4, 5, and 6), which contains over two-thirds of the entire electorate. In this space, the five parties of the center-left coalition, and even the PCI, are mentioned by a large number of voters as possible voting choices. This suggests that the segmentation of the political market, though still in existence, is becoming less rigid than it once was.

The point is made more explicit by an examination of the possible voting choices considered by various groups of voters. Since the primary partisan orientation of these voters is also known, this amounts to asking the following question: In what proportions and in what directions would the voters shift *if* they decided to abandon what appears to be their first choice? The complete answer to this question requires analysis beyond the scope of the chapter, but the gist of it can be summarized as follows. First, the percentage of the voters so strongly identified with a party that they do not even consider any other possible choice is relatively low. Only the PCI and the DC appear to have a sizable body of strong identifiers, but even in the case of these two parties, this core of voters does not exceed one-third of their parties' total electorate. Second, most of the voters are apparently open to two or three secondary choices. Third, most of these choices are oriented toward neighboring parties; they adhere, that is, to the traditional criterion. There are also, however, some nonnegligible potential flows of voters that cut across traditional blocs (table 2-10). In brief, there appears to be a widening of the political market, along with the beginning of a breakdown of the old boundaries. The relative degree of openness of the centrist *laici* (secular) voters toward the PCI, and vice versa, is the most significant aspect of this development. Lack of fully comparable data for earlier times makes it difficult to ascertain precisely how much of a change these patterns really represent. The impression that some change exists is corroborated, however, by other items drawn from the same survey, which reflect the voters' views of the nature of the Communist party and their opinions concerning possible future coalition alignments different from those of the past.[20]

The data reviewed in this chapter suggest that future changes in the behavior of Italian voters are more likely to be general and zigzagging than they are to be abrupt and unidirectional. The potential for change revealed by the data on the voters' second choices is indeed there. But considering a party as a possible alternative is not the same thing as taking the crucial step of making the decision to shift. Second choices are, after all, second choices, and they might never become reality. Long-standing habits are hard to break, even when voters are unhappy with the parties they have chosen in the past. Change may be more likely as the older generations of voters are gradually replaced by younger people who were socialized in a less dramatic period of history, are less affected by the taboos and fears of the past, and are more open to a pragmatic style of politics.

Notes

1   These expressions are from the *Corriere della Sera*, June 28, 1983.
2   Ibid.
3   *Corriere della Sera*, June 5, 1983.
4   See the results of surveys by *Demoskopea* and *Makno*, reported in *L'Espresso*, May 22, 1983.
5   An example of these difficulties is provided by a study carried out by the Doxa Institute in April 1983. Respondents were first asked, "If there were elections tomorrow, for which of the following parties would it be right to vote?" In an attempt to get a sense of the voters' leanings, the following question was asked of those who did not answer the first: "Among the parties included in this list which one has fewer defects, which one is least culpable, which one do you distrust least?" In spite of this probing, which by itself says a lot about the public's mood at the time, over 25 percent of the people interviewed could not be assigned a party preference.
6   For a sample of opinions and comments on this point, see *L'Espresso*, May 22, 1983.
7   The mean scores for the various politicians included in the list evaluated by the voters were as follows: Pertini, 8.1; Berlinguer, 4.2; Spadolini, 4.2; Craxi, 3.8; De Mita, 3.7; Fanfani and Zanone, 3.6; and Longo, 3.5.
8   The mean scores for parties were as follows: PCI, 4.1; PSI and DC, 3.9; PSDI, 3.1; MSI, 2.1. The mean evaluations of other groups were: *carabinieri*, 7.0; *polizia*, 6.9; big business and small industries, 5.8; clergy, 4.9; shopkeepers, 4.5; and unions, 4.0.
9   This dissatisfaction is clear from four surveys of the Eurobarometer Series conducted between October 1981 and April 1983. Italians ranked last in all four surveys in terms of their "satisfaction with the way democracy works." *Eurobarometer*, no. 19 (June 1983): 28.
10   Ibid., 44.
11   *Corriere della Sera*, June 28, 1983.
12   In the entire province of Treviso, for example, the *Liga* (League) received 7.4 percent of the vote, while in the city of Treviso it received only 6.5 percent. Comparable differences were also obtained in the provinces of Padova, Vincenza, and Verona.

13   Maria Weber has estimated that approximately one-fifth of the voters who abandoned the
      DC moved to the PSI. *Sole-24-Ore*, July 19, 1983.

14   According to the information contained in the Doxa survey of April 1983, the DC was
      overrepresented by 11 percentage points among voters sixty-five years of age or older and
      underrepresented by 5 percentage points among voters eighteen to thirty-five years old.

15   This thesis is discussed in a number of works, such as Arturo Parisi, ed., *Mobilita' sensa
      movimento: le elezioni del giugno 1979* (Mobility without movement: The elections of June
      1979) (Bologna: Il Mulino, 1980); Arturo Parisi and Gianfranco Pasquino, eds., *Continuità
      e Mutamento Elettorale in Italia* (Electoral continuity and change in Italy) (Bologna: Il
      Mulino, 1977); Alberto Martinelli and Gianfranco Pasquino, eds., *La Politica nella Italia
      che cambia* (Politics in changing Italy) (Milan: Feltrinelli, 1978); Percy Allum and Renato
      Manheimer, "Electoral Volatility in Italy," 1984, mimeographed.

16   Differences in the criteria of classification make it difficult to compare the 1983 data with
      earlier findings. The general pattern emerging from the table is not, however, very different
      from the one I reported in "The Italian Electorate in the mid-1970s: Beyond Tradition?" in
      Howard R. Penniman, ed., *Italy at the Polls: The Parliamentary Elections of 1976* (Wash-
      ington, D.C.: American Enterprise Institute, 1977), table 3-10, 111.

17   For data on changes in the left-right locations of voters from the late 1960s to the early
      1980s, see Giovanna Guidorossi, *Gli Italiani e la politica* (Italians and politics) (Milan:
      Franco Angeli, 1984), especially table 3.1, 107; similar data are also presented in Ivo H.
      Daalder, "The Italian Party System in Transition: The End of Polarized Pluralism?" in
      West European Politics 6 (July 3, 1983): 227.

18   For a concurring view on the continuing importance of the left-right dimension, see Guiliano
      Urbani and Maria Weber, *Cosa pensano gli operai* (What workers think) (Milan: Franco
      Angeli, 1984), especially p. 72.

19   See Allum and Manheimer, "Electoral Volatility in Italy," and other works cited there.

20   Between 1976 and 1982 the percentage of voters who believe that the PCI is different from
      the Communist parties of other countries has increased by some 17 percentage points. This
      changing view is shared by Socialist, Christian Democratic, and centrist voters. See Guido-
      rossi, *Gli Italiani e la politica*, especially pp. 122, 133.

3 The Christian Democrats: The Big Losers

DOUGLAS A. WERTMAN

————The Christian Democratic party (DC), which for thirty-eight years had been the major government force in Italy, was the big loser in the 1983 parliamentary elections, and its losses were much larger than expected. In the five national elections from 1963 through 1979 the DC lost in some regions while gaining in others, maintaining an incredible degree of electoral stability in the country as a whole; it varied between 38.3 percent and 39.1 percent. In 1983 the polls and virtually all observers and political leaders predicted only limited change once again for the DC: at most a loss of 1 or 2 percentage points. Instead, the DC lost more than 5 percentage points in these elections and reached a historic low of 32.9 percent. Why this occurred is the major question of the election and the primary focus of this chapter.

The DC's Role after 1974

The first shocks to the DC's dominance of the Italian political system came in the 1974–75 period.[1] In May 1974 the Catholic church's (and the DC's) position against the divorce law was defeated by a wide margin in a referendum. In June 1975 the combination of DC losses and sizable Communist gains in the regional and provincial elections narrowed what had been a gap of more than 10 percentage points between these two parties to less than 2 percentage points. In 1976 and 1979, however, the DC was able to overcome this first crisis period—or, more accurately, to postpone the effects of the party's problems on its vote in national elections. In the 1976 parliamentary elections the DC, aided primarily by the fear that the Communist party (PCI) would pass the DC to

The views expressed herein are those of the author and do not necessarily represent the views of the United States Information Agency or the United States government. I would like to thank Jim Marshall for his comments on much of this manuscript.

become Italy's largest party, won the same 38.7 percent it had received in the 1972 parliamentary elections. In 1979 the DC won 38.4 percent, while the Communists, after thirty years of gains in national elections, fell 4 percentage points to 34.4 percent, solidifying the position of the DC as the largest party.

The DC has remained the most important and powerful government party since 1974. Despite the victory in 1976, however, and the stability in 1979 (though somewhat disappointing given the expectation that the DC would make gains), the DC's dominance in the Italian political system was no longer as firm after the 1974–75 period as during the previous thirty years.

In early 1976, following the 1974 divorce referendum and the left's gains in the 1975 regional elections, the center-left formula, which had governed Italy for most of the period between 1963 and 1976, entered a period of crisis. The Socialist party (PSI) withdrew its support from the center-left formula, and this led to early elections and to a period of almost four years in which no stable majority existed. Between mid-1976 and early 1979, the answer to this lack of a political majority was the "national solidarity" strategy. All cabinet positions were held by Christian Democrats, but, for the first time since 1947, the Communist party, together with the DC, the Socialists, and a few smaller parties, was associated with the government majority. The DC-PCI confrontation in late 1978–early 1979 came after the PCI, whose electorate and rank and file were increasingly restive with this arrangement, was again refused seats in the cabinet. This conflict, combined with the 1979 election results and the changes in the political strategies of the Christian Democrats, the Communists, and the Socialists, ended the "national solidarity" phase and led to one in which a new form of the center-left formula was instituted.

A new center-left has existed since 1980. In June 1981 it became the five-party (pentapartito) coalition composed of the Christian Democrats, the Socialists, and the three small lay parties, the Republicans, Social Democrats, and the Liberals (who were not in the original center-left). The DC, while retaining much of its power, has not however, dominated the political system as it did before 1974. There were a number of important indications that the DC's role in the Italian political system had changed somewhat even prior to the 1983 elections. First, in 1979 Republican Ugo La Malfa and Socialist Bettino Craxi were the only non-DC leaders since 1945 to be given the chance even to try to form a government, though both were unsuccessful. Second, in the Forlani government formed in October 1980, the Christian Democrats, though representing two-thirds of the government's parliamentary strength, accepted equality in the number of cabinet seats between themselves and the other government parties combined for the first time. Finally and most importantly, in June 1981, after holding the prime ministership for thirty-nine successive governments since December 1945, the Christian Democrats agreed to support someone other than a Christian Democrat, specifically Republican Giovanni Spadolini, as prime minister.

The DC between 1979 and 1983

The major questions about the DC in the period between the 1979 and 1983 elections are its relations to other parties, especially the Communists and the Socialists; the pressures for reform of the DC itself; and the nature of Ciriaco De Mita's year as party secretary between his election in May 1982 and the parliamentary elections of 1983.

The DC's Relationship to Other Parties   Between 1976 and 1980 the dominant question in the DC's political strategy was its relationship to the Communist party and what role in the majority or the government the PCI might have. During both the 1976 and 1979 election campaigns, the DC's major theme was anticommunism. "In 1976 it had been the fear of the Communists' passing the DC to become the largest party; in 1979 the DC tried to make the election as much as possible into a referendum on its opposition to Communist entry into the Government together with the DC."[2]

The 1980 DC National Party Congress was divided primarily over the party's approach to the Communists, with the DC's relationship to the Socialist party an important, though secondary, consideration and largely a function of the DC's strategy toward the PCI. The final document approved by the DC National Congress marked a defeat for the political strategy of outgoing party secretary Benigno Zaccagnini and the late Aldo Moro. This pro-Zaccagnini minority, which included ex-Prime Minister Giulio Andreotti's faction, wanted to make an effort to continue the "national solidarity" policy through some cautious opening to the Communist party, first over policies and then possibly over government formulas. The 57 percent majority, however, consisting of the factions led by Amintore Fanfani, Arnaldo Forlani, Flaminio Piccoli, Antonio Bisaglia, Carlo Donat Cattin, Emilio Colombo, and Mariano Rumor, included a "preamble" in the final resolution of the congress that, in effect, rejected further cooperation with the PCI. The primary points of this preamble were: (1) while not criticizing the political strategy followed by the DC between 1976 and 1979, it excluded any opening to or "co-responsibility" with the Communist party; and (2) the emphasis was to be on government with the Socialists and the small centrist parties.[3]

This preamble was aimed primarily at the Communist party, but one result of it was to increase emphasis on the development of DC-Socialist relations. Two additional factors are important in the shift that occurred between 1980 and 1982 as the DC-Socialist rivalry replaced DC-Communist relations as the center of attention: (1) the increased assertiveness by the Socialist party and its reentry in the cabinet; and (2) the weakened position of the PCI and its movement away from the "historic compromise" strategy toward an "alternative of the left" strategy.

In April 1980 with the formation of Francesco Cossiga's second government, the Socialist party reentered the cabinet for the first time since early 1976. The Socialists and the Christian Democrats remained together in this and four subsequent governments (Forlani's from October 1980 to June 1981, two led by Spadolini from June 1981 to November 1982, and the Fanfani government formed in December 1982) leading up to the 1983 elections. All but one of the government crises in this period were brought about by the Socialists, who were anxious, especially after their successes in the 1980, 1981, and 1982 local elections, to have early parliamentary elections in which they hoped to be the major winners. Craxi's assertiveness toward the Christian Democrats, aimed at strengthening the PSI's electoral performance as well as its share of national and local power and, ultimately, at gaining the prime ministership, considerably exacerbated DC-PSI relations and also made the Socialists the major threat to the DC.

In addition, the DC's concern about the Communist party diminished significantly following the PCI's poor showing in the 1979 parliamentary elections and in the local elections between 1980 and 1982. A weakened PCI whose leadership often appeared drifting and uncertain in both its domestic and foreign policies was not the kind of threat to the DC that it had been in the second half of the 1970s. On the domestic side, the PCI's political strategy, though moving toward the "alternative of the left," was ambiguous and did not have the necessary support to be a realistic option. On the international side, even though PCI-Soviet relations became more tense as a result of the Soviet invasion of Afghanistan and, in particular, the imposition of martial law in Poland, these events and other foreign policy questions such as the deployment of cruise missiles further complicated the PCI's position in Italy by bringing renewed attention to the question of PCI-Soviet relations.

For these reasons, by the time of the DC National Party Congress in May 1982, the central issue was the style of the DC's relationship with the Socialist party.[4] The conflict, which became personalized at the congress in the contest for party secretary between Arnaldo Forlani and Ciriaco De Mita, was basically over how assertive the DC should be toward Craxi's PSI. De Mita was considered a much more dynamic and combative individual than Forlani, and he also took a more hardline position toward the PSI. In a speech at the congress, De Mita said that the Socialist party should not "imagine that it will be dealing with an acquiescent DC."[5] De Mita's victory indicated a choice by a majority at the DC congress for a tougher stance toward the Socialist party. His supporters, who won about two-thirds of the seats in the DC's National

Council, consisted of two broad groups: (1) the coalition of pro-Zaccagnini factions on the party's left, including De Mita's *Base*; and (2) the swing group at the congress, composed of the factions of three long-time leaders of the party, Giulio Andreotti, Flaminio Piccoli, and Amintore Fanfani (who abandoned Forlani after the two had been together in the same faction for twenty-five years). The strengths of individual factions at the congress had changed very little since 1980, but a realignment in alliances took place that resulted in a new majority within the DC as well as the splitting apart of two of the most long-standing factions: the *Fanfaniani* (between Fanfani and Forlani) and the *Dorotei* (between Piccoli and Bisaglia).

Reform Within the DC By 1975 the Italian public's view of the DC had considerably deteriorated, primarily as a result of the wear and tear on the DC's image from its thirty years in power.[6] By the mid-1970s the DC was widely perceived as a deeply divided and corrupt party that was ineffective in dealing with Italy's problems and was largely interested only in retaining its hold on power. The intense factionalism within the DC and the lack of turnover in the party's top leadership group furthered the image of a party unwilling and unable to reform itself.[7] The 1975 regional elections, the first major elections in which the growing dissatisfaction with the DC became manifest, made the question of party reform a central concern within the DC, especially because of its electoral implications.

Following the DC losses in these 1975 regional elections Benigno Zaccagnini, long a leader in the DC but widely seen as sincerely interested in reforming it, was chosen to replace Amintore Fanfani as party secretary. Zaccagnini was reelected by a narrow margin at the March 1976 DC congress, which was proclaimed as the congress of *refondazione* ("refounding") of the DC. Zaccagnini was chosen to give the DC a new image at a time of crisis, and his picture, together with the theme of the "new DC," appeared prominently in the 1976 DC campaign.[8] Zaccagnini remained DC party secretary for almost five years, from mid-1975 until early 1980. His genuine efforts to end the divisiveness of faction and to bring about fundamental change in the DC generated considerable enthusiasm within the DC's rank and file, but Zaccagnini's attempts to reform the DC ultimately failed.

The theme of reform of the party, therefore, continued to be a central issue in the DC. Though political strategy toward the Communists and the Socialists was the dominant concern of DC leaders in the late 1970s and early 1980s, the internal pressures for reform of the party organization did not go away. Strong attacks on the factional system of power within the DC and expressions of a desire for "refounding" of the DC continued to come from the party's rank and file, from some of the younger DC members of parliament of all factions, and from organizations and individuals within the Catholic world.

Both lay Catholic intellectuals and some clergy, most prominently Bartolomeo Sorge, the editor of the Italian Jesuit journal *La Civiltà Cattolica*, spoke out about the urgent need for the DC to reform itself if it wanted to regain the confidence of and maintain the electoral support of the Catholic subculture.[9]

This widespread dissatisfaction, combined with the DC's giving up the prime ministership in June 1981 after thirty-six years, and the critical, worsening weakness of the DC in Italy's urban areas, created pressures that led to the DC National Assembly in November 1981. Party leaders, party members, and, in the real innovation, the so-called *esterni*, or "outsiders," participated in this four-day meeting to discuss in public the "revitalization" of the DC. These *esterni* included well-known Catholic intellectuals as well as members and leaders of many organizations in the Catholic subculture. This meeting supported a number of changes in the party's rules, the most important being the direct election of the party secretary at the party congress and the reservation of 10 percent of the votes at the party congress for the *esterni*.[10] Though many of the top DC leaders very reluctantly accepted the idea of direct election of the secretary, the assembly's proposals were adopted by the DC National Council in January 1982 for use at the DC congress of May 1982.[11] Neither this assembly nor the participation of the *esterni* at the DC party congress, however, brought about significant changes in the way decisions were made within the DC.[12] In fact, De Mita's election was largely the result of behind-the-scenes maneuvering by three individuals—Andreotti, Fanfani, and Piccoli—who had been top factional and party leaders in the DC for twenty-five years or more.

De Mita as Party Secretary   In the year between his election as secretary at the May 1982 congress and the parliamentary elections in June 1983, Ciriaco De Mita was an activist leader who took a number of important and sometimes controversial initiatives aimed at putting the DC on the offensive again, especially against the Socialists, and at reasserting the DC's "centrality" in the political system. He wanted to give the DC a more aggressive image and overcome any sense that the DC's policies and strategies were only a reaction to the ideas and initiatives of other parties.

Consequently, the 1982–83 period was marked by continuing, intense polemics between the DC and the PSI. Conflicts persisted over the stability of governments and whether to hold early elections, over governmental policy and power at the national level, over Socialist participation in local government alliances with the left where a center-left coalition was also possible, and over De Mita's definition of Italy's two largest parties, the DC and the PCI, as the alternatives for governing Italy.

In speeches and interviews in 1982 and 1983, De Mita developed his ideas on the role of the PCI and the DC in Italy's political system. He said that the lay parties, including the PSI, must choose between the two major parties in Italy, who, because of their natures, could not govern together. A major purpose, undoubtedly, of De Mita's espousal of the bipolarism of the Italian political system was to undercut Craxi's effort to establish the central role for the Socialists in Italy. Probably even more important, the leader of the DC was talking about the PCI in a way different from any other DC secretary. De Mita in effect was saying that there were no longer any ideological preconditions against PCI participation in the government. De Mita added, however, that though the PCI should not be excluded from the government on ideological grounds, it was not yet ready to be a party of government. The PCI, he argued, lacked a culture of government (the disposition to govern and to enact concrete policies) and, therefore, the only real choice for the four lay parties was to continue the center-left with the DC.

De Mita's role as secretary should not be seen only in terms of the DC's relations with the PCI, the PSI, and the small lay parties. His efforts also focused on rebuilding the image of the DC as an honest party that was ready to propose and enact concrete solutions to the problems of Italy in the 1980s. He hoped to do this, and possibly to gain new sources of support for his party, through: (1) giving the DC a more coherent economic policy by espousing fundamental reform of the welfare state and economic austerity to attack Italy's huge budget deficit and its double-digit inflation; and (2) creating a "new DC" through rebuilding the party organization, most urgently in Italy's major cities, limiting the role of the factions, and, in the election campaign, replacing some DC incumbents with *esterni*. De Mita's style and many of his methods may have been different from those employed by Benigno Zaccagnini when he tried to build a "new DC" in the aftermath of its 1974–75 crisis. Nevertheless, there is clearly a strong parallel between these two attempts.

One aspect of De Mita's program was his effort to reach out to the industrialists and to the "emerging" middle classes, that is, the managerial, technocratic, middle class. De Mita talked frequently in 1982 and 1983 about the need to reform the liberal democratic state and to have a more "rigorous" economic policy. He spoke, for example, of attacking built-in inflationary aspects of government spending, such as "automatic spending mechanisms" in social welfare programs, or of strengthening private competition in areas such as health care.[13] De Mita's close ally, Giovanni Goria, whom De Mita was able to install in late 1982 as treasury minister, expressed sympathy for some controversial positions held by *Confindustria*, the association of private industry, on issues such as slowing down the effects of Italy's wage indexation system.

De Mita's repeated call for economic discipline (*rigore*) did win him some applause from Italy's industrialists, but it also sparked some conflict within the DC over whether De Mita was changing the "popular" (and interclassist) nature of the DC appeal to a more conservative one. The fear of some DC leaders was that the DC, which has always combated the efforts of others to portray it as a traditional conservative party, would be tagged with an image that would undercut parts of its electoral base. The DC in fact has maintained its position in Italy in part by avoiding clear choices and serving as a mediator among social groups. In other words, the concern was whether De Mita was trying to give a too clearly defined economic policy to a party that had always done well with a "mushy" economic policy.

De Mita's efforts at building the image of a "new DC" were aimed not only at industrialists and managers, but also toward reforming the DC's organization and overcoming the effects of factionalism. Among the actions he took were: (1) putting professionals into some important positions in the party and in the public corporations;[14] (2) beginning a campaign to restructure the party's organization where the DC is weakest, that is, in the major metropolitan areas such as Turin, Milan, Rome, Naples, Bari, Palermo, Bologna, and Florence;[15] and (3) replacing a significant number of incumbents with prestigious independents during the selection of candidates for the 1983 elections.

De Mita, in other words, did more than talk about reform. He met considerable resistance to some of his initiatives, however, and he did not have sufficient time before the election to carry through fully on these efforts. Real change in a complex organization like the DC, especially one with a long-entrenched leadership class, cannot be brought about in a short time. Some first steps were taken, but De Mita's claims of overcoming the excesses of factionalism and creating a "new DC" were clearly exaggerated. For example, in the formation of both the Fanfani government in late 1982 and the Craxi government in mid-1983, the DC positions in the government were divided among the party factions in about the same way—in relation to their percentage at the preceding party congress—that has long been true, and this was accompanied by the same kind of in-fighting among factions.

The DC and the Election Campaign

The question of future governmental alliances and the rivalry between the DC and the PSI dominated the newspaper headlines and the speeches of political leaders in the 1983 campaign. Of secondary importance was the debate over future economic policy. Despite the efforts of the Communist party to make the cruise missile deployment a major issue, this and other foreign policy questions were nonstarters during the campaign. Of special concern to the DC were: (1) a DC campaign that continued the themes of De Mita's first year as party secretary; (2) the importance given to nominating prestigious "outsiders" as DC candidates; and (3) as in 1979, the lack of strong church support for the DC.

Campaign Themes The major themes of the DC election campaign were largely the same ones that dominated De Mita's year as secretary prior to the campaign: the Christian Democratic–Socialist polemics, the emphasis on economic austerity, and the "new DC." This was a major departure from the 1976 and 1979 campaigns in which anticommunism was the dominant DC theme.[16] Unlike in these previous campaigns, in 1983 the PSI, not the PCI, was the DC's principal target. This was not surprising after a year of almost constant conflict between the DC and the PSI following De Mita's election, which was meant to be a clear signal of DC readiness to assert itself against a PSI that was in ascendance between 1980 and 1982. De Mita's approach to the PSI during the campaign, while generally approved within the DC, was by no means supported unanimously; some DC leaders, including then foreign minister Emilio Colombo, criticized De Mita for the intensity of his attacks on the PSI and for, thereby, drawing attention away from the DC's traditional anti-Communist appeal.

The most important DC-PSI polemics during the campaign were over future governmental alliances.[17] The DC, supported to a certain extent by the Republicans, Liberals, and Social Democrats, consistently pressured Craxi to indicate what kind of postelection government coalition the PSI preferred. Near the end of the campaign, when Craxi finally did make a proposal for a three-year postelection pact among the parties of the center-left, De Mita criticized this proposal as still leaving many doubts, such as why Craxi wanted a three-year alliance when a parliament is elected for five years.[18]

In this debate over alliances, some in the DC supported the idea of a neocentrist coalition including the DC and the three small centrist parties but excluding the PSI, and some in the PSI preferred the PCI's proposal of an alternative of the left including the PSI but excluding the DC. Both the DC and the PSI used these proposals during the campaign in an attempt to put the other party on the defensive. It was clear throughout the campaign, however, that: (1) most of the top leaders in the DC and the PSI did not favor these proposals; and (2) neither a neocentrist coalition nor the alternative of the left was likely to have a solid majority after the election.

DC Candidate Selection The other major strand of the DC campaign was the DC's "new course," with De Mita asking support for the "new DC" based on its courage in calling for economic austerity and in undertaking reform of the party itself. Central to this appeal was the DC's selection of candidates, both in dropping some incumbents and in adding new faces.

The "new DC" theme played a role in the 1976 campaign, when Benigno Zaccagnini's face and the slogan "the new DC has already begun" were prominently featured on the DC's posters. In 1979, when the crisis of the DC seemed to have passed, this was not a central theme. By 1983, however, it was again a major focus. Directly related to this, the DC's candidate selection was a central issue in 1976 and in 1983, but not in 1979. In fact, 1976 and 1983 stand out as the two elections out of the nine parliamentary elections since 1948 in which the largest number of DC incumbents were refused renomination. While between 1948 and 1972 only 10 percent or fewer of the DC incumbent deputies and senators were not renominated and in 1979 only 6 percent were not renominated, in 1976 and 1983 more than 20 percent were not renominated.[19]

This large turnover in the 1983 DC candidate lists was a direct effort to further the image of a "new DC" and was a result of De Mita's attempt to revitalize the party. As usual, the DC National Executive Committee met in virtually continual session for nearly a week to finalize the candidate lists.[20] The major emphasis was put on "operation *esterni*," that is, adding to the DC lists a considerable number of prestigious "outsiders," especially prominent Catholic intellectuals, leaders of organizations from the Catholic subculture, and, to build DC credibility among industrialists and managers in parallel to the DC's election program calling for economic austerity, representatives of the business community. A primary means for doing this was through nominating "outsiders" in more than thirty "safe" DC senatorial seats, especially in large cities such as Rome, Milan, Turin, and Naples to build the DC's image where the party's social presence is weakest. For example, several DC cabinet members and other incumbent senators were moved from safe seats in Rome to safe seats elsewhere in Italy and were replaced in the Rome districts by prominent independents. While there were many refusals, the DC was able to bring a number of prominent independents from both the church and business worlds on to its candidate lists. The most publicized DC success was Guido Carli, ex-president of both the Bank of Italy and *Confindustria* and long sought by several parties as a parliamentary candidate.

The Church in the 1983 Campaign   In contrast to its strong and open support for the DC in the 1940s and 1950s and again in 1976, the church expressed lukewarm and indirect support of the DC in 1979 and 1983.[21] Pope John Paul II, as a non-Italian and, probably as important, a Pole, has been much less interested in Italian politics than his postwar predecessors, and this was abundantly clear in 1983. He was willing to involve himself deeply in the 1981 referendum on abortion because this is a social issue of great concern to the church, but he was unwilling to intervene in the 1979 or 1983 election campaigns in support of the DC. The DC's loss in 1983 caused some concern in the Vatican, but it did not create the great consternation there that it would have under previous popes or that the loss in the abortion referendum did.

As it had done prior to every other parliamentary election, the Italian Bishops' Conference issued a statement to Catholics about the 1983 elections.

This statement, like the one in 1979, did not include the traditional pro-DC phrase calling for the "unity of Catholics." In response to the widely expressed concern that many voters would abstain, the bishops first said that it was the duty of Catholics to do their part in promoting the "common good" by voting in the elections. This communique then, in commenting on what should guide Catholics in their choice of party, made at most only an oblique statement of support for the DC by asking that: "believers in Christ and in His Word must find in their faith the criteria for the formation of their conscience as Christian voters and in their evaluation of which men and programs to choose."[22] Unlike the widespread criticism in 1981 about the deep involvement by the pope and the church in the abortion referendum, the 1983 preelection statement by the bishops aroused little press comment or political controversy.

The Election Results

The big DC loss was the surprise of the 1983 elections. Nearly every expert and political leader expected the DC to remain at about the same level as in 1979 or to fall at most 1 or 2 percentage points. Similarly, all polls taken during the campaign predicted between about 36 and 38.5 percent for the DC.[23] Contrary to this virtually unanimous expectation of minimal change, the DC was the big loser of 1983 when its share of the votes dropped to an all-time low of 32.9 percent.

The DC's biggest losses were in the largest cities in both northern and southern Italy, in its traditional Catholic stronghold of the Veneto, and in a number of southern provinces, including Bari, Messina, and Reggio Calabria. The central feature of the DC losses, however, is that they were spread virtually across the entire country with only moderate variation in the size of losses from one area to another. With the exception of the four provinces in the two small southern regions of Molise and Basilicata, the DC lost in every province in the country. In eighty-five of the ninety-five provinces, the DC lost more than 3 percentage points. And in fifty-eight out of ninety-five the losses were between 4 and 7 percentage points, or within only 1.5 percentage points above or below the overall national result.

In the 1979 election, and to a lesser extent in the previous elections in the 1970s, the DC remained at the same level in Italy as a whole, compensating for losses in some parts of the country, especially the northwestern industrial triangle, with gains in most parts of southern Italy. This "southernization" trend did *not* continue in 1983. The relative dependence of the DC on different parts of Italy changed in only a limited way in 1983. For example, the DC lost more heavily in the Veneto, but the Veneto remains one of the DC strongholds.

No single party was the recipient of all or even most of the DC's losses.[24] Rather, there was apparently a substantial fragmentation, with the DC losses probably going to at least eight other parties. Some of these parties gained votes from the DC in most parts of Italy, while others took votes from the DC in only limited areas of the country. Likely recipients of DC losses throughout much of Italy, though in varying degrees in different parts of the country, were the Republicans (PRI), who gained 2.1 percentage points over 1979; the Liberals (PLI), who gained 1.0 percentage point; and the neo-Fascist MSI, who gained 1.5 percentage points. In addition, the *Partito dei Pensionati* (Pensioners' party) probably took votes from the DC in most parts of Italy. Running in its first election, the Pensioners' party won 1.4 percent of the vote but won no seats because its support was too evenly dispersed throughout the country.[25] More localized winners at the DC's expense include the regional parties in the Veneto and Sardinia, and, in some areas of the South, the Socialist party and the Social Democratic party. Finally, the DC may have lost more than its proportionate share from abstentions and spoiled and blank ballots.[26]

Regional Patterns   In much of Italy, including most of the Northwest, the Red Belt, large parts of the South, and much of the islands of Sicily and Sardinia, DC losses were either at or near the national average. DC results were most uneven in the South. While there is variation in the DC losses around the country, there are a number of clear patterns in different parts of Italy.

In the Northwest (Lombardy, Piedmont, and Liguria), DC losses in the nineteen provinces ranged from 3.6 to 7.4 percentage points, all within 2 percentage points of the national average. It appears that much of the DC losses went to the PRI, the PLI, and the MSI. In all but two of the nineteen provinces and in about 80 percent of the senatorial districts, the combined gains of these three parties were about equal to or greater than the losses of the DC. Furthermore, there is a fairly consistent relationship between the size of DC losses and the total of combined PRI-PLI-MSI gains. With only a few exceptions, PRI gains were between 2 and 4 percentage points, PLI gains were around 1 percentage point, and MSI gains were between 1 and 2 percentage points. Patterns in Friuli and Trentino Alto-Adige were roughly the same as those in the Northwest.

While voting patterns in the Veneto in northeastern Italy and the island of Sardinia differed somewhat, these two regions share an important characteristic: A regional party was the major winner and undoubtedly the recipient of a substantial portion of the DC losses. In the Veneto, combined PRI-PLI-MSI gains varied little from one province to the next or from one senatorial district to another and averaged about 4 percentage points. DC losses, however, which were in the range of at least 7 to 8 percentage points in much of the Veneto, were considerably larger. A sizable number of ex-DC voters apparently went to the Veneto's regional party, the *Liga Veneta* (Veneto League), which won about 4 percent of the vote in Veneto while contesting its first parliamentary election.[27] In Sardinia, combined PRI-PLI-MSI gains totaled only a little more than 1 percentage point, considerably below both their national average and the DC losses of 6.4 percentage points in Sardinia. In addition, the left as a whole lost a few percentage points. A substantial majority of these votes lost by both the DC and the left clearly went to the *Partito Sardo d'Azione* (Sardinian Party of Action), which jumped from 1.9 to 9.5 percent.

In most of the Red Belt (the regions of Emilia-Romagna, Tuscany, Umbria, and the Marches), DC losses were at or a little below the national average. In Emilia-Romagna the pattern was similar to that of the Northwest, with combined PRI-PLI-MSI gains, though generally a little smaller than those in the Northwest, close to the total of DC losses. In the other regions, combined PRI-PLI-MSI gains totaled 2 to 3 percentage points in most provinces, ranging from 1 to 2 percentage points less than DC losses in most cases, with some DC losses apparently dispersed among a number of other parties, including the Pensioners' party.

In Sicily and the continental south, where the DC gained in nearly every province in 1979, there was no single consistent pattern in 1983. Of the thirty-five provinces, the DC result was more than 1 percentage point better than the national average in fourteen, within 1 percentage point in thirteen, and more than 1 percentage point worse in eight. The parties that profitted most from DC losses differed substantially from one province or senatorial district to another in the South, but, depending on the province, included the MSI, the Socialists, the Pensioners' party (PNP), and the three centrist lay parties, the Republicans, the Liberals, and the Social Democrats (PSDI). Compared to 1979, the MSI gained 1 percentage point or more in twenty-two of thirty-five southern provinces (2 percentage points or more in twelve of the twenty-two), the PSDI gained 1 percentage point or more in sixteen, the PRI in eleven, and the PLI in eight. None of these parties lost support in more than a handful of the southern provinces.

The Socialists did much better in the South than elsewhere, winning more votes in virtually every southern province and gaining 3 percentage points or more in half of them. The PSI may have taken a small number of votes from the DC in most southern provinces, but the bulk of the PSI gains undoubtedly came at the expense of the Radicals and other parties on the left. Analysis of voting patterns in each southern province and senatorial district, however, suggests that the PSI had more significant gains at the expense of the DC in about a quarter of the southern provinces, particularly in much of Sicily and Puglia.[28] The Social Democrats, who lost or remained stable in nearly every province north of Rome, gained 1 percentage point or more in about half of the provinces of the South, concentrated in the regions of Puglia, Calabria, and Campania. Though the MSI gained 1 percentage point or more in two-thirds of the southern provinces, its results varied from gains of as much as 3 to 4 percentage points in some areas to only small gains or even small losses in others. The Republican and Liberal results also varied substantially across the South.[29]

The DC in the Largest Cities   In 1979 the DC won 31.3 percent in the ten largest cities, compared to 39.9 in the rest of Italy. In 1983 the gap widened even further to fully 10 percentage points: in the ten largest cities the DC lost 6.6 percentage points to fall to 24.7 percent, while in the rest of Italy the DC lost 5.2 percentage points to fall to 34.7 percent.[30] The DC's weakness in many of Italy's largest cities has progressively worsened since the DC losses in the 1975 local elections, and 1983 only made the situation even more acute. De Mita's first efforts to adapt the DC's party structure to social realities in Italy's large cities, efforts which were frequently resisted, did not have enough time or support to make a difference.

As with the rest of Italy, the parties that profited most from DC losses varied from city to city. In Milan and Turin, combined PRI-PLI-MSI gains were larger than DC losses. The Republicans alone increased their share by 6.9 percentage points in Milan and 4.7 percentage points in Turin. The PRI also gained most in Genoa, Bologna, and Florence. The gainers in some other large cities were the MSI in Naples, the Socialists in Bari, and the *Liga Veneta* in Venice.

The Bases of DC Support

Surveys done in Italy over the past ten years, including a survey three months before the 1983 election and one a few weeks after, suggest that, apart from the continuing shift of the DC electorate away from the large urban areas discussed above, there has been in recent years, including 1983, neither a significant change in the characteristics of DC supporters nor a more accentuated dependence of the DC on any particular social group. In other words, the DC losses appear to be broadly spread across most groups in Italian society rather than coming to a markedly disproportionate degree from any single social group. The DC electorate remains predominantly religious and female, and the DC continues to be stronger among older rather than younger voters and among rural and small town voters than among urban voters, especially those in the largest cities. While the evidence on social class is not sufficient to examine changes in the degree of DC support among an important subgroup, such as urban, northwestern, middle-class voters, in which the DC may have lost more heavily than average, nationwide the pattern of support for the DC among different occupational groups appears to have altered relatively little in recent years.[31]

Despite the continuing secularization in Italian society and the church's more limited commitment to the DC, a majority of DC voters are regular church attenders. The DC remains the only party with a predominantly religious electorate. A March 1983 Doxa survey found that, similar to the results of other surveys over the past fifteen years, 62 percent of DC voters said they attend church regularly (51 percent every week or almost every week and 11 percent two to three times a month), while only 26 percent of non-DC voters (18 percent and 8 percent, respectively) did so. In fact, regular churchgoers make up a small minority of the supporters of any other Italian party. Furthermore, not only does the DC electorate remain predominantly religious, but the DC, in 1983 as earlier, also continues to be the party of a substantial majority of those who attend church weekly or almost every week: 67 percent of weekly church attenders voted for the DC in 1975, 70 percent in 1980, and 63 percent in March 1983.[32]

Closely related to this religious base, the DC also remains the *only* party with a predominantly female electorate. This has been true throughout the DC's history; surveys since 1948 always show that about 60 percent of the DC electorate were women. In the many surveys published over the past ten years, the DC's electorate has consistently been between 59 and 62 percent women. In March 1983, 60 percent of DC voters were women, and in July 1983, 59 percent were.[33]

In 1983, in very similar proportions to other surveys of the past decade, the DC:

- remains weakest among voters aged eighteen to thirty-four and strongest among voters aged fifty and older, in particular those aged sixty-five and older (in a July 1983 survey, among those giving a party preference, the DC gained 49 percent of those sixty-five and older, but only 24 percent of those twenty-five to thirty-four and 28 percent of those eighteen to twenty-four); and
- continues to be considerably stronger among farmers, somewhat weaker than average among the working class, and near its average among most other occupational groupings, including professionals, executives, and white collar workers.

Why the DC Losses?

The size of the DC's losses was the biggest surprise of the 1983 elections. The surprise was not that the DC lost some support. In fact, despite its remarkable electoral stability nationwide in the 1960s and 1970s, many have hypothesized, especially since the mid-1970s, that the DC would gradually lose due to long-term trends such as secularization of the society, depolarization of the political system, and generational change. The surprise was that the DC lost so much all at once.

Major Factors in the DC *Losses*   Why then did the DC lose heavily in the 1983 elections? The answer to this question is elusive. No survey or electoral data gives us an exact answer, and certainly no single factor explains all the DC losses.[34] This question has been the source of much debate within the DC itself following the election and prior to the DC National Congress in early 1984. In this debate, De Mita and his supporters have argued that the loss was primarily the result of the DC's loss of credibility from its "long years" in power. By contrast, De Mita's opponents place much of the blame for the DC losses on De Mita's year as party secretary. They argue that too much emphasis was placed on self-criticism and changing the DC, on economic austerity, and on attacking the PSI rather than on the traditional DC's anticommunist appeal while remaining a "mediator" without a clearly defined economic policy.[35]

I argue that De Mita's view is much closer to the truth. In other words, the DC losses in 1983 cannot be seen simply as a result of one DC election campaign or of De Mita's leadership.[36] De Mita's style and messages may have helped the DC a little in some ways and hurt it a little in others, but to a large extent the DC losses in 1983 are a continuation of its crisis of the mid-1970s: Losses were only postponed in 1976 and 1979 by anticommunism and, in 1979, also by the Moro assassination. While those who have gained from the DC losses have varied considerably from one part of Italy to another, the losses were largely the result of one set of nationwide factors rather than of a variety of local explanations. In particular, the DC's losses in 1983 are viewed here as primarily a result of the combination of the long-standing and profound disillusionment with the DC's rule in Italy and the diminished usefulness of the anti-Communist appeal in 1983.

Profound dissatisfaction exists among the Italian public with the ineffectiveness of governments in dealing with Italy's problems and with the system of *partitocrazia*, that is, the pervasive system of patronage and domination of policy making by political parties. Many Italians believe there is widespread corruption in their country's political system. The Lockheed and petroleum scandals of the mid-1970s, the P2 scandal concerning the Masons and their influence in the political system, and the long-standing question of ties of political parties to the Mafia and its Neapolitan version, the Camorra, are only a few of the scandals in the 1970s and 1980s that have fed this image.

In fact, recent surveys show that 80 percent or more of Italians believe the Italian people have little or no faith in the political parties, are dissatisfied with the way democracy functions in Italy, and think that things are going poorly with relation to "the seriousness and honesty of the people in government."[37] This dissatisfaction with the way democracy works in their country is considerably more widespread in Italy than elsewhere in Western Europe.[38] Most importantly, this disillusionment is shared by Christian Democratic voters. Though their own party has long been the dominant force in Italy's political system and has been in the government continuously for thirty-eight years, large majorities of Christian Democratic voters, like the voters of other parties, are dissatisfied with the functioning of the state and with the honesty of the people in government.[39]

The DC is the party most hurt by the political alienation. The greatest blame for Italy's problems is put on the Christian Democratic party, the originator though not the only beneficiary of the system of *partitocrazia*. Even more important, many Christian Democratic voters share the view that the DC has a major responsibility for Italy's problems. For example, in a late 1982 survey of university graduates, 71 percent (68 percent of DC supporters) agreed that "the primary responsibility for Italy's problems rests with the political parties." Of those agreeing, 64 percent named the DC, 39 percent the PSI, and 30 percent the PCI, while no more than 10 percent named any other single party. Among Christian Democrats, fully 47 percent named their own party; by contrast, 22 percent of Socialists mentioned their own party, and no more than 10 percent of the supporters of any other party named their own party.[40]

Public perceptions about the Italian political system, Italian political parties in general, and the DC in particular worsened considerably between the late 1960s and the early 1970s.[41] In other words, profound disillusionment with the DC, even among its own voters, had already developed by the time of the DC's first crisis in the mid-1970s. By 1975, as Aldo Moro argued in a speech following the 1975 regional elections, a portion of the DC electorate was "tired" of the DC.[42] Survey evidence presented by Robert Putnam, Robert Leonardi, and Raffaella Y. Nanetti clearly demonstrates what happened to the public image of the DC: (1) there was "during the 1970s the draining of that massive reservoir of public esteem that the DC had acquired during the 1950s and 1960s as the guarantor of Italian democracy and the godfather of the Italian economic miracle"; (2) paralleling the general worsening in the Italian public's image of their political system, the DC loss of sympathy was "heaviest during the period 1972–1975" but the erosion continued at a slower rate into the 1980s; (3) during the 1970s, the sympathy for the DC dropped more than the sympathy for almost any other party or political force; and (4) very important for the DC's electoral support, the decline in sympathy for the DC was greater among its supporters than its opponents.[43]

Similarly, Giacomo Sani has argued that between 1967 and 1976 there was "a systematic and severe deterioration in the popular view of the DC."[44] By 1976, most of those with an opinion viewed the DC as dishonest, divided, and not very modern. The DC image worsened between 1967 and 1974 and, especially on the question of honesty, even further in the 1975–76 period, primarily because of the Lockheed and petroleum scandals, both involving some important DC figures.[45] It is at this image of a scandal-ridden, power-hungry, factionalized party that the DC's various—but thus far largely ineffectual—efforts at party reform were aimed. Despite these efforts, this image of the DC, which had developed to a large extent by the mid-1970s, remained in 1983.

Even with this profound dissatisfaction, widespread DC losses could not have occurred in 1983—as they did not in 1976 or 1979—if the anti-Communist factor had not been of diminished importance. As we have seen, much of the DC's support stems from its religious basis, anticommunism, or clientelism and has long come *despite* rather than because of the DC's governmental performance. As Baget-Bozzo has argued, however, the 1983 election may have been the first "normal" election in postwar Italy, in that anticommunism played a minimal role.[46] Unlike 1976 or 1979, the Christian Democratic–Socialist rivalry, not the Christian Democratic–Communist conflict, was at the center of attention in 1983.

The deemphasis on the Communist question in 1983 was a result of a number of factors. First, most expected that the PCI would either lose a little or stagnate in 1983 and that the DC would lose only a few percentage points at most, thereby keeping a substantial gap between the two. This parallels somewhat the 1979 election, in which all expectations were for DC gains and substantial PCI losses. In other words, the anti-Communist appeal, while central to the DC campaign in 1979 as in 1976, was probably not as effective the second time around.[47] Second, the serious difficulties of the Communist party since 1979 meant that it was perceived as less of a threat not only by many DC leaders but also by many DC voters. Third, De Mita's way of speaking about the PCI in the 1982–83 period, in effect saying that there was no longer any ideological barrier against Communist participation in the government, and the choice of the DC leadership to emphasize the polemics with the PSI rather than attempting to make the 1983 campaign another crusade against communism, tended to downplay the anti-Communist appeal. Related to this, during the election campaign De Mita, in a first for a DC leader, appeared in a televised debate with the PCI leader Enrico Berlinguer.[48] Finally, of long-term importance, there has been a gradually developing depolarization of the Italian political system. The "pool of fervent anti-Communists" has been shrinking in the 1970s, so that, while the PCI is far from fully legitimized, the number of Italians intensely disliking and fearing the PCI has declined somewhat.[49]

In sum, by 1983 there were fewer anti-Communists to mobilize; 1983 was not an election in which they could be easily mobilized; the DC strategy did not center on mobilizing them; and the disillusionment with the DC among a substantial number of DC voters proved to be a stronger motivating factor than did fear of the PCI. In 1983 many centrist and rightist voters who voted in the past for the DC as the bulwark against communism cast a vote of protest or a vote for another party, especially the PRI or the PLI, that they had long preferred.

This explanation of the DC's losses in 1983, which puts primary emphasis on the DC's negative image combined with the diminished role of anticommunism in 1983, is further supported by looking at the likely recipients of many of the ex-DC votes. First, more than 3 percentage points, much of it probably from the DC, was won by four parties that must be considered free of scandal and, therefore, good candidates to receive protest votes because they were totally outside the system of power: the MSI, the Pensioners' party, and the regional parties in Sardinia and Veneto.[50] Second, abstention or casting spoiled or blank ballots may have been other forms of protest for some ex-DC voters. Third, two other likely gainers at the expense of the DC, the Republicans and the Liberals, both have a long-standing image of respectability though they have been part of many postwar governments. The prestige and credibility of the Republicans was further enhanced by the year and a half that Giovanni Spadolini served as prime minister, especially with the comparison many voters made to DC-led governments.[51] Finally, the failure of the PSI and the PSDI to make gains in much of northern Italy and their inability to benefit from the DC losses except in some parts of the South also support this explanation because both parties, compared to the PRI and PLI, are more widely perceived to have many of the same negative qualities as the DC.

Secularization over the past twenty-five years, particularly as a result of generational change, has meant that the pool of practicing Catholics available to the DC has become smaller. For example, the number attending church weekly has dropped from two-thirds to one-third of the population.[52] This, combined with the weakening of the church's commitment to the DC, has begun to hurt the DC and will continue to eat away slowly at the single most important base of DC support. The secularization probably has hurt the DC most in the large cities, where church attendance is lowest and where the church, like the DC, has the weakest social presence. The gradual process of secularization, however, while contributing to the loss, is not the primary explanation of the big losses the DC suffered all at one time in the 1983 election.

One other long-term factor which, though not a major explanation of the DC losses, may be of limited importance, especially in parts of southern Italy, is that the DC is being penalized by its somewhat lessened ability to control resources at the local and national level and by the simple fact that, with the crisis of the welfare state, there are fewer resources to control. This is, of course, the most difficult explanation of all to assess. Unlike the North, however, some of the DC votes lost in parts of the South probably went to the Social Democrats and the Socialists, the other two parties most identified with the system of political patronage.

The Impact of the DC Campaign and De Mita   The DC electoral losses have been viewed here primarily as a result of the DC's negative image combined with the diminished role of anticommunism in 1983, secondarily as a result of secularization, and, in some parts of the South, to a limited degree as a result of the undercutting of some clientelistic support. The DC campaign and De Mita had only limited positive or negative effects.

While losing a sizable chunk of voters in 1983 who had supported it in previous elections, the DC apparently won few new voters from other parties. De Mita's efforts to overcome the negative image of the DC by creating a "new DC," one perceived as modern, honest, and effective, either did not have enough time to work or were simply not credible.[53] Many among industrialists and the "emerging" middle class may have applauded De Mita's economic program, but they voted for the Republicans or the Liberals as more credible alternatives. Even in most of the senatorial districts where the DC put up well-known, attractive "outsiders" as candidates, the DC losses were no more contained than in the rest of the country.

De Mita's campaign and his efforts to create a new DC may have hurt the party among some of its traditional supporters, but these were not the primary reasons so many voters left the DC. As many of De Mita's opponents within the DC would argue, his deemphasis on anticommunism was probably most important. De Mita's discussion of the place of the PCI in Italian politics was only one of several reasons why the communist issue played a minor role in the 1983 election. De Mita may have worried some DC supporters who were opposed to the program of economic austerity. There is no evidence of massive desertion from the DC by working-class voters. Further, a sizable number of ex-DC voters cast their ballots for the PRI and PLI, two parties whose commitment to economic austerity was clear and strong.

Conclusion

The 1983 election results directly raised the question of the future of the DC in the Italian political system, with many seeing the DC's large losses as the beginning of an irreversible decline. In addition, the long-discussed possibility of the PCI passing the DC in national elections to become the largest party in parliament seemed more real after the DC's 1983 losses (and to even a greater degree after the PCI's gains in the 1984 European parliament elections brought the two to about the same level).

However, the two major electoral tests since 1983—the June 1984 European parliament elections in which the DC held its 1983 level of about 33 percent and the May 1985 regional, provincial, and communal elections in which the DC, playing heavily on the anticommunist theme, regained somewhat to 35 percent—have shown that the 1983 losses were not the beginning of a continual and irreversible decline. Furthermore, the PCI's political isolation and electoral weakness, especially after the losses in the mid-1985 local elections, which suggested that the PCI's 1984 gains were transitory, and the defeat in June 1985 of the PCI-sponsored national referendum on wage indexation, make it appear less likely that the PCI will pass the DC in the next parliamentary elections.

The DC's role in the political system was clearly hurt in 1983. Craxi became prime minister not so much because of his triumph but because of the DC losses. At the same time the DC remained by far the largest party in the government coalition, and part of the price Craxi paid was to give many of the key ministries to the DC. From mid-1983 to mid-1985, despite many conflicts among the government parties, Craxi's government was able to survive in part because the DC was ultimately unwilling to bring it down and remained at least a reasonably loyal ally.

The DC's success in the May 1985 local elections and De Mita's ability to secure the election of Francesco Cossiga as president of Italy on the first ballot strengthened the DC's position in the political system and De Mita's position within the DC. The DC has gained a relatively secure political position until the parliamentary elections of 1987 or 1988.

The question of the DC's electoral (and consequently political) future was, however, by no means definitively answered by the 1985 elections. If the 1983 losses did not mean the beginning of an irreversible DC decline, the 1985 results did not necessarily mean that the DC will do well in the next parliamentary elections. There are a number of alternative possibilities that remain for the DC's short-term and long-term future. For the next parliamentary elections these possibilities range from a partial DC recovery compared to 1983 (something along the lines of the 1985 results) to a further small loss compared to 1983. If the DC should stay near the 35 percent level it won in 1985, this would not be so bad for a party which many in 1983 thought faced permanent decline. More extreme possibilities of, on the one hand, DC recovery to its 1979 level of 38 percent or, on the other hand, a substantial decline compared to 1983 are much less likely. Factors such as the role and efficacy of the anti-Communist card; the ability of the DC (limited thus far) to reform itself; the strength of the Catholic organizational network in Italy; the speed with which the secularization process, which will certainly not be reversed, continues; and the image and political strategy of the other Italian parties will all strongly condition the DC's electoral future.

Even if it is not the dominant party it was before the mid-1970s, the DC, which has been in every government for more than forty years, will clearly stay there for a good bit longer. It will likely remain the largest party in the country for a substantial period and will certainly by a wide margin be the largest party in any government coalition in the near future. The DC also stands a good chance of regaining the prime ministership within the next several years. In other words, the prospects for the DC and De Mita, while by no means without real limitations and uncertainties, are much better in 1986 than they appeared in 1983 to most observers of the DC and to its own leaders.

Notes

1   Several works on the DC that discuss its history and development, including the 1974-76 period, are Giorgio Galli, *Storia della* DC (The history of the DC) (Bari: Editori Laterza, 1978); Giuseppe Di Palma, "Christian Democracy: The End of Hegemony?" in Howard R. Penniman, ed., *Italy at the Polls: The Parliamentary Elections of 1976* (Washington, D.C.: American Enterprise Institute, 1977), 123-54; Douglas A. Wertman, "The Christian Democrats: Masters of Survival," in Howard R. Penniman, ed., *Italy at the Polls, 1979: A Study of the Parliamentary Elections* (Washington, D.C.: American Enterprise Institute, 1981), 64-103; and Gianfranco Pasquino, "Italian Christian Democracy: A Party for all Seasons?" *West European Politics*, 2, no. 3 (October 1979): 88-109.

2   Wertman, "The Christian Democrats," 93.

3   *La Stampa*, February 21, 1980, 1-2.

4   See, for example, the discussion about the 1982 DC congress by Enzo Marzo, "La 'questione socialista' ha dominato interventi e polemiche prima del voto" (The "socialist question" dominated the speeches and polemics before the vote), *Corriere della Sera*, May 6, 1982, 2. See also Guido Gerosa and Gigi Moncalvo, *De Mita Il Nuovo Potere* (De Mita the new power) (Milan: Sperling and Kupfer Editori S.p.A., 1982), 223-78. Detailed summaries of the debate at the congress can be found in *Il Popolo*, May 4, 5, 6, and 7, 1982.

5   *Il Popolo*, May 6, 1982.

6   Evidence of this is presented in the section titled "Why the DC Losses?" in this chapter.

7   There is a substantial literature on DC factionalism. See, for example, Alan Zuckerman, *The Politics of Faction: Christian Democratic Rule in Italy* (New Haven, Conn.: Yale University Press, 1979), or Wertman, "The Christian Democrats," 77-83.

8   Di Palma, "Christian Democracy," 134-35.

9   See, for example, two unsigned articles from *La Civiltà Cattolica*: "Crisi e rinnovamento della Democrazia Cristiana" (The crisis and revitalization of the Christian Democratic Party) (September 19, 1981), and "Dibattito sul rinnovamento della DC. Verso l'Assemblea di novembre" (Debate on revitalization of the DC: Toward the November Assembly) (October 3, 1981).

10   See *Il Popolo*, November 26, 27, 28, and 29, 1981, for details on the National Assembly. A good summary on the National Assembly is in "Italy's new model party," *The Economist* (December 5, 1981).

11   *Corriere della Sera*, January 24, 1982.

12   One reason for the limited impact of the *esterni* at the congress is their heterogeneity; that is, they represented a variety of organizations and viewpoints. See *L'Espresso*, April 25, 1982, 21. Interestingly, the DC National Council decided in November 1983 to exclude the *esterni* from voting on the party secretaryship at the 1984 national congress. *Corriere della Sera*, November 15, 1983, 4.

13   See, for example, interviews with De Mita in *La Repubblica*, November 24, 1982, 3, and December 23, 1982, 6-7.

14   For example, De Mita chose Professor Francesco D'Onofrio to head the local governments office at the DC headquarters and Professor (and ex-Minister of Industry) Romano Prodi to head the big state holding company IRI.

15 De Mita discussed the weakness of the DC party organization in the major cities in an interview published in *La Repubblica*, April 10-11, 1983, 4-5. Articles on De Mita's efforts to restructure the DC in the major cities—and the subsequent negative reaction in the local party organizations—appeared in *L'Espresso*, April 17, 1983, 9; and *La Repubblica*, April 19, 1983, 12, and April 21, 1983, 4.

16 On the 1976 and 1979 DC campaigns, see respectively Di Palma, "Christian Democracy"; and Wertman, "The Christian Democrats."

17 Two useful articles on the conflict over alliances are Antonio Padellaro, "La polemica sulle future alleanze al centro del contronto elettorale" (The polemics over future alliances at the center of the election confrontation), *Corriere della Sera*, May 9, 1983, 2; and Gianni Baget-Bozzo, "La sortita di Craxi" (Craxi's statement), *La Repubblica*, June 22, 1983, 10.

18 See the interview with De Mita in *Panorama*, June 27, 1983, 57, 59-61.

19 On the 1948-76 period see Maurizio Cotta, "Il rinnovamento del personale parlamentare democristiana" (The turnover of DC members of Parliament), *Il Mulino*, no. 259 (September-October 1978): 723-42. On 1979 see Wertman, "The Christian Democrats," 97-98. On 1983 see *Corriere della Sera*, May 24, 1983, 1; and *La Repubblica*, May 26, 1983, 3.

20 See the many articles on candidate selection in *Corriere della Sera* and *La Repubblica*, May 17-26, 1983; and *L'Espresso*, June 5, 1983, 12-13.

21 For a discussion of the Catholic church's role in Italian politics between 1945 and 1981, see Douglas A. Wertman, "The Catholic Church and Italian Politics: The Impact of Secularization," *West European Politics* 5, no. 2 (April 1982): 87-93.

22 Excerpts of the bishops' statement are given in *Corriere della Sera*, June 5, 1983, 1; and *La Repubblica*, June 5-6, 1983, 3.

23 There is no firm evidence as to why all the polls overestimated the DC result. Some factors that may explain it in part include: (1) there was a high rate (40 to 50 percent) of refusals and nonresponses on party preference questions; (2) the last surveys were finished ten days before the election and therefore did not catch the final changes and crystallization of opinion; (3) the DC may have been overrepresented among the 16 percent of the electorate who either failed to vote or cast a spoiled or blank ballot; and (4) some respondents may have lied and given the DC as a socially more acceptable choice (for example, this may be true of some MSI voters).

24 The patterns of electoral results and likely beneficiaries of DC losses discussed in this section are based on an analysis of election statistics at the level of the 95 provinces, the almost 250 senatorial districts, and, in some cases, the commune and neighborhoods within cities. Some caution must, of course, be used in interpreting aggregate statistics such as these. They are the best source available to us, however, for examining the destination of DC losses.

25 The Pensioners' party and its results are discussed in "Doccia fredda per i pensionati: tanti voti ma neanche un seggio" (Cold shower for the pensioners: So many votes but not even one seat), *Il Giornale*, June 29, 1983, 4; and "I pensionati: miracolo con pochissima spesa" (The pensioners: A miracle with little spent on the campaign), *Corriere della Sera*, June 28, 1983, 8.

26 The percentage of valid votes in Italy has always been among the highest for any Western democracy. This was true again in 1983. In the 1983 elections, however, the total percentage either abstaining or casting a blank or spoiled ballot increased by more than 4 percentage points from 1979.

27 A good discussion of the Veneto League is given in Edgardo Bartoli, "Italiani invasori ci avete traditi, ora ridateci il Veneto" (Italian invaders you have betrayed us, now give us back Veneto), *La Repubblica*, June 24-25, 1983, 5.

28 This discussion of the Socialists is based on an analysis in each southern province and

senatorial district of the relationship between: (1) the patterns of PSI gains coupled with the losses by the parties to its left; and (2) the patterns of DC losses compared to the gains of other nonleft parties.

29   Provinces in which these parties made their greatest gains were: for the Republicans, 4.0 percentage points in Messina and 3.9 percentage points in Reggio Calabria, and, for the Liberals, 4.2 percentage points in Messina and 2.6 percentage points in Benevento. Overall, however, neither of these parties did as well in the South as in other areas of Italy.

30   The ten largest cities are Rome, Milan, Turin, Naples, Genoa, Bologna, Florence, Palermo, Bari, and Venice. These results are based on the author's calculations from city-by-city results reported in *Il Giornale*, June 29, 1983, 6.

31   I would like to thank Alfonso Del Re of Doxa for the results of the 1983 surveys that are analyzed in this section. The portrait of the DC electorate drawn here from 1983 surveys is virtually the same as the ones presented in: (1) Giacomo Sani, "The Italian Electorate in the Mid-1970s: Beyond Tradition," in Howard R. Penniman, ed., *Italy at the Polls: The Parliamentary Elections of 1976* (Washington, D.C.: American Enterprise Institute, 1977), 111, 113, which uses 1975 data; (2) "Caratteristiche demografiche e socioeconomiche dei probabili votanti per i diversi partiti e degli elettori indecisi" (Demographic and socioeconomic characteristics of the probable voters for the various parties and of the undecided voters), mimeographed paper distributed by Doxa in April 1979 and based on the combined results of 24,000 respondents from Doxa surveys done in 1977 and 1978; and (3) *Bollettino della Doxa* 36, nos. 15–16 (October 27, 1982), which reports on the sociodemographic profiles of the electorates of the various parties based on a combined sample of approximately 10,000 cases from five surveys conducted in 1981 and 1982.

32   The 1975 data were provided by Giacomo Sani. The 1980 data come from the April 1980 *Eurobarometer*. The 1983 data come from a March 1983 survey conducted by Doxa and provided to me by Alfonso Del Re.

33   Earlier results on the sex composition of the DC electorate are discussed in Wertman, "The Christian Democrats," 74, 76. Data from the 1975–80 period are presented in a table on page 75 in that chapter.

34   An interesting analysis of the DC losses is in Alberto Ronchey, "Ricaduta o decadenza della DC?" (Relapse or decline of the DC?), *La Repubblica*, September 27, 1983, 10.

35   For a discussion of the analyses presented by De Mita's critics during the precongress debates in late 1983, see *Corriere della Sera*, December 5, 1983, 1; and *La Repubblica*, December 6, 1983, 9; December 8, 1983, 10; and December 14, 1983, 6.

36   A good discussion on this point is presented in Gianni Baget-Bozzo, "Una sconfitta di tutta la DC" (A defeat of the entire DC), *Mondoperaio*, nos. 7/8 (1983): 4–6.

37   Eighty-eight percent said Italians have little or no faith in their political parties, according to a Demoskopea survey reported in "Mai cosi arrabiati" (Never so angry), *Panorama*, January 24, 1983, 25. In the April 1983 *Eurobarometer*, 80 percent of Italians said they were dissatisfied with the way democracy functions in Italy. Eighty-five percent believed things were going poorly "with relation to the seriousness and honesty of the people in government," according to a December 1980 Doxa survey reported in *Bollettino della Doxa* 35, nos. 5–6 (March 1, 1981), 43.

38   In the April 1983 *Eurobarometer* survey, when 80 percent of Italians said they were dissatisfied with the functioning of democracy in their country, the number dissatisfied ranged from 22 to 54 percent in the other European Community countries. Italians, however, remained as committed to democracy as other West Europeans; as in the other EC countries, only about one in ten or fewer has supported revolutionary change in Italy in *Eurobarometer* surveys since 1973.

39   Seventy percent of Christian Democrats (compared to 82 percent of the entire sample)

thought things were going poorly "with relation to the functioning of the state," and 73 percent of Christian Democrats (compared to 85 percent of the entire sample) thought things were going poorly "with relation to the seriousness and honesty of the people in government" in a December 1980 Doxa survey reported in *Bollettino della Doxa* 35, nos. 5–6 (March 1, 1981), 42–46.

40 The data come from a national survey of 1,000 university students and graduates aged twenty to sixty-four, conducted in October–December 1982 for the United States Information Agency.

41 For example, in 1967, 35 percent of Italians thought things were going poorly with relation to the functioning of the state, while 22 percent said things were going well and 22 percent said neither well nor poorly. By 1974, 83 percent said things were going poorly. Similar results occurred on the question of "the seriousness and honesty of the people in government." These results are reported in *Bollettino della Doxa* 35, nos. 5–6 (March 1, 1981), 42–43.

42 This quote is reported in Aniello Coppola, *Moro* (Milano: Feltrinelli, 1976), 139–40.

43 Robert D. Putnam, Robert Leonardi, and Raffaella Y. Nanetti, "Polarization and Depolarization in Italian Politics, 1968–1981" (Paper presented at the 1981 Annual Meeting of the American Political Science Association, New York, September 1981), 39, 44–45, 69–70.

44 Giacomo Sani, "The Italian Electorate in the Mid-1970s," 105.

45 On the question of the honesty or dishonesty of the DC: in 1967, 36 percent said the DC was honest, 13 percent said dishonest, and 51 percent did not answer; in 1974, 22 percent said honest, 24 percent said dishonest, and 54 percent did not answer; in 1975 21 percent said honest, 27 percent dishonest, and 52 percent did not answer; and in 1976, 23 percent said honest, but 51 percent said dishonest, and the don't knows dropped to 26 percent. *Bollettino della Doxa* 30, nos. 17–18 (September 1, 1976), 141.

46 Gianni Baget-Bozzo, "Il piacere di votare" (The pleasure of voting), *La Repubblica*, June 7, 1983, 8.

47 Wertman, "The Christian Democrats," 100.

48 The text of the debate, which was televised nationwide a week before the election, is reported in *La Repubblica*, June 18, 1983, 6–7.

49 Putnam, Leonardi, and Nanetti, "Polarization and Depolarization in Italian Politics, 1968–1981," 70.

50 Giorgio Galli presents similar reasoning with relation to the MSI in discussing the possibility of future MSI gains in "E la destra approfitta" (And the right profits), *Panorama*, April 18, 1983, 35.

51 In fact, the strength of the Republicans was unchanged in the 1980 elections and up some in the 1981 elections, but up much more in the 1982 elections after Spadolini had been prime minister for a year.

52 On the secularization process, see Wertman, "The Catholic Church and Italian Politics," 99–104.

53 The view that time worked against De Mita in 1983 is held by many, including Father Bartolomeo Sorge, the director of *La Civiltà Cattolica*, whose views are reported in *La Repubblica*, July 15, 1983, 2.

4 The Ambiguous Alternative: The Italian Communist Party in the 1983 Elections

MARCELLO FEDELE

————The leadership of the Italian Communist party (PCI) was only slightly altered in the general elections of June 1983 from the one that had led the party throughout the 1970s.[1] This fact itself is thought-provoking, particularly if we compare it with the innovations that occurred at the same time within the Christian Democratic party (DC), the PCI's great adversary over the previous decade.

On the other hand, the 1983 elections were in a sense exceptional for the Communists, second in significance only to the historic confrontation of June 20, 1976.[2] The unusual aspect in this case was that the party leadership had managed to remain intact while a new "political cycle" replaced the one that had ended forever on May 9, 1978, when the Red Brigades terrorists handed over the lifeless body of Aldo Moro.

Certainly May 9, 1978, was a day of mourning for the whole Italian political system. Because Moro had been the only Christian Democratic leader capable of piloting the DC through the troublesome phase of national solidarity, his death held special meaning for the PCI. In other words, Moro's assassination marked the end of the "historic compromise" strategy and the beginning of a wearisome race against the clock to rediscover the "Communist identity" that had inevitably been obscured by the possibility of government participation.

After the PCI won the 1976 elections hands down, the historic-compromise policy soon proved inadequate, particularly from the perspective of the other parties participating in national solidarity. For them the uninterrupted series of institutional mediations represented chiefly the chance to control the social conflict to which the 1960s had given rise.

As we know, in the end it was all pointless, because the problem of

This chapter was translated into English by Kristin Jarratt.

government stability was never solved. As the DC and the intermediary parties caught their breath and regrouped, however, taking full advantage of the temporary social peace that prevailed, the PCI found itself caught in a crossfire. The crossfire, as we shall see, was not entirely the other parties' doing. In no time at all, relations with the PSI (Italian Socialist party) went sour. Later there were conflicts with the labor unions, and in the end the very notion of the left fell victim to the mortal blows of Red Brigades terrorism.[3]

This is not the place to discuss a period that may deserve more attention than it is normally allotted in a summary analysis.[4] We ought not to forget, however, that the elimination of national solidarity left the Communist leadership without a strategy while it confronted the prospect of losing many of the new voters it had acquired in 1976.

Chronologically, but especially politically, the 1979 elections were still part of the season that had begun with the historic compromise. When the PCI's forward march was brought to a standstill in these elections, another alarm bell sounded. In just three years, the party had lost most of the new consensus gained at the 1976 polls, and its careful avoidance of a political outlook had locked it into sterile opposition, thereby negating the leadership's efforts to gain acceptance of the PCI as a "government party."[5] How could the leadership now overcome the impasse that threatened to trigger a process of authentic political regression?

To answer this question we must focus on the most interesting problem that has emerged from the 1983 elections. Every party, and particularly the PCI, tends to consider each election "decisive" and "different," because votes represent an important party "resource" that it would be irresponsible to waste. For the PCI, however, the 1983 elections actually were different, above all because the party viewed them as part of a much larger process, whereby the leadership closed the old historic-compromise cycle and established the credibility of the "alternative" strategy that would mark its entire electoral campaign.

Indeed, when the "Salerno switch" gave birth to the alternative in 1980, the PCI was straining under the problems left unresolved by the years of national solidarity.[6] Some individuals blamed the party's failure during that period on the DC's recurring tendency to isolate the PCI or on the PSI's competitiveness with its stronger leftist partner. Today, however, these interpretations appear simplistic and unsatisfactory. Apart from the party's conflicts with its allies in those days, secondary troubles were due to the limits shown by the PCI itself in its government participation.

At the international level, during the national solidarity stage the party had not yet distanced itself from the Soviet Union. When it did so later on, the rift confirmed the PCI's decision to take its place within a Western frame of reference.[7] By the same token, the economic crisis struck before the PCI was able to rid itself completely of the burden caused by previous demagogic policies in the labor unions.[8] More generally, the "government party" vocation had rarely been accompanied by a thorough discussion of reform in the context of a pluralistic and democratic country.[9] Doubtless these considerations all confirm that hindsight is the best sort of vision. As far as the passage from opposition to government was concerned, however, there were still two problems that the leadership had to face if it wanted to keep its political and electoral strength intact. The first was the internal organization of the party; the other was the definition of a new political strategy.

It was impossible to avoid serious discussion of the party's role, on the one hand because the electors were clamoring for greater internal democracy and on the other because it was imperative to devise forms of organization that would involve the intermediary and professional cadres who had voted Communist in 1976 and had thereby given credit to the PCI's proposals of programs for "good government." For the first time the PCI was forced to deal with the consensus of a particular opinion group. Furthermore, this group could not be organized along the traditional lines, according to which every elector was a potential card carrier and every party member was a militant to be mobilized.[10] For the moment, the party chose to transform its "Feste dell'Unità" into great shows of collective enthusiasm, but the real issue was whether and how to change the party's rule of democratic centralism.[11]

As for strategy, after the historic compromise had been dumped, the PCI had to determine how it could be an opposition force without blocking the future prospect for government participation. For some time it was unsure how to proceed, and even when the alternative proposal was suggested, the means of evaluating the different majority coalitions remained essentially unaltered. In other words, the opposition's "strength" and "responsibility" varied in accordance with the amount of space given to the PCI by parties of the majority.

Such complicated entanglements could plainly be unraveled only by searching for a radically different identity. The Communist leadership, however, showed perhaps more adherence to party tradition than the situation might have called for and thus faced these problems with extraordinary caution. According to the slogan, the leaders set out to find "change within continuity."

Let us overlook the logical difficulty represented by the fact that sooner or later any true change will lead to a break with the past, so that it is impossible to maintain any true respect for continuity. Far more meaningful is the general characteristic that tended to emerge from a reconstruction of the early 1980s. On the one hand, the party's supporters continued to call for the deritualization of political life and the modernization of the party organization; on the other, the strongest party of the left tended to block this request in the name of a "diversity" that was considered worthy of preservation.

Although the dynamics of these developments may seem contradictory, there actually were general considerations and contingent political processes. Only by understanding these forces can we evaluate the way in which the PCI faced the 1983 elections. No one, for instance, can seriously deny that the PCI has changed over the past few years. Even the most benevolent outside observers, however, have concluded that the PCI has not changed enough. Furthermore, it is clear that the entire Italian political system has not changed, and its stasis has contributed substantially to the delay in further Communist evolution.[12] In the second place, during the 1980s the conflict between PSI and PCI has worsened, as the Socialists have consistently used the PCI's troubles as the excuse for a bitter demand that the right lead the left.

Finally, another factor perhaps best explains the contradictions inherent in a policy based on change within continuity. After the phase of great expansion touched off by the historic compromise, the Communist leadership has been preoccupied with the need to maintain control over its traditional electorate, even if doing so means reducing the party's influence within the wider electoral range that the PCI had been able to claim after the 1976 elections.

As we shall see, the PCI was split on medium-range prospects, worried by the electoral competition of the PSI, and troubled by the country's new political climate, which manifested less politicization than had the previous decade. As a consequence, the PCI's proposed policy in the 1983 elections was strong enough on the general level but weak—if not altogether absent—in the area of analytic instrumentalization and particularly in its inability to confront the problems of reorganizing the party, acquiring new votes, and forging alliances with intermediary lay forces.

We have already attempted to identify the basis for the uncertainty of the PCI leadership. Policy proposals actually developed along two lines. At the most general level, the declared objective was to affirm the "alternative" strategy. In reality, however, in one sense the PCI gave up trying to create the conditions that would give it the means to obtain more persuasive affirmation, while in another sense the PCI ensured above all that the elections would confirm its ability to control its electorate. If, as we believe, such "duplicity" did indeed exist, this aspect of the electoral campaign is worth examining more closely.

We shall also try to discover why an election that had originally been set up as a defensive battle eventually turned into an unexpected success for the so-called alternative, which had been the most ambiguous part of the Communist platform during the 1983 election campaign. At that point we should understand the paradoxical character of the election results, from which the

PCI gained some indirect political benefits, despite the fact that the gains were originally feared more than welcomed.

From the Convention to
the Electoral Campaign

In January 1983 the Communist central committee (*comitato centrale*) approved its fundamental statement, to be submitted to the party's provincial organs in preparation for the sixteenth national convention. Because early elections were already in the air, it was only natural for the orientation of the leadership to be at least somewhat affected.

In accordance with the party's operational methods, the statement presented by Secretary Enrico Berlinguer touched upon all the most significant political issues, although the main preoccupation of the committee was to ensure that the subject of relations with the Soviet Union did not eventually split the party. Indeed, many party members had expressed skepticism about the propulsive function of socialism; this had divided the Communist leadership, thereby creating its first true internal opposition, led by Armando Cossutta, a prominent member of the national committee (*direzione nazionale*) who had opposed the anti-Soviet rift from the outset.

The mass media immediately focused on the friction; surveys and studies confirmed the existence of widespread support for the Soviet Union among the rank and file of the PCI; finally, Cossutta published a book just before the convention.[13] These developments accentuated the feeling that it might be possible to split the party on the issue of relations with the USSR. Provincial conventions showed at once that such worries were unfounded, however: the amendments proposed by Cossutta or inspired by his stance never drew more than 10 or 15 percent of the votes, with the minor exceptions of the Isernia and Vicenza gatherings.

The problem of democratic centralism, or, more generally, the internal organization of the party, however, led to bitter disputes everywhere.[14] This subject had been broached by Pietro Ingrao when the preconvention platform was submitted for approval. Without specifically contesting the model of organization based on democratic centralism, the party leader's motion shifted the axis of internal decision-making power from the national committee to the central committee. Ingrao's amendments, which had initially been rejected by a mere four votes when put before the central committee, were reconsidered and approved by all the provincial conventions, despite the tacit opposition of the leadership. Later, when this resistance became explicit (for instance, in Florence, where Giancarlo Pajetta, one of the party's founding leaders, openly expressed his doubts about the wisdom of expanding party democracy), the national committee's motion was most astonishingly defeated. Nor were better results forthcoming for the initiative directed by the party's number two man, Alessandro Natta, who invited the party to reflect upon the fact that the central committee could not be the "only organ" to decide because "there are areas of decision that more properly belong to organs such as the National Committee or the Secretariat."[15] Indeed, the lower-echelon demand for greater power was approved in all the large cities and at the majority of the conventions, thereby reversing the expectations of the national committee.

Although the PCI leaders originally worried that they would be forced to confront a nonexistent demand for rapprochement with the USSR, in the end they were faced with appeals for greater democracy from diverse factions that in many cases had gone so far as to use the secret vote in electing delegates, often with surprising results. In Prato, the whole local leadership lost out; in Naples, the first delegate elected was a worker who unseated Luciano Lama, the secretary general of the CGIL (the Communist-affiliated Federation of Italian Labor Unions), while the eminent national leader Giorgio Napolitano was twenty-first among thirty delegates; in Rome, the Senate party leader, Edoardo Perna, was sacrificed along with Antonello Trombadori, Marisa Rodano, and other lesser leaders.

The caution that had prompted party leaders to aim for change with continuity was so totally at odds with the mood of the delegates that the latter hardly paid any attention to the problem of continuity as represented by PCI-Soviet relations. The leaders' energy was almost entirely dedicated to anything that would accelerate renewal—that is, greater internal democracy—and this was implicit confirmation that the leadership's "control" of the base had been badly damaged.

By comparison with the years of national solidarity, the entire structural organization of the party was greatly altered. There was now an enormous turnover among card-carrying members, with almost 100,000 recruits annually replacing the same number of members who failed to renew their cards. There were only half as many members under age thirty as there had been in 1977, while party members between the ages of fifty-one and sixty had increased their share of the party membership from 14 percent to 21 percent. Members older than sixty had risen from 18 percent to 23 percent.[16]

As for the "administrators" (meaning the individuals elected to serve in public organizations), members between thirty and thirty-nine years of age were grossly overrepresented; they held 32 percent of municipal posts, 26 percent of provincial posts, and 19 percent of regional posts. Thus in terms of generations the recruits of the 1970s now constituted half of the party's administrators, whereas the old guard of the 1950s held only 11 percent of the posts.

All the unwritten rules of democratic centralism had reached the inevitable breaking point, and these rules, used in the formation of leadership groups, had guaranteed a balance between the different components of the party. As long as there was an effective means of mediating power relations among these elements, discussions involving the leaders of the party could be shrouded in obligatory secrecy, and the militants could be asked to support the party line through an open vote. When this means of mediation no longer existed, however, the whole power system broke down. The consequent division between leadership and supporters was at times a generation gap but at other times more specifically a political gap.

With respect to the problem of the alternative, for instance, the party was actually less united than might have been surmised, because of the almost total absence of discussion in preparation for approval of the strategy. It was not surprising, however, that at least three positions emerged at the provincial conventions. The Rome convention approved an amendment supported by several prominent members of the national committee, demoting the alternative from a "strategy" to a "policy line" and attributing decisive worth only to "the unity of Communist, Socialist and Catholic masses in their struggle to achieve socialism." In other words, the prospect of the historic compromise had been abandoned only for the moment. There were other observers who considered the alternative only insofar as it referred to solidarity with the PSI, thus giving priority to the problem of political alliances. Finally, there was the leftist version, which argued that the alternative ought to be construed as a social pact subordinate to the "new needs" of women, young people, ecology, and so on, with all possible institutional consequences left to be considered as they arose.

Naturally, it was not always possible to clearly distinguish these three factions of the PCI from one another because priority was still given to presenting a unified appearance, particularly since the elections were around the corner. Furthermore, first the generational division between base and summit and then the political jostling of the leadership itself explain why at the 1983 elections the PCI as a whole was more concerned with preserving the party's strength than with advancing any new strategies.

The general political situation was further aggravated by predictions that preceded the elections and were amplified by preelection surveys. In the first place, a large number of voters were discovered to be "undecided"; in addition, one left-wing party, the tiny Radical party (PR), had shown an interest in riding the winds of protest by encouraging abstentionism. This phenomenon was of particular concern to the Communists, who feared their greatest loss of votes among the young. On the other hand, it was almost taken for granted that there would be a drain of issue-influenced votes. Such votes would, according to most surveys, now be oriented toward the intermediary secular parties and, in smaller numbers, toward the PSI. Moreover, because no one had predicted the DC collapse, the PCI leaders were beginning to believe that they were facing an extremely difficult electoral campaign marked by "class" considerations (as Berlinguer would later tell a postelection central committee meeting dedicated to analyzing the vote) and that they would have to compensate for what the PCI was now calling the "New Right" politics of the DC.[17]

Finally, if we take into account the fact that the *Confindustria* (General Confederation of Italian Industry) was trying to postpone the signing of labor contracts that affected the major industrial categories until after the elections, it is easier to understand why the campaign based on the alternative was little more than a slogan, whereas in reality the party still favored its traditional membership and catered to the political formations now found on its left.

Indeed, a campaign that tended to stress the alternative strategy would first have required the party to concentrate its attention on center or issue-influenced votes and later to establish closer connections with the whole Socialist constituency. The PCI feared the possible consequences of absten- tionism, and it was concerned with the possibility that the PSI might grow too much. It was also disarmed by the DC leadership, which was no longer claim- ing that the PCI lacked democratic legitimacy but was "challenging" the PCI with respect to the "things to be done." In view of these factors, the PCI adopted a position that would be comprehensible at least later. It threw open its left flank to embrace every possible malcontent while it openly attacked the PSI, and of course the DC. Here the so-called alternative was a sort of plebi- scite, which in essence proposed a choice: either go with us or go against us.

If it was to accomplish its goal, however, the PCI was going to have to improvise somewhat during the electoral campaign. Its improvisations did not pass unobserved: In substance, the party claimed that the alternative had al- ready come about, whereas in reality all the Socialists and Communists in parliament represented only 40 percent of the seats.[18] Why, then, should the PSI immediately support the alternative if to reach the fateful 51 percent it would have to rely upon the consensus of forces such as the Radicals, Social Democrats (PSDI), or Republicans (PRI), who not only had little desire to accept such a program but were not even considered real partners?

Obviously, such a situation indicates not so much an error of logic or mathematical ineptitude as a different evaluation of the political setup, which once again had set the leaders of the left at odds. Both Socialists and Commu- nists were essentially convinced that the votes accumulated by the left in 1976 would be lost unless each party did everything in its power to take advantage of the new situation. The Socialists wanted to establish a new balance among all forces of the left, and thus they stressed their own detachment from the PCI. The PCI wanted to reconfirm its own political importance and therefore con- centrated on compiling combined ballots that would embrace the entire left on the basis of the code word "alternative," which by now was clearly more a slogan than a policy.

This perspective explains several characteristics of the ballot sheets and the electoral platform. In 1983 the PCI used a new type of combined ballot, with minor left-wing formations such as the PDUP (Party of Proletarian Unity) appearing alongside traditional left-wing independents, most of whom were reelected. In a situation dominated by the fear of losing votes, two other subtle processes were adopted. In the first place, party bureaucrats displayed a new tendency to consolidate ballots, contradicting past experience that showed that party activity brought greater prestige and power than did election to the public assemblies. Second, the friction between the national committee, which was demanding candidates from the center, and the peripheral forces straining for positions on the ballot inevitably damaged the weakest components, that is, the old-time intellectuals and the Communist representatives of "new wisdom," whose presence was often sacrificed.

As the party platform was conceived, it embraced three broad themes: the moral issue of healing the state, the establishment of an economic policy aimed at assuring greater employment, and finally the preservation of the social services that the crisis was threatening to kill, with the adoption of more equitable fiscal and redistributive criteria.

In any electoral campaign the platform's primary value is the number of votes it can attract. Still, there is no doubt that, by ignoring the determining factors of the economic crisis, thus making it appear to be the fault of the New Right, such a platform tended to significantly bolster the pillars that had fostered the growth of the left in previous years—in other words, labor union clout, welfare policy, and the complaint that after the war the DC had "occupied" the national government. In this light, it is clear why *Rinascita*, the PCI weekly, dedicated its supplements to the "revolution of the movements" or to the "moral issue" rather than, for example, to the "welfare crisis" or to "institutional reform." Indeed, the problem facing the Communists in these elections concerned not reducing but rather accentuating their uniqueness with respect to possible allies in a hypothetical alternative alliance.

The PCI Wins, but Is It a Real Victory?

In the overall political climate that attended the 1983 elections, one somewhat new factor favored the Communists. For the first time since the war, the DC did not set off on the campaign trail urging fear of the PCI's lack of democracy. In the past, the subject of Communist illegitimacy, whether for internal or international reasons, had always been exploited to the utmost by the Christian Democrats as an appeal to voters looking for a last stand against communism.[19] Naturally, during the 1970s this interpretation had already begun to lose credibility.[20] Still, its very existence always activated a "DC or PCI" plebiscitary element, which normally operated in favor of the Christian Democrats. However, Ciriaco De Mita's election as secretary of the DC and the PCI's decision to stay clear of the USSR defused the issue of the PCI's illegitimacy, so that the Communists were able to go into the campaign unburdened by the need to document their Western sympathies.

As strange as it may seem, the PCI nonetheless used this opportunity to reinstate a plebiscitary element in the electoral choice. In this case it served the opposite purpose of gathering the party's electorate back under the umbrella of the alternative. The PCI leaders repeated ad infinitum that they proposed an alternative to the DC and not just to its system of power, thereby making it difficult for the intermediary secular parties to sustain their positions. The Socialists in particular were continually scolded for a "lack of clarity" and a tacit willingness to discuss the postelection eventuality of governing with the DC.

The PCI line was accepted only by the DC, which was also proposing a choice between two alternative alliances. The result was a double process, the interpretation of which represents the most problematic aspect of the entire electoral outcome. The DC did indeed experience one of its most serious electoral declines in the postwar period, losing heavily on its right flank, where the MSI (Italian Socialist Movement) passed from 5.3 to 6.8 percent of the votes. In part, the reason was that many traditional Christian Democratic voters felt released from the obligation to defend democracy against the Communists, inasmuch as losses in 1979 and the PCI-PSI disputes appeared to be sufficient obstacles to any advances the Communists might otherwise make.

The MSI gain cannot be interpreted as a victory for the alternative. Nevertheless, the decline of the central positions justified the PCI view that the outcome confirmed its proposal. Whereas the DC had lost votes, furthermore, the plebiscitary element introduced during the electoral campaign resulted in a strengthening of the Communist mandate. So in the end the alternative was victorious, thanks more to the weakness of the DC than to the strength of the PCI. Any thorough analysis of the votes must demonstrate this point.

The 1983 overall Communist results were only 0.5 percent lower than those of 1979, that is, they involved about half a million fewer votes. This statistic, however, takes on quite a different light if we consider that in 1983 the PCI combined its ballots with the PDUP, a small, extreme left-wing party that had garnered 1.5 percent of the votes in 1979. What is more, the PDUP candidates won by substantial margins in 1983. Luciana Castellína was elected in Milan by 30,000 votes, Lucio Magri in Turin by 46,000 votes, and Luca Cafiero in Naples by 40,000 votes. In other words, the PCI lost more than 0.5 percent in 1983. Indeed, if the PDUP's votes were fully absorbed by the combined ballots, the Communists lost at least 1.9 percent. In reality the Communist party suffered the same type of slide as the Christian Democrats, particularly in view of the much greater losses of 1979, when the PCI relinquished another 4 percent of the electorate it had acquired in 1976.

In short, although the DC may have been in deep trouble, the crisis did not benefit the PCI as much as it did the intermediary secular parties and the panoply of "civil ballots" presented at the polls in 1983. Thus the undecided electors gave their votes above all to the secular forces—the Republican, Liberal, and Social Democratic parties—which, together with the PSI, gained 5 percent. In addition, there was also a move to the far right (MSI) and to the far left (PDUP); in the latter case, the candidates obtained much stronger personal successes than did the Communists with them on the PCI ballot. Finally, the PCI lost heavily to such forces as the "senior citizens' ballot," the "Venetian League," and other small groups, which combined with a steep rise in abstentionism as well as the casting of blank and spoiled ballots to become the "third party," with 18 percent of the votes.

Some Communists remarked soon after the election that the outcome had rewarded the PCI; this assertion is hard to support without maintaining that the "third party" of protesters and undecided voters was first and foremost founded upon dissatisfaction with the DC power system. Was this really the case?[21]

The identification of this electoral force is crucial for the whole political system in Italy but especially for the Communists. Never before had there been a party of abstention and protest aimed so directly at the PCI.[22] Pre-election surveys had revealed some voters undecided about whether to support the PSI, the PRI, or the DC, but still another faction was catalyzed by the Radicals' calls for protest votes, and the main target of this campaign was the PCI, accused of secretly keeping the party system alive. During the previous legislative term, numerous warning signals had left little doubt that Radical Secretary Marco Pannella was determined to make the most of the dissent and tedium that existed throughout the entire political system in Italy, but above all among the forces of the left. Even the candidature of Toni Negri was an open challenge to the Communists; indeed, it was repeatedly billed as such.

The growth of the MSI demonstrated that party's ability to attract a good part of the undecided right-wing voters. Although the Radical electoral campaign failed to produce a total success, it nevertheless showed that a sizable portion of left-wing voters were indeed indifferent to the alternative. On the day after the elections, however, the Communist leadership ignored those signs, claiming not merely a victory but also a reinforcement of the entire left.

While the first assertion seems improbable for reasons indicated above, the second implies a gross stretching of the truth that is most difficult to accept. Not only had the combined forces of the PCI, PSI, PR, PDUP, and DP (Proletarian Democracy) been set against each other, but their combined votes had dropped from 45.9 percent in 1979 to 45.0 percent in 1983. When asked why the national committee insisted upon calling this a victory, Renato Zangheri, a prominent member of the PCI party secretariat, answered, "I would include more than the votes of these four parties [in that evaluation]. Part of the votes that went to the Social Democrats and Republicans should also be considered left-wing votes, albeit a moderate left-wing." [23]

There may well be some truth in this assessment, but it is hard to accept the PCI's claim that supporters of the alternative were converging on the general area covered by the parties of the left. The absence of such a convergence, of course, does not automatically exclude its future existence. It is certain, however, that before the 1983 elections the PCI had never attempted to draw a similar conclusion, whether with respect to political forces or to popular support, despite the fact that the alternative could appear realistic only if the PCI gave much greater attention to the "center" of the political system.

I have discussed probably the most controversial aspects of the election results, but other factors deserve mention because they indicate a deep-rooted feeling about communism that can remain impervious to short-term variations. In the first place, the PCI performed well in all the large cities in the center and North of Italy, home of the country's most politically aware constituencies. Here the political geography seems to have been permanently modified, a change that demands even greater understanding in view of the difficult objections that the Communists faced in the very places that were governed by left-wing coalitions.

On the other hand, the overall picture of large geographic areas and single regions is somewhat different. Although decline in the North and center was only slight, the loss of votes in the South was greater, particularly in Sardegna (−2.9 percent), Molise (−2.2), and Abruzzi (−1.7), showing that the serious hemorrhages of 1979 had not been stemmed. The same was true in such traditional DC strongholds as Fruili (−1.4), where the DC lost anyway. Trentino (+0.1), Tuscany (+0.7), and Sicily (+0.5) were the sole regions in which the PCI gained, albeit only slightly.

Finally, although the PCI managed to keep its hold in industrial areas, it faced problems with young people voting for the first time, as can be deduced from the difference between its results for the House (29.9 percent) and the Senate (30.8 percent). The higher percentage in the Senate is significant because new voters can vote only for House members.

In view of the political system's tendency toward splintering and disintegration, it would be wrong to underestimate the insight into social orientation offered by these statistics, which indicate the role that the Communists will continue to play in Italy's political life in the near future. Clearly, the fast drain that hampered the PCI at the end of the 1970s as a consequence of the national-solidarity experience has slowed down. It is equally certain, however, that this can be called neither a new phase of expansion nor a decisive affirmation of the alternative strategy. Furthermore, inasmuch as the PCI's further development will depend in great part upon its leadership's ability to interpret the 1983 elections, as well as upon the leaders' skill in adapting the party line and in organizing the consensus gathered thus far, we shall conclude our analysis with a look at the way in which the party's decision-making bodies have directed their investigation of the vote and its implications.

The Ambiguous Alternative

In the elections of June 20, 1976, the DC managed to hold its ground, but the PCI crossed the 30 percent threshold for the first time. In response, no less important a DC leader than Aldo Moro spoke of "two winners" and appealed to his party to enter a "third phase," during which the Christian Democrats would no longer hold the political future of the country in their hands alone.[24]

Apart from the mere numerical outcome of the vote, 1976 proved to be the moment of maximum Communist expansion. Now as never before the PCI could contest the DC's central role in Italian politics. To do this, however, the PCI had to retain support in an area that most likely had never before voted Communist.

Naturally, things were not quite so simple. It soon became clear that the historic-compromise policy was curbing rather than accelerating transformation of the party system, thanks above all to a never-ending chain of institutional mediations. At this point the PCI touched off the abrupt Salerno switch, from which the so-called alternative was born.

In the meantime, during the second half of the 1970s the PCI's image and its credibility as the reforming party were tarnished. Although the fight for a central role in politics had reached the final round, with the DC unable to attain its former preeminence, the PCI was also progressively weakening. Its loss of strength threatened to destroy all the possible benefits it might derive from the change in policy. The alternative was thus the brainchild of a leadership mainly concerned with keeping the credibility it had gained in the past. Furthermore, no deep change had actually occurred inside or outside the party so far as newly acquired voters were concerned.

Divided about the long-term prospects for the party and damaged by a debate about organization that had dragged on for too long with no appreciable results, the PCI faced the 1983 elections with no real backing for the alternative, whether in the realm of platforms, of popular support, or of possible allies. When the time came to face the music, the alternative lost the appearance of being a political objective and became principally a tool for opposing the formation of new government alliances that would tend to minimize the role played by the Communists. The discussion that kept the sixteenth convention concerned with internal democracy, and later with the results of the election, confirmed that the leaders considered their alternative to be a trench from which they could defend themselves in a tough political fray rather than an expansive proposal that would facilitate the solution of problems inside and outside the party.

Thus the ambiguity of the Communist vote in 1983 can be viewed in light of a paradox. The vote did confirm a DC decline, which the PCI leadership interpreted as a victory for the alternative. On the other hand, not only did the PCI not advance, but it was unable even to stave off the losses it had so feared and had so ferociously fought against. Thus in 1983 the two winners of 1976 had become one loser (the DC) and, at the very least, a "nonwinner" (the PCI), inasmuch as the crisis with respect to a central political role and the party system had not resulted in the strengthening of the Communist party.

Such a situation obviously makes it clear why the PSI—the only party that managed to achieve the objectives it had proposed—with barely 11 percent of the votes was later able to take advantage of the DC-PCI weakness and to force the acceptance of the nation's first Socialist prime minister of the republic. As unimposing as the electoral strength of the Socialists may be, it was nonetheless enough to give them at least temporary access to the central role that the DC was forced to abandon following its defeat. The PCI could not form a government because of its isolation from the other political parties.

I would like to emphasize that the PCI leadership's postelection reflections still contained some uncertainties that had characterized the party line during the campaign. The statement that summarized the first national committee meeting was devoted entirely (if understandably) to the evaluation to be given the new political setup that followed in the wake of the DC's unexpected defeat. Indeed, the statement says: "[That] for the first time it might . . . be possible to create a democratic majority without the DC changes the whole political outlook and severely handicaps the old Christian Democratic centrality," thereby giving a whole new image to the problem of governing.

Although the observation was true in general terms, it was later supplemented by Berlinguer's opening remarks at the central committee meeting devoted to the elections. The PCI secretary said, "Since the PCI has survived essentially intact through years of attacks and maneuvers aimed at reducing it to a marginal and voiceless entity," the overall result of the vote, "apart from the mere count of percentages, marks a strategic victory for our policy of the 'alternative.'" [25]

Thus the most desirable aspects of the 1983 elections—DC defeat and slight PCI gains—became the means to interpret the vote as confirmation of a goal (the alternative) that the campaign had instead shown to be mainly instrumental in maintaining control over the party's electorate. Even Berlinguer's explanation of the growth of secular and Socialist forces only went so far as to observe that the Republicans and Liberals had gained because during the campaign they had not forgotten to emphasize the importance of the "moral issue," the warhorse of the Communist campaign.

As usual, the secretary was using his speech to appropriate an intermediary leadership position. Although he showed that he was aware of the troubles that these elections forecast with respect to the other social forces in the government, he went on to use the external event (the defeat of the DC) to establish the internal unity needed to develop the alternative, inasmuch as that unity did not exist within the party. The internal disunity was made painfully clear by the debate that followed Berlinguer's remarks. Cossutta, for one, protested to the point of contesting even the skeletal platform offered in Berlinguer's speech. In questioning the incorrect conclusion (which had been taken for granted, in view of the DC defeat and the PCI gains), he was one of the very few to admit that the left (especially the PCI) had not only not taken advantage of the DC's losses but had also gone on to lose more from the 1979 level.[26]

Even two traditional factions, represented on the national committee by Giorgio Napolitano and Pietro Ingrao, advanced cautious reservations from their opposite corners of the ring. The former refused to use the alternative "merely as a banner or a party badge" and interpreted the strategy "as a policy in the full sense of the word,"[27] thereby emphasizing the importance of some rapprochement with the other forces of the left and center. On the other hand, Ingrao, who stood for the left-wing interpretation of the alternative, proposed a dialogue with the other social forces and closer attention to party organization.[28]

Despite calls for unity—which in such difficult times may appear anachronistic even more than liturgical—the uncertainties of PCI leadership remained. Although the favorable postelectoral period was wasted almost entirely on day-to-day squabbles over government coalitions, it still was not decided how the PCI would ever manage to overcome the obstacles represented by its kind of inner organization or by the outlook for possible political or social allies.

To interpret everything said so far as indicating that the PCI has set off on a dead-end street would probably be erroneous, because the cycle that followed the historic compromise is still far from exhausting all its possibilities. The Communists did, however, emerge from the 1983 elections with no more votes and with the same problems that they have had since they launched the policy of the alternative. Whether this policy can gradually shed the chiefly defensive connotations that it has held so far, thereby going on to help create a real alliance for reform, will depend not solely upon the PCI but also upon the future evolution of the entire political system in Italy.

Notes

1   This point has been made by Franco Cazzola in "Le difficili identita dei partiti di massa" (The identification difficulties of the mass parties), *Laboratorio politico* (September–December 1982): 35. According to Cazzola, "only one member in four of the present Communist party leadership was not part of that group during the historic compromise phase or at the beginning of the decade." (Ibid.)

2   See Steven Hellman, "The Longest Campaign: Communist Party Strategy and the Elections of 1976," in Howard R. Penniman, ed., *Italy at the Polls: The Parliamentary Elections of 1976* (Washington, D.C.: American Enterprise Institute, 1977), 122–54. Along more general lines, see Arturo Parisi and Gianfranco Pasquino, eds., *Continuità e mutamento elettorale in Italia* (Electoral continuity and change in Italy) (Bologna: Il Mulino, 1977).

3   The best reconstruction of the period appears in Paolo Franchi, "Per una storia del compromesso" (A story of compromise), *Laboratorio politico* (March–June 1982): 44–62. Within the PCI itself, the most organic analysis comes from Giorgio Napolitano, *In mezzo al guado* (Caught in midstream) (Rome: Editori Riuniti, 1979).

4   An attempt to trigger a systematic analysis is evident in the monographic issue of *Laboratorio politico* (March–June 1982) dedicated to the historic compromise. The vast range of contributing authors makes this issue worthy of mention. An evaluation of it by Luigi Graziano appears in "Il compromesso storico ed i dilemmi dell'Eurocommunismo" (The historic compromise and the dilemma of Eurocommunism), *Democrazia e diritto* (January–February 1983): 89–110.

5   For more on 1979 election outcomes, see Joseph LaPalombara, "Two Steps Forward, One Step Back: The PCI's Struggle for Legitimacy," in Howard R. Penniman, ed., *Italy at the Polls, 1979: A Study of the Parliamentary Elections* (Washington, D.C.: American Enterprise Institute, 1981), 104–40. The title of the essay indicates the author's position.

6   No one had predicted the switch. As late as the November 3–5, 1980, central committee meeting, Berlinguer said, "The government's goal of wide democratic union" should be respected, at least until the party accepted a different goal "of equally innovative importance." Then on November 27 the national committee held a special meeting, in which it decided to adopt a radically different policy, which Berlinguer explained the next day in Salerno, where he proposed the "democratic alternative" for the first time. For the first issue, see E. Berlinguer, "Scendere in campo con nuove iniziative unitarie versos la sinistra e le forze democratiche" (To enter the field with a new unifying initiative toward the left and the forces of democracy), *L'Unità*, November 7, 1980, 1. The national committee decision is announced in "Un'altra Italia deve governare" (Another Italy must govern), *L'Unità*, November 28, 1980, 1.

7   The reference here is to the critical attitude with respect to the USSR that came as a specific reaction to the turn of events in Poland in 1981.

8   A discussion of the limits shown by the labor unions at this time can be found in Aris Accornero, "Sindacato e rivoluzione sociale" (Unionism and social revolution), *Laboratorio politico* (July–August 1981): 5–34. Along more general lines, see also Marino Regini, *I dilemmi del sindacato: Conflitto e partecipazione negli anni settanta e ottanta* (The dilemma of unionism: Conflict and participation in the 1970s and '80s) (Bologna: Il Mulino, 1981).

9   A universally valid example appears in *Proposta di progetto a medio termine* (Proposal for a medium term project) (Rome: Editori Riuniti, 1977). This theme, together with the debate that later followed regarding "the third way," was soon forgotten.

10   The question of area is addressed in Marcello Fedele, "La dinamica elettorale del PCI, 1946–1979" (The electoral dynamic of the PCI, 1946–1979), in Massimo Ilardi and Aris

Accornero, eds., *Il Partito Communista Italiano: Struttura e storia dell'organizzazione* (The Italian Communist party: Structure and history of the organization) (Milan: Feltrinelli, 1982), 293–312. For a different view of the problem, see Arturo Parisi and Gianfranco Pasquino, "Relazioni partito-elettori e tipi di voto" (Relationship of party-electorate and type of votes), in *Continuità e mutamento elettorale in Italia* (Bologna: Il Mulino, 1977), 215–49.

11   This problem has been addressed by Salvatore Sechi in "L'austero fascino del centralismo democratico" (The rigid attraction of democratic centralism), *Il Mulino* (May–June 1978): 408–53. For a different evaluation, see also Marcello Fedele, "Il partito di massa e l'equivoco dell'organizzazione" (The party of the masses and the uncertainty of the organization), *Laboratorio politico*, no. 2–3 (1982): 241–57, as well as Gianfranco Pasquino, *Organizational Models of Southern European Communist Parties*, Occasional Paper 29 (Baltimore: Johns Hopkins University, April 1980).

12   This evaluation is given in Gianfranco Pasquino, "Il PCI nel sistema politico degli anni '70" (The PCI and the political system of the 1970s), in S. Belligni, ed., *La giraffa ed il liocorno: Il PCI dagli anni '70 al nuovo decennio* (The giraffe and the unicorn: The PCI from the 1970s into the next decade) (Milan: F. Angeli, 1983), 78–79.

13   On this subject see the results of the research conducted by Marzio Barbagli and Piergiorgio Corbetta in "La svolta del PCI" (The turning point of the PCI), *Il Mulino* (January–February 1981): 95–130, which discusses the effects on the party as a result of the leadership's dilemma: wanting to "change policy line" without having to "change its secretary." Armando Cossutta, *Lo strappo: USA, USSR e movimento operaio di fronte alla crisi internazionale* (The fragmentation: The USA, USSR, and the labor movement at the head of the international crisis) (Milan: Mondadori, 1982).

14   The problem had already been "officially" discussed in the open-minded speech that Giorgio Napolitano gave at the central committee meeting on January 7–8, 1981. During the period before the convention, Pietro Ingrao's position was not the only one. See also Luigi Berlinguer, "Partito di massa e forme snodate di organizzazione" (The party of the masses and the equivocation of the organization) and Antonio Baldassarre, "Un nuovo partito di massa?" (A new party of the masses?), *Democrazia e diritto* (January–February 1983): 19–40 and 41–64, respectively. The two viewpoints differ but are equally interesting.

15   Alessandro Natta, "Le democrazie nel partito" (Democratization of the party), *Rinascita*, no. 8 (February 25, 1983): 1–2.

16   These statistics were quoted in Enzo Marzo, "PCI: Chi conta ha 40 anni" (The PCI: The ones who count are forty years old), *La Stampa*, February 23, 1983, and were later partly collected in the PCI-edited volume *XVI congresso nazionale: Organizzazione, dati, statiche* (Rome: PCI, 1983). For the problem of the transformations that have occurred within the party during the 1970s, see Aris Accornero, Renato Manheimer, and Chiara Sebastiani, eds., *L'identità Communista* (Rome: Editori Riuniti, 1983).

17   Enrico Berlinguer, "L'iniziativa del PCI per l'alternativa nelle nuove condizioni dopo il voto" (The initiative of PCI for the alternative and the new conditions of the vote), *L'Unità*, July 19, 1983, 1.

18   It should be noted that the alternative was forced to seem "timely" to such an extent that even PDUP leaders such as Lucio Magri rejected it angrily. See Magri, "Le basi reali di un'alternativa" (The real bases of an alternative), *Rinascita*, May 27, 1983, 7.

19   The most recent treatment of this problem appears in Giovanna Zincone, "Il PCI e un partito antisistema?" (The PCI and an anti-system party?), in S. Belligni, ed., *La giraffa ed il liocorno*, 83–110.

20   It should be kept in mind that a "new image" had been in the works for some time; see Giacomo Sani, "La nuova immagine del PCI e l'elettorato italiano" (The new image of the

PCI and the Italian electorate), in Donald Blackmer and Sidney Tarrow, eds., *Communism in Italy and France* (Princeton, N.J.: Princeton University Press, 1975), 323–56.

21 One evaluation that presents, at least in part, a more balanced view is Claudio Petruccioli, "Una spinta profonda a rinnovare il sistema politico" (A profound push to renovate the political system), *Rinascita*, July 8, 1983, 112.

22 One of the earliest analyses was Stefano Rodota, "Quei voti di protesta non sono tutti uguali ma prendiamoli sul serio" (The protest votes are not all equal but let us take them seriously), *L'Unità*, July 3, 1983; see also Gianfranco Pasquino, "La protesta dei senza voto" (Protest without voting), *Rinascita*, July 1, 1983, 15–16.

23 Interview with Renato Zangheri in *La Repubblica*, July 2, 1983, 3.

24 A good reconstruction of Aldo Moro's viewpoint is given in Aniello Coppola, *Moro* (Milan: Feltrinelli, 1976), 130–53.

25 Enrico Berlinguer, "L'iniziativa del PCI per l'alternativa" (The initiative of the PCI for the alternative), 1.

26 Armando Cossutta, "Intervento al Comitato Centrale" (Intervention by the Central Committee), *L'Unità*, July 26, 1983, 8.

27 Giorgio Napolitano, "Intervento al Comitato Centrale," *L'Unità*, July 21, 1983, 8.

28 Pietro Ingrao, "Intervento al Comitato Centrale," *L'Unità*, July 21, 1983, 9.

5 The Italian Socialist Party: An Indispensable Hostage

K. ROBERT NILSSON

───────In the early years of the Italian Republic, coalitions among the Christian Democratic party (DC) and smaller secular parties to its left and right, including the Social Democratic (PSDI), Republican (PRI), and Liberal (PLI) parties, succeeded one another under Christian Democratic prime ministers, thereby laying the groundwork for a Christian Democratic regime. The Socialist party (PSI), led by the late Pietro Nenni, continued throughout those years in "unity of action," with the larger Communist party (PCI) perpetually in opposition from the time of the PSI/PSDI schism to the "opening to the left" of the early 1960s.

Socialist and Demochristian leaders alike realized that a PSI share in power could come about only if the PCI took the place of the Christian Democratic party as the pivotal force in government, or if the PSI were induced to form a centrist coalition, sundering the Marxist alliance. The Fernando Tambroni episode of 1960 made the center-left formula workable, introducing a largely working-class PSI to the circles of power, thanks to Aldo Moro's skillful exploitation of the Tambroni crisis to persuade dubious observers that there was no stable alternative to an "opening to the left." Tambroni's flirtation with the right had provoked a public response of virulence—greeted in its turn by heavy-handed repression—that brought Italy as close to civil war as it had been since the attempt on Palmiro Togliatti's life.

Beginning in 1963 then, the PSI has been included in no fewer than fifteen of twenty-three governments, with an accumulated tenure of 155 months, or thirteen years. The party's share of power and (even limited) access to patronage had obvious advantages but came at a price: governmental ineffectiveness in resolving Italian problems was attributable to *all* coalition partners, including the PSI. The party's more militant members charged the leadership with preferring the perquisites of power to the transformation of society. In short, middle-class prudent reformism had displaced, according to the militant view, proper Socialist zeal.[1]

After the exhaustion of the opening to the left and its inevitable compromises, a new Socialist leadership sought to escape such criticism through opening even further to the left, by inducing the PCI to shed its identification with the Soviet Union and the Soviet party.

The PSI's dilemma has thereby intensified. Whether in alliance with the PCI or with the DC, the PSI—unless its electoral fortunes change dramatically—must be either a subordinate or a destabilizing element in any center-left coalition it joins (see table 5–1). The PSI can veto any unwelcome DC initiatives without being able to impose its own will on its partners. On the other hand, a new governing formula that would exclude the DC altogether by PSI collaboration with the PCI on the national level could only mean for the Socialists permanent subordination to a larger, less faction-ridden, and more disciplined PCI. For the PSI to rejoin the PCI in opposition might invigorate militants but would alienate the middle-class electorate so important to the PSI. The PSI's pirouettes to avoid either horn of this dilemma have repeatedly brought down governments and have done nothing to attract voters.[2]

Craxi as Leader   The center-left experiment "shook the tree while others gathered the fruit."[3] Disappointment over the meager pickings was crowned by the losses of the 1976 general election that led to the repudiation of Francesco De Martino's leadership. Bettino Craxi, a right autonomist, defeated Antonio Giolitti to become party secretary, after having forged an alliance between his own reformist supporters and those of the "lion of the Left," Claudio Signorile. Together, Craxi and Signorile eliminated central committee rivals, as the "revolt of the forty-year-olds" unfolded. Their judicious patronage appointments consolidated their grip on the party.[4] By 1983, a full 25 percent of Italy's banks were run by PSI appointees, as contrasted with 5 percent two years earlier.[5]

Craxi and Signorile split in January 1980 over the ENI (National Hydrocarbon Agency)–Petromina question. Thus when Riccardo Lombardi, long the left conscience of the party, resigned his post as president, the hold of Craxi's neoreformist forces over the party was complete. His erstwhile enemies, especially in the southern regions from which De Martino, Giacomo Mancini, and Signorile drew their strength, hastened to climb aboard lest the bandwagon leave them behind altogether. "Once they were all De Martiniani, and now they're all Craxiani."[6]

Craxi's surge to power symbolized the passage of the party's leadership into younger, steadier hands: those of leaders who were reformist, modernizing, secular, distanced from both the DC and the PCI, but no better able than

Table 5-1 Percent of National Votes by Party, Chamber of Deputies, 1948–1983

Party	1948	1953	1958	1963	1968	1972
Center						
DC	48.5	41.2	43.0	38.3	39.1	38.8
PSDI	—	4.5	4.6	6.1	—	6.1
PRI	2.5	1.6	1.4	1.4	2.0	2.9
Right						
PLI	3.8	3.0	3.5	7.0	5.8	3.9
MSI	2.0	5.8	4.7	5.1	4.5	8.7
DN						
Major left						
PCI	31.0 [b]	22.6	22.7	25.3	26.9	27.2
PSI		12.7	14.2	13.8	14.5 [c]	9.6
Minor left						
PR (Radical party)						
PDUP (Democratic Party						
of Proletarian Unity)						
DP (Proletarian Democracy)						

a. Total seats = 630.
b. Including PSI.
c. PSI and PSDI combined to make the PSU in 1968–69.

their predecessors to fulfill the Lombardian vision of the PSI's historic role as a left party aiming at undermining DC hegemony to accelerate the creation of a PCI/PSI, all-left government. To maintain the PSI autonomy necessary for the realization of such a long-range objective, new short-term directions were identified and appropriate slogans coined: governability, conflictual democracy, European socialism with a human face.

By the spring of 1980 Craxi's leadership was uncontested, despite the party's failure in 1979 to raise its voter share to above 10 percent and to win over either the individuals who had left the PCI or the progressive, secular middle class.

A Changing Role   The PSI's tactical shifts, from "center left" to "never again without the Communists," from the "democratic alternative" to the "alternation for governability," were produced by the contradictory goals of sharing power (with a larger mass party to either right or left) and retaining PSI autonomy. The fundamental dilemma has not been resolved even with Craxi's appointment as prime minister. The forty-first PSI congress (held in Turin in 1978) and the "Socialist Project" elicited from party intellectuals set out party aspirations that were reiterated and refined at the forty-second party congress (held in

1976	1979	1979 Seats	1983	1983 Seats[a]	Change in Seats, 1979–83
38.7	38.3	262	32.9	225	−37
3.4	3.8	20	4.1	23	3
3.1	3.0	16	5.1	29	13
1.3	1.9	9	2.9	16	7
6.1	5.3	30	6.8	42	12
	0.6				
34.4	30.4	201	29.9	198	− 3
9.6	9.8	62	11.4	73	11
1.1	3.5	18	2.2	11	− 7
1.5	1.4	6	—[d]		
1.5	0.8	—	1.5	7	7

[a]. PCI.

Sources: *Il resto del Carlino*, June 26, 1983, 1; *La Stampa*, June 6, 1979, 1; *La Repubblica*, June 29, 1983, 1; *Rinascita*, July 1, 1983, 2.

Palermo in 1981), and at the PSI planning conference (held at Rimini in the spring of 1982), where Craxi's courting of the managerial elite of the "Third Industrial Revolution" and of the youth of the "Electronic Challenge" was embraced by party leaders.[7] As we will see below, the PSI entered the 1983 general elections on a platform set forth in documents prepared on these occasions.

Those documents describe the democratic future of the nation as depending on ending the DC's political hegemony, best done by a secular cluster (PSI-PSDI-PRI) as the only alternative to the PCI, to which the small lay parties want to be neither subordinate nor auxiliary. The governability of Italy, in its turn, requires the "effective capacity of the executive to decide and to control" and therefore requires institutional reforms able to bring Italy closer to the European social democratic model. (We can only imagine how the inversion of the Communist-Socialist power balance of François Mitterrand's Socialists must consume Mr. Craxi.)

The same documents continue an essentially social democratic discourse when they turn to economic first principles: Private enterprise is not incompatible with socialism unless it creates "hegemonic power over the social and economic system." Nationalizations that produce "bureaucratic collectivism"

Table 5-2 1973 PSI Membership by Social/Economic Class (percent by region)

Region	Worker	Clerk	Self-employed	Agricultural Worker	Inactive	Other
North	40.6	21.3	7.4	7.5	15.0	8.2
Center	37.0	23.8	8.2	9.2	12.3	9.5
South	30.1	19.4	7.2	18.9	12.8	11.6
Italy	35.2	20.9	7.4	13.0	13.5	10.0

Source: "Il Partito Socialista Italiano: Strutture e organizzazione," *Socialismo Oggi* (Venezia: Marsilio Editori, 1975), 330, 343.

and threaten efficiency and innovation are rejected by the PSI, the party of the future. The "old myths" of the left have, indeed, been shattered and a new, modern, Western image of the PSI has been offered in contrast to that of the PCI, which is held to be rigidly inflexible and doctrinaire. Party intellectuals such as Alessandro Pizzorno, Norberto Bobbio, Paolo Sylvos Labini, and Federico Mancini played a major role in this pursuit of autonomy and availability. Craxi himself wrote an essay on Proudhon's thought, prompting a debate with the PCI, as it was meant to do.[8]

Despite the misgivings of people who found the leader's "instinct for the jugular" and arrogance unsettling, the majority recognized the need for aggressive leadership of a party known not to be a workers' party in the fashion of other European Socialist parties, yet offering itself as simultaneously European, working class, and a spokesman for the progressive elements of other classes.[9] Table 5–2 uses the only available figures to show the party's variations in social composition by region. Those figures reveal that in 1973 the PSI members in the South already came primarily from the lower middle class and from the ranks of agricultural workers. Moreover, studies done since that time agree that the party's southernization has accelerated with the growth and spread of available patronage.[10]

Shortly before the 1983 election, a survey of the 523,000 card-holding members of the PSI revealed that 9.1 percent were university graduates (three times as many as in 1973), 18.9 percent were secondary school graduates (twice as many as in 1973), 6 percent fewer were workers than in 1973, and 4 and 3 percent more were professionals and technicians, respectively.[11]

A Demoskopea poll with 7,500 respondents checked the congruence between parties' electorates and campaign imagery, revealing that, as shown in tables 5–3 and 5–4, the PSI is sustained primarily by voters drawn from among the middle-aged and the lower middle class.[12]

The Party Tested   The spring of 1983 seemed an unwise moment for the PSI to force a general election by withdrawing support for the Amintore Fanfani government. Craxi had already failed in an earlier bid to become prime minister (Giovanni Spadolini instead became the first non-Demochristian to occupy that office). Moreover, Craxi led a party weakened by scandal in Turin and Savona (involving allegations of corruption touching Socialist city councillors) and unified by feudal baronetcies rather than by militance. Yet Craxi, confident of his new, young cadres and reassured by his "brain trust," led the party to an election that, when the votes were tallied, was less profitable than had been hoped. Why, then, had the risk been taken?

One reason seems to have been related to changes in the dominant DC, and the second reason concerned the DC's relationship with the PCI. The DC,

Table 5-3 Sex and Age of Voters by Party (index: Italy = 100)

	Sex		Age					
	Male	Female	18–24	25–34	35–44	45–54	55–84	84+
DC	87	112	93	83	98	104	104	120
PCI	116	85	131	131	107	82	81	68
PSI	115	86	80	104	103	112	109	83
PRI	116	85	60	121	125	105	99	71
PR	105	95	223	158	81	56	60	47
PSDI	129	73	66	70	93	154	113	97
PLI	110	91	116	102	98	85	95	111
MSI/DN	127	75	145	77	84	81	96	139
PDUP/DP	131	73	180	250	106	34	9	16

Source: C. Valentini, "Con quella faccia da straniero" (With that foreign face), *Panorama*, June 20, 1983, 55.

Table 5-4 Educational Level of Voters by Party (index: Italy = 100)

Party	University Degree	High School	Junior High	Elementary School	Less than Six Years
DC	78	94	83	110	119
PCI	66	82	121	102	95
PSI	88	104	120	103	60
PRI	360	162	113	49	39
PR	188	209	125	38	42
PSDI	170	120	116	72	94
PLI	268	217	93	48	35
MSI/DN	72	131	133	79	69
PDUP/DP	456	219	95	31	8

Source: C. Valentini, "Con quella faccia da straniero" (With that foreign face), *Panorama*, June 20, 1983, 55.

led by Ciriaco De Mita, was regaining self-confidence, and its new leadership had chosen the unambiguous role of representing the most modern and progressive entrepreneurs of *Confindustria* (employers' association), even if this meant modifying the clientelistic practices that had, in large part, accounted for the party's interclass appeal (a modification for which the DC was to pay a heavy electoral price). Such a DC, if given time for regrouping, might very well be in a position to create a center-right "Euromoderate" government similar to those of Helmut Kohl and Margaret Thatcher.[13]

PSI leaders reasoned that it was better to face down a resurgent DC in 1983 than in 1984, by which time Pershing and Cruise missiles would be installed at Comiso, with a Socialist defense minister (Lelio Lagorio) responsible. A 1984 election run against a center-right DC and—simultaneously—a PCI able to exploit whatever public disquiet might result from the missile deployment would have left the PSI facing another test of the proposition that, when the DC and PCI are polarized, the PSI suffers because it must choose between the two, thus compromising its claims to distinctness and paying the loss electorally.[14] Craxi thought it best to avoid the test.

The tactical question of timing involved calculation. Longer range attitudes to the DC involved fears. Fears of the DC's potential for an "authoritarian involution" were expressed by Craxi as early as the Palermo congress, where he warned "against the risks of a test-tube capitalistic, technocratic . . . , conservative, integralist, bureaucratic" authoritarianism. When FIAT (Fabbrica Italiana Automobili: Torino) spokesman Cesare Romiti deplored political parties in a speech to the graduating class of the Carabinieri academy, and when Giovanni Agnelli of FIAT told the chiefs of staff of the North Atlantic Treaty Organization (NATO) that Italy should be run by those who are most competent —that is, by its industrialists—the entire left became alarmed.[15]

Moreover, the possibility that De Mita would outflank the PSI by agreeing to deal directly with the PCI as a wholly Italian and Western party, legitimate enough to alternate with the DC, left Craxi with little choice. If he was to occupy the anti-Communist center as an alternative to a corrupt DC, the time to act had come.

The Campaign

Organization　Mindful of the 1976 experience, PSI leaders by and large avoided immoderate attacks on the DC lest they produce a swing to the PCI (the anti-DC party par excellence). Moreover, even the most optimistic Socialist forecasts could not mask the likelihood that any postelection coalition would turn on the DC. To exacerbate PSI-DC relations, therefore, would be to reduce PSI negotiating strength.

The slogan, "Rigor, Fairness, Growth" (*Rigore, Equita, Sviluppo*) offered appeals to each targeted segment of the electorate: "Rigor" for the middle-class professionals, "fairness" and renewed "growth" for the labor unions and the rank and file. Craxi's speeches and interviews and party publications frequently stressed eagerness for identification with the Socialist parties of France, West Germany, and the Scandinavian countries.

More revealing of the party's strategy is the memorandum sent by Craxi in the opening days of the campaign to all party candidates "suggesting" that they emphasize *not* coalition prospects (necessarily involving collaboration with the DC) but *program*.[16] Let us now direct our attention to that program.

Substance The 105-point concrete proposals can be placed, for our purposes, in either of two categories, institutional reform or economic policy, which aimed together at confronting Italy's long-range governability and solvency.

Institutional reforms A bicameral committee was proposed to study the changes to be implemented.[17] It would prepare proposals concerning the selection of the president of the republic, to be chosen directly by the electorate rather than by the parliament and for a term shorter than that provided under the 1947 constitution. Similarly, the president of the Council of Ministers— that is, the prime minister—was to be chosen independently of his cabinet by the parliament. Thus the vote of confidence would be given to him and his program without reference to the delicate balancing of factions within supportive parties. Party secretaries' decisive hold on Italian political life—the "partitocracy"—would be weakened, if not broken altogether. The addition of a cabinet council made up of major ministers, it was hoped, would place the prime minister in a better position to coordinate the formulation of his government's policies. The ministries of the budget, the treasury, and finance should be subsumed by a single Ministry of Economics. Similarly, the ministries of state participation, southern development, and industry and commerce should form a single Ministry of Industry and the South. It would have at its disposal the Fund for Investment and the Promotion of Industry. The *Cassa per il Mezzogiorno* (Southern Development Fund) should be reorganized to serve regional authorities and their territorial development programs. The Ministry of Labor should control the Fund for Employment and Labor, to be financed by increased tax revenues. Moreover, the National Agency for Labor and Employment, responsible for worker training and for organizing socially beneficial projects, should be equipped to provide income maintenance during periods of labor redundancy.

In parliamentary business the West German institution of the "constructive vote of no confidence" would be introduced for possible adoption. It would allegedly prevent the joining together of parliamentary forces seeking to bring down a government unless they were able to transfer their confidence to another coalition, which they would agree to sustain. Crises, presumably, would occur less frequently, and executive stability would be assured. The PSI also advocated reducing the number of deputies and senators to a total of eight hundred and redefining the competencies of the upper house. The Difensore Civico Nazionale would be appointed, with functions similar to those of an ombudsman. Finally, the practice of holding floor votes by secret ballot should be ended, the better to ensure governmental disciplinary control over the MPs who are members of the coalition parties. (The insistence on such discipline, as expressed by Prime Minister Craxi, led a PCI deputy to charge him with attempting to "domesticate a sovereign assembly.")[18] Party members thus tried to keep back-bench snipers from voting against their party's leadership under cover of the secret ballot, as they have in the past.

Few of these innovations would require constitutional revisions, although the method of selection and the tenure of the president of the republic of course would. Other constitutional revisions would be needed to attain some of the economic objectives outlined summarily below. Articles of the Constitution that deal with the organization of labor, the right to strike, and worker participation in economic policy formulation would require revision advocated by the PSI. Relative to the judiciary and its eventual reform, the position of the PSI included: procedural revisions aiming at accelerating investigative and trial procedures; the introduction of the justice of the peace to decongest the calendars of lower courts in dealing with minor civil controversies; and the redrawing of jurisdictional lines. Together, these revisions would make Italian justice conform to "the model" of the major Western democracies. The public administration was, of course, to be reformed: every Italian government for the last twenty years has vowed that it would be, often assigning ministerial rank to a secretary for bureaucratic reform.[19]

One of the last areas for institutional reform was local government. Here, too, the Socialists favored the direct election of mayors by city populations so that local needs rather than national party considerations would be paramount among local political notables. (Apparently no thought was given to the problems this provision might present to Socialist advocacy of centralized control over party "barons.") In the large metropolitan areas, the institution of a new level of government would be considered.

Economic policy   Rational planning and efficiency require dealing with questions of productivity, labor costs, and mobility for maximum resource use. PSI positions on budget cuts, revenue increases, and industrial relations reflected these concerns. Although it opposed "monetarism of the Euroamerican Right," the PSI envisaged rationalizing income supplements to reduce the deficit by lowering spending, increasing tax revenues, and more vigorously policing tax evaders.[20] An incomes policy and an (undefined) reorganization of government funds would release new investment, most especially for the

South and for young entrants to the labor force who have yet to find their employer. New Labor Agencies, to be established regionally, would be financed by funds now used for workmen's compensation (*Cassa Integrazione Guadagni*, or CIG) and would be administered with union participation to determine labor market needs and to regularize the practice of "black" labor or "cottage industries" (the "submerged" economy).

In this way and by regulating the right to strike, PSI policies would increase productivity. The PSI was also committed to establishing instruments for the formulation and supervision of industrial policy (understood as government measures to promote or to prevent structural industrial change) and to implement the European Community's Fifth Directive (inviting member states to legislate two-tier company boards, one of which includes worker representatives to participate in decision making, the very "codetermination" long rejected by Italian unionists and leaders alike).

That industrial democracy is one of the central themes of European socialism explains the PSI's readiness to risk the rank-and-file hostility that confronted earlier proponents of worker collaboration in the administration of a reinforced capitalism.[21] Together, these political and economic proposals constituted the Great Reform, which became one of the pillars of the PSI campaign.

Three-Year Pact   Entering the campaign with such a program, hoping to attract voters on the left and on the right, Craxi proposed to the DC—ten days before the elections—an agreement to sustain an acceptable postelection coalition for three years, thus guaranteeing that effective, long-range measures would be given an opportunity to have their intended impact. To many observers on the left, both in the party and outside it, the proposal meant only two things: that the DC would be cemented in power, and that the leftist alternative would be postponed. To the leaders of the DC, the proposal ensured the relative isolation of the PSI from the left and thereby raised the price to be asked of the Socialists for the status of "privileged interlocutor." The pact affirmed the DC's centrality by stabilizing the status quo of the coalition brought down on Socialist initiative.[22]

January 22 Accord   The Socialist program to increase productivity, reduce inflation, lower the deficit, and deal with unemployment could not be implemented without the cooperation of organized labor, especially as regards labor costs.

Agreements (for which the PSI took major credit) painfully negotiated during 1982 were signed in January 1983 by a representative of the major employers' association, *Confindustria*'s Vittorio Merloni; the separate union-federation components CGIL (General Confederation of Italian Workers), CISL (Catholic Trade Union Association), and UIL (Italian Workers' Union); and Labor Minister Vincenzo Scotti (a Christian Democrat in the Fanfani government).[23] The accord put an end to salary leveling, which highly skilled and supervisory workers had long resented; held out the hope of reducing inflation to 13 percent for 1983 and to 10 percent by 1984; and courted union leaders by its affirmation of trilateral "concertation" such as that which the negotiations themselves signified. Family allowances were to be made inversely proportional to gross income, and transport, postal, and other utility rates were set to rise. The accord also sought to reduce the collectivity's health costs by reducing the number of pharmaceuticals subsidized by the state.

The main feature of the accord was the revision of the wage indexation system—the escalator clause, or *scala mobile*, which pegs automatic wage increases to regular readings of the cost-of-living index. The logic was that automatic increases (1) had reduced the scope of collective bargaining, because the increases brought about by the escalator clause absorbed the whole of what might have been negotiated; (2) had demoralized the most skilled workers by reducing wage differentials; and thereby (3) had discouraged the acquisition of new skills and the mastery of new techniques. The revision of the indexing system reduced wage increases by 15-18 percent, thereby lowering the cost of labor.

To persuade the CGIL, CISL, and UIL to swallow such medicine, some sweetening was added in the form of guarantees that, should the inflation rate continue above the programmed level of 13 percent, the loss in workers' real income would be offset by increased tax deductions. Moreover, industry agreed to concessions concerning contracts up for renewal: an across-the-board increase of LIt. 100,000 monthly to be spread over 1983-85 ($62 monthly).

For their part, the employers were accorded the right to hire individuals for on-the-job training programs and to take on part-time workers without recourse to the local labor office lists: That is, individuals can be *named* for hiring, a practice formerly forbidden under Italian labor law. The accord also invited its signatories to regulate the right to strike and reduced the work year by forty hours by mid-1985.

The party claimed that this trilateral agreement on economic policy demonstrated its ability to deal with modern industrial society without recourse to the "mythology of the past—the collision between classes." Similarly relegated to the past is the "myth of the inviolability of the escalator clause." By attacking it, the PSI risked losing its (modest) working-class support, dividing the largest of Italy's unions, and splitting the interunion federation. Not to have mounted the attack would have meant yielding the field to continued high inflation and the loss of overseas markets and of domestic governability.[24]

Foreign policy   PSI proposals noted that solidarity with NATO and with the United States would not preclude the advocacy of East-West arms limitations agreements, continued trade with the Eastern bloc countries, or friend-

Table 5-5 Percent of Votes for PSI in Major Cities, 1979–83

Region	General Election 1979	General Election 1983	Change
NORTH			
Turin	9.9	9.2	−0.7
Milan	11.6	11.0	−0.6
Trento	10.2	10.5	0.3
Venice	11.9	13.3	1.4
Trieste	3.7	6.3	2.6
Genoa	12.0	10.3	−1.7
Bologna	7.8	8.4	0.6
CENTER			
Florence	10.1	10.2	0.1
Perugia	10.8	11.6	0.8
Ancona	9.0	11.1	2.1
Roma	8.3	8.6	0.3
L'Aquila	7.9	11.7	3.8
SOUTH			
Naples	5.9	8.9	3.0
Bari	10.7	18.4	7.7
Potenza	7.0	7.8	0.8
Catanzaro	10.5	14.5	4.0
Palermo	7.0	9.8	2.8
Cagliari	8.7	9.1	0.4

Source: Adapted from *La Repubblica*, June 29, 1983, 15.

ship and cooperation with other nations of the Mediterranean basin, both European and Arab. Italian initiatives in Middle East negotiations, which were to include a mediating role, would facilitate the restoration of "Arab lands to the Arabs" while ensuring Israeli security. The foreign policy positions of the party seem intended as much to reassure Italy's major transatlantic ally regarding Socialist reliability and loyalty as to mollify opinion within Italy.

The Results   Clientelism, corrupt practices, and scandals—so long attributed to the DC—have tainted the PSI, giving weight to pessimists' predictions. Outside the party, observers complained that the party was irresponsibly bringing down successive governments and seemed to lust after ministerial power. The gap between the party's actual voting support and its pretensions was reportedly growing, as an increasingly middle-aged, middle-class party, administered by white-collar workers and clerks, addressed the new professionals of the Electronic Age.

Figure 5-1   Percent of Vote for PSI by Region (Chamber of Deputies, 1983), and Change from 1979. Source: *Rinascita*, July 1, 1983, 10.

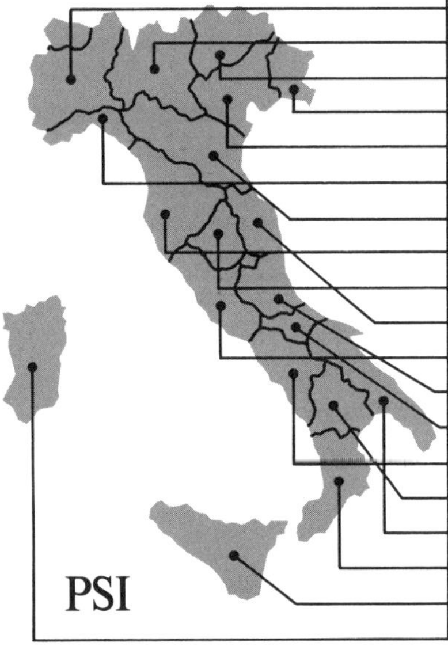

Region	1983 Vote	1979-83 Change	
Piedmont	10.5	0.2	
Lombardy	12.0	0.7	
Trentino A.A.	6.8	0.2	
Friuli V.G.	10.8	3.2	North
Veneto	10.6	1.1	
Liguria	10.1	−1.5	
Emilia R.	9.9	1.4	
Tuscany	11.0	1.3	
Umbria	12.2	1.0	Center
Marche	9.8	1.8	
Lazio	10.0	1.3	
Abruzzi	9.7	2.2	
Molise	7.9	0.5	
Campania	12.8	3.4	
Basilicata	11.0	0.1	South
Puglia	14.4	4.2	
Calabria	16.1	3.3	
Sicilia	13.3	3.3	
Sardinia	10.1	−1.2	

PSI

Pessimism seemed no less called for on tactical grounds. Although the possibility existed of a DC/PCI "arrangement," the Three-Year Pact proposal was meant to parry attack from that quarter. The main preoccupation was another matter: The essentially conservative, "rigorist" program risked antagonizing Socialist workers—already slipping away—as well as party ideologues, who repudiated the goal of ensuring capitalism's survival and who could be heard grumbling that, if the Liberal party's policies were to be advanced, Liberal leaders might as well do the work.[25] Craxi's "new party" was indeed being tested.

When the votes of June 26 and 27 had been counted, therefore, the party had reason to be relieved, if not exultant. Although PSI gains in major cities were indeed more conspicuous in the southern regions, modest gains were registered in many cities in the North (and in *all* central cities). Table 5–5 contrasts PSI votes in the 1979 general election with those of 1983.

The same proved to be true on the regional level, as figure 5–1 demonstrates. In only two Italian regions did the PSI suffer a net loss relative to 1979: Liguria (1.5 percent) and Sardinia (1.2 percent). In all other regions, the registered change showed a net gain: modest, to be sure, but a gain increasing by eleven the number of seats to which the PSI was entitled in the Chamber of Deputies.

Why, then, was Socialist enthusiasm over the outcome so restrained? For one thing, the losses in Milan and Turin (Milan is Craxi's home district, and his preferential votes there were fewer than Spadolini's) meant that the "emerging classes" had been unsuccessfully courted. In fact, every analysis showed that these were the voters primarily responsible for the impressive showing of the PRI, which was apparently more readily accepted as a credible party of rigor by the secular center. Craxi's attempt to forge a New Deal "Keynesian coalition" had failed just as surely as did his attempt to enter the club of modern, Western, reformist Socialist parties commanding a relative majority. The PSI was still 6.8 million votes removed from the PCI. Yet having been punished for its association with (and even emulation of) the DC, it still found itself re-forming a government very like the one that it had just brought down, but this time with Craxi at its head.

Party publications called the elections a "discreet electoral success and a great political success," an electoral success because the PSI alone among the three mass parties increased its vote, if only by a small percentage, and a great political success because "the neo-centrist De Mita line that aimed at reducing

Table 5-6 Percent of Votes by Party for Chamber of Deputies, 1976–1983

Party	General Election			Change 1979–83 (percent)	Seats[a]	Change 1979–83 (seats)
	1976	1979	1983			
PCI	34.4	30.4	29.9	−0.5	198	− 3
PSI	9.6	9.8	11.4	1.6	73	11
PR	1.1	3.4	2.2	−1.2	11	− 7
PDUP/DP	1.5	2.2	1.5	−0.7	7	7
Left	46.6	45.8	45.0	−0.8	289	—
DC	38.7	38.3	32.9	−5.4	225	−37
PSDI	3.4	3.8	4.1	0.3	23	3
PRI	3.1	3.0	5.1	2.1	29	13
PLI	1.3	1.9	2.9	1.0	16	7
SVP*	0.5	0.6	0.5	−0.1	—	—
Center-Right	47.0	47.6	45.5	−2.1	293	—
MSI/DN	6.1	5.9	6.8	—	42	12

a. Total seats = 630.

*German-language DC party in Alto Adige.

Sources: Rinascita, July 1, 1983, 2, 4; Sani, "Italian Voters, 1976–1979," in Howard R. Penniman, ed., Italy at the Polls, 1979: A Study of Parliamentary Elections (Washington, D.C.: American Enterprise Institute, 1981), 44.

the [PSI] role was beaten."[26] Craxi's own calculations contrast the fortunes of
the lay allies of the PSI with those of its larger rivals on the right and the left.
Thus the combined DC and PCI votes of 1976 were 73 percent and fell to 62.8
percent in 1983, whereas the combined votes of PSI, PSDI, PRI, and PLI increased from 17.4 percent in 1976 to 23.5 percent in 1983 (see table 5–6).[27]

"The real alternative," said Giorgio Benvenuto in a postelection interview,
"is the lay and Socialist one."[28] But that alternative, like the formula heretofore, can reach its majority only in alliance with either Demochristians or
Communists. In fact the coalition that supported Fanfani in the six months of
his preelection government is similar to that supporting Craxi, despite its components' loss of three seats in the Chamber of Deputies and four seats in the
Senate. As table 5–6 shows, no alternative was possible, either on the left or
on the right. No one can rule without the center; the center can govern only by
raiding the left or the neo-Fascist Italian Social Movement-National Democracy (MSI-DN) right.

The Craxi-Martelli analysis of the party's showing recognized the power
of the *signori delle tessere* (the manipulators of membership cards used in
seating congress delegations) and their preoccupations with patronage, which
nourishes factionalism and protects the autonomy of the party less than that of
its barons.[29]

Within the party, it has been openly asked whether the PSI should continue to identify itself in the person of the leader. Campaign commercials on
private television channels seemed more appropriate to a personalized American presidential campaign than to a parliamentary contest among parties. The
left wing of the party especially has insisted that a clear program must be
"open to the contributions of the Communist opposition." The end of DC
hegemony, if indeed that is what the elections portend, should be used to
facilitate "PCI reformist evolution."[30]

In view of the arithmetic of the electoral results, with the PRI clearly
stealing a march on both the DC and the PSI in the three-way race to appeal to
the entrepreneurial bourgeoisie and to the emerging classes, how did Craxi
rather than Spadolini become prime minister? In at least one observer's
opinion, Spadolini's very success led the DC to block his return to the prime
minister's office. In fact it is more desirable for the DC for the PSI to be given
the assignment, "in the hope that they will use it poorly."[31]

The Current Status of the PSI

The price exacted—and readily paid—for Craxi's accession to the office of
chief executive included the PSI's yielding the influential ministries that were
headed by Socialists in the last Fanfani government in favor of fewer and less
prestigious seats. Under Fanfani, Socialists had headed defense (Lelio Lagorio),

Table 5-7 Cabinet Seat Distribution: Composition by Party
of Fifth Fanfani Government and First Craxi Government

Party	Fanfani V Seats	Percent of Total	Craxi I Seats	Percent of Total
PSI	8	29.6	6	20.0
DC	13	48.0	16	53.3
PSDI	4	14.8	3	10.0
PLI	2	7.4	2	6.6
PRI	0	0	3	10.0
Total	27	100.0[a]	30	100.0[b]

Note: Figures may not add to totals because of rounding.
a. 99.8 percent.
b. 99.9 percent.
Source: Author's compilations.

finance (Francesco Forte), state participation (Gianni De Michelis), and southern development (Claudio Signorile). In contrast (see table 5–7), the major Socialist ministries in Craxi's first government were transportation, labor, tourism, foreign trade, and European Economic Community relations.

Not only has the PSI suffered a reduction in its share of cabinet seats, but the cabinet's composition is additional cause for concern in that it is likely to increase rather than diminish factional tensions (and thus sniping) within the Demochristian majority. The inclusion of a "technician" (Filippo Maria Pandolfi); of a "Young Turk" (Giovanni Goria) at treasury; of Oscar Scalfaro, an old Scelbaiano (any supporter of the DC faction once led by right-wing Mario Scelba) at the interior; and of Nino Gullotti, old *doroteo* (DC centrist) at culture, provides a cross section of a party describable as a "federation of ideologies."

Apt as such a description is when applied to the DC, it seems even more appropriate to the Pentapartito itself. The negotiations leading to Giulio Andreotti's appointment to the foreign ministry and to Spadolini's installation at defense simultaneously ensure DC and PRI interest in sustaining the government, reassure the United States and NATO concerning the "reliability" of yet another Socialist-led member government in the Mediterranean, and—from the DC's perspective—can be read as meant to preclude a U.S. shift toward the PSI as an acceptably moderate governing party to the exclusion of the DC.[32]

Yet despite the power disparities of the coalition parties and despite the centrifugal dynamics built into the cabinet itself, the PSI program has been put in motion. A parliamentary committee of forty has formed under the chairmanship of the PLI's Aldo Bozzi (after an unseemly squabble with Fanfani that ended only when the PLI threatened to withdraw from the Pentapartito) and has begun to consider the institutional reforms proposed by the PSI. The cabinet council, comprising Craxi, Arnaldo Forlani (DC), Spadolini (PRI), Luigi Longo (PSDI), and Renato Altissimo (PLI), meets and functions, negotiating the extent to which each coalition member is prepared to sustain the joint proposals. In sum, initiatives advanced by the PSI at Turin, Palermo, and Rimini are being considered. The 1984 budget, moreover, reflected the PSI's priorities.

The mathematics are inexorable, however: The PSI commands no majority. Craxi's ascendancy is a consequence of the impossibility of a center-right government forming around a DC wounded at the polls. His policies will be considered and adopted as long as the outcome is not perceived as destabilizing, and opposition can be expected from several sources. Early use of the secret ballot to defeat the government on a procedural question (concerning construction licensing and taxation) suggested that Craxi would not find it easy to have his way. One Demochristian, reacting to Craxi's anger at the *franchi triatori* (snipers: a term used to describe those parliamentarians who, under cover of the secret ballot, vote against measures that their party is committed to support), described the projected reform as a coup de main (*colpo di mano*).[33]

The party also finds itself locked in battle with its DC ally on the question of local *giunte*. The DC has insisted that national legislation proposed by the Pentapartito be implemented by local administrations that reproduce the national governing formula. Its insistence forces the PSI to consider abandoning its historical associations with the left in favor of the moderate right. The PSI seems highly unlikely to accede to demands that could lead to divorce from its traditional constituencies in those cities where leftist *giunte* (PCI/PSI) long rules. Moreover, local Socialists, who do not perceive themselves as "colonies in a Socialist empire," are hardly likely to accept marching orders from the party's headquarters in Rome.[34]

In other program areas the chief opposition will come from the workers' ranks, not because of the votes they might deny the party, but because anti-government protest demonstrations and strikes would define the government's helplessness in dealing with industrial relations, labor costs, and economic policy—cornerstones of the Socialist Project and of the January Accord. Incomes policy, reduced wage indexing, spending cuts, and tax revisions constitute a policy of rigor seemingly imposed by economic circumstances, whether in Mitterrand's France or in Craxi's Italy. A labor consensus supportive of such sacrifices can come only if there are clear countervailing gains. The burdens of the Craxi government will include persuading the work force that a new industrial policy (legislation is being drafted by Minister of Industry Altissimo) and the implementation of the Fifth Directive (being studied by Giuliano Amato and Mario Dido) offset the sacrifices of lowering labor costs.[35]

If the Pentapartito is able to steer the budget and the program through parliament, Craxi's standing in the eyes of the public will no doubt rise. Public distrust of parties and of professional politicians, has reached extreme levels, at least in the polls. A Demoskopea interview of 2,000 voters in November 1982 revealed that 87.9 percent had "no faith" or "little faith" in the parties or their leaders. No coalition formula (Pentapartito, National Solidarity, Left Alternative, or Lay Government) had wide popular support. Yet 48.1 percent preferred a Socialist prime minister and 28.3 percent were opposed.[36]

Craxi's future, like that of his party, will depend on his ability to disarm critics and opponents within his own party, within the government he heads, and among extraparliamentary forces able to frustrate policies. Close observers have already noted that Craxi has changed from an irascible, aggressive, arrogant campaigner and party leader to a man "prudent, formalistic, even vague."[37] The exercise of power weighs more heavily than its pursuit.

The evidence suggests that he is pragmatic rather than inflexible, prudent as well as calculating, and quicker to exploit an opening to power than to organize its effective use. He may prove to fit Fidel Castro's definition of the most effective revolutionary—the "principled opportunist"—or he may prove to be the leftist secular component of a moderate majority.

Conclusions

Many contradictory elements of the PSI's position will present difficulties of their own. A PSI contribution to the "governability" of Italy satisfies one of the party's proclaimed objectives but only by stabilizing a system in which the central role is perforce played by a DC that has been its chief architect and beneficiary and whose alleged excesses produced the "crisis of governability" in the first instance. Similarly, the party's pursuit of autonomy from the PCI leads it to attack its Communist cousins for their tenuous Soviet ties while courting them in the name of solidarity on the left and the transformation of a society increasingly stabilized with each advance in governability.[38]

In dealing with the union federation, too, the PSI's policies of "rigor" run afoul of recollections of the EUR Accords of 1978 (named for the Esposizione Universale Romana, a convention center outside Rome); that is, union leaders and party leaders alike risk losing the support of the rank and file when they counsel austerity, moderation, and worker restraint in order to salvage a capitalist system of accumulation. To militate for moderation is not only a contradiction in terms but also means the pursuit of policies that most unionists have found to be dysfunctional. In their experience, militance pays; moderation does not.

Thus if Craxi can cajole parliament into adopting a program of necessity, he might gain in middle-class support but at the risk of seeing his party divide over the issues separating reformists from Lombardiani, advocates of the sound administration of capitalism from proponents of systemic transformation. The PSI's schismatic tradition—despite the bandwagon effect to which I earlier alluded—may be revived by the "search for power" guaranteeing the governability of a system that traditional Socialist ideals are committed to transforming.[39] The "consensus of the center" may come at a very high cost.

Throughout the effort, a jealous DC and other lay rivals can be expected to impede those solutions most certain to accrue to Craxi's advantage. Just as the left within his party insists that saving capitalism should not be a Socialist preoccupation, so his coalition partners do not define the resolution of Socialist problems as their primary concern.

When Craxi was invited to form a government, in the face of palpable PSI coolness, the Milan Stock Exchange actually gained. "Imagine," said Giorgio Galli, "a Socialist makes the Stock Exchange euphoric and may have to break with the unions."[40] Business leaders—including Vittorio Merloni of *Confindustria*—praised the economic policies of the PSI, hoping that they would include the two-year income freeze proposed by MIT's Franco Modigliani.[41]

Arrayed against reform are other individuals who form an antiausterity coalition that governments confront at their peril: The nonprivileged classes, the skilled workers, and the new bourgeoisie—all elements wooed heretofore by the PSI—derive advantages from the failure of governmental efforts to stem the redistributive effects of inflation.[42] Immobility is not to everyone's disadvantage.

The irresistible conclusion is that the Craxi government will prove as immobilized as its DC-centered predecessors and that Craxi will be able to hold on only by means of compromise designed to placate the DC. Craxi's personal optimism is expressed in his comment to a journalist: "The day after they've voted me out, they'll need my votes. Then we'll see."[43] The secretary and prime minister is right. His party is indispensable to the DC in a center-left government, to which there seems to be no alternative, and is equally indispensable to the left coalition with the PCI. In either eventuality, however, the party's electoral strength is totally inadequate for playing the role to which its dominant figures aspire. If the party is to share in power at all, the apportionment will be done by other individuals.

Thus for the foreseeable future, despite a Socialist and activist president in the king's former palace and a Socialist government head in a former Fascist state, the forces arrayed against change and the preoccupation with internecine factional struggles will combine to preclude change that goes beyond the cosmetic. "Se vogliamo che tutto rimanga come e, bisogna che tutto cambi."[44] (If we want everything to stay as it is, everything has to change.)

Notes

1 Sidney Tarrow, "Three Years of Italian Democracy," in Howard R. Penniman, ed., *Italy at the Polls, 1979: A Study of the Parliamentary Elections* (Washington, D.C.: American Enterprise Institute, 1981), 21.

2 P. Pons, "M. Bettino Craxi: L'art de s'imposer" (Mr. Bettino Craxi: The art of imposing himself), *Le Monde Hebdomadaire*, August 10, 1983, 3.

3 De Martino as cited by F. Mussi, "Un risultato scomodo per le ambizioni di Craxi" (An inconvenient result for Craxi's ambitions), *Rinascita*, July 1, 1983, 6.

4 See Gianfranco Pasquino, "The Italian Socialist Party: An Irreversible Decline?" in Howard R. Penniman, ed., *Italy at the Polls: The Parliamentary Elections of 1976* (Washington, D.C.: American Enterprise Institute, 1977), 221; also David Hine, "The Italian Socialist Party under Craxi: Surviving but Not Reviving," *West European Politics* (special issue edited by P. Lange and Sidney Tarrow) (October 1979): 135; and G. Pansa, "E venne il giorno di Bettino" (And Bettino's day came), *La Repubblica*, July 22, 1983, 3.

5 F. Ceccarelli and B. Manfellotto, "Bettino rischiatutto" (Bettino bets it all), *Panorama*, May 9, 1983, 43.

6 G. Valentini, "Ho sbagliato tante, troppe volte" (I've erred many, too many times), *La Repubblica*, November 8–9, 1981, 4. A revealing discussion of the shifts of loyalty among southern notables is found in Judith Chubbs, *Patronage, Power, and Poverty in Southern Italy: A Tale of Two Cities* (Cambridge, Mass.: Harvard University Press, 1982), 25.

7 Partito Socialista Italiano, "Per il 'Progetto Socialista'" (For the 'socialist project'), Documenti 41° Congresso (Torino: PSI, March 29–April 2, 1978); "Le Tesi per il 41° Congresso del PSI presentate del segretario del partito Bettino Craxi" (The thesis for the 42nd PSI Congress presented by Party Secretary Bettino Craxi) (Palermo: PSI, April 22–26, 1981); *Avanti!*, April 6, 1982, 2.

8 P. Mieli, "Bettino, che silenzio c'e stasera: Gli intellettuali e il governo Craxi" (Bettino, how quiet it is tonight: The intellectuals and the Craxi government), *L'Espresso*, September 19, 1983, 68–75.

9 G. Giugni, "Craxi, secondo tempo" (Craxi: Second reel), *La Repubblica*, April 1, 1982, 6.

10 Compare, for example, Gianfranco Pasquino, "The Italian Socialist Party," *Italy at the Polls, 1976*, 213, where he rejects the assertion that the PSI has been southernized, with "The PSI," *Italy at the Polls, 1979*, 163, where he records the impressive southern showing of the PSI, and with Giacomo Sani, "Italian Voters, 1976–1979," *Italy at the Polls, 1979*, 47, in which he describes the PSI as losing where it should be strong and advancing in the most backward areas.

11 Ceccarelli and Manfellotto, "Rischiatutto," 43.

12 C. Valentini, "Con quella faccia da straniero" (With that foreigner's face), *Panorama*, June 20, 1983, 52–55.

13 F. Recanatesi, "Dibattito a quattro" (Four-way debate), *La Repubblica*, September 9, 1983, 8; see also G. Galli, "Perche Craxi e ottimista" (Why Craxi is an optimist), *Panorama*, May 9, 1983, 36; and Mussi, "Un risultato scomodo," 6.

14 Hine, "The Italian Socialist Party under Craxi," 140.

15 C. Valentini, "Le paure di Berlinguer" (The fears of Berlinguer), *Panorama*, May 30, 1983, 38; and Pons, "M. Bettino Craxi," 3.

16 C. Valentini, "Uno sguardo dal basso" (A look from below), *Panorama*, June 27, 1983, 42.

17 Such a committee has been created under the chairmanship of Aldo Bozzi (PLI). Gianfranco Pasquino, a regular contributor to the series covering *Italy at the Polls*, serves on the committee in his capacity as newly elected senator of the independent left. See *La Repubblica*, December 14, 1983, 2, for a discussion of his contributions.

18   P. Mieli, "Quanto durera Bettino?" (How long will Bettino last?), *L'Espresso*, October 30, 1983, 14.

19   Amintore Fanfani's first government, formed in 1954, assigned the post to Umberto Tupini, who retained it in Mario Scelba's first cabinet. Each government for the next fifteen years included this ministry, and after a brief hiatus, it was reintroduced in Mariano Rumor III (1970). The first non-Demochristian in the post was Schietroma (PSDI) in Fanfani V. In Craxi's first government, a Demochristian — Remo Gaspari — held the assignment.

20   *La Squilla* (The trumpet blast), June 6, 1983, 3. This is a newsletter of the Bologna Federation-PSI.

21   See K. Robert Nilsson, "The EUR Accords and the Historic Compromise: Italian Labor and Eurocommunism," *Polity* (Fall 1981): 29-50.

22   F. Mussi, "Un risultato scomodo," 6-7; M. DeAngelis, "Una proposta che colpisce l'autonomia del PSI" (A proposal that undercuts PSI autonomy), *Rinascita*, June 24, 1983, 4.

23   Partito Socialista Italiano, "Costo del Lavoro: Un accordo che premia la volonta riformista" (Labor costs: An accord that rewards the reformist will) (Milano: PSI, 1983) describes the January Accord. G. Giugni, chief author of the Labor Statute of 1970, is recognized as architect of the accord. Half of the Italian labor force (about 60 percent organized) is enrolled in the CGIL; about a third in the CISL, and less than half that in the UIL. Lucio Lama (CGIL) is on the central committee of the PCI; Piero Carniti's CISL is in the Catholic trade union tradition, and Benvenuto (UIL) is a member of the PSI's executive committee.

24   G. Carli, "Rigoristi, vil razza dannata" (Rigorists, damned and vile race), *La Repubblica*, September 16, 1983, 10.

25   G. Galli, "La fantasia non basta" (Imagination is not enough), *Panorama*, August 8, 1983, 27.

26   *La Squilla*, September 12, 1983, 1.

27   G. Pansa, "E venne il giorno," 3.

28   P. Buongiorno, "Basta con gli Yes-Men" (That's enough of the yes-men), *Panorama*, July 18, 1983, 45.

29   G. Baget-Bozzo, "La sfida di Craxi" (Craxi's challenge), *La Repubblica*, October 5, 1983, 8.

30   "La sinistra socialista bolognese" (The Bolognese socialist left), *La Squilla*, September 13, 1983, 2.

31   R. di Rienzo, "E Spadolini diventa Spadolone" (And Spadolini becomes the great sword), *L'Espresso*, July 10, 1983, 13.

32   P. Franchi and B. Manfellotto, "Fu vera svolta?" (Was it a real turning point?), *Panorama*, August 15, 1983, 30-31.

33   Mieli, "Quanto durera?" October 30, 1983, 14.

34   *La Repubblica*, September 7, 1983, 8.

35   Amato, former boy wonder of Antonio Giolitti's staff, is undersecretary to the prime minister. Tensions separate Amato from Gennaro Acquaviva, PSI secretariat-functionary, and from Giorgio Giovannini, newly appointed chef du cabinet. Staff appointments have been delayed as a result, and Craxi's critics have delighted in underscoring the hesitations and inefficiencies of the self-styled "party of the electronic age." See C. Valentini, "Sua eminenza rosa" (His pink eminence), *Panorama*, October 24, 1983, 54.

36   B. Manfellotto and C. Valentini, "Mai cosi arrabbiati" (Never before so angry), *Panorama*, January 24, 1983, 25.

37   P. Franchi and B. Manfellotto, "In practica" (In practice), *Panorama*, August 8, 1983, 33.

38   G. Pasquino, "Sources of Stability and Instability in the Italian Party System," *West European Politics* (January 1983): 103.

39   F. Coen, "Tutte le carte del PSI" (All the Socialist party's cards), *La Repubblica*, September 4-5, 1983, 6.

40 Galli, "La fantasia non basta," 27.

41 *La Repubblica*, October 7, 1983, 3.

42 See G. Galli, "Cento giorni per Bettino" (A hundred days for Bettino), *Panorama*, August 15, 1983, 27. See also chapter 7 of Giuseppe Di Palma, *Surviving without Governing* (Berkeley: University of California Press, 1977).

43 Mieli, "Quanto durera?" 15.

44 Tancredi to his uncle, in Giuseppe Tomasi di Lampadusa, *Il Gattopardo* (Milan: Feltrinelli, 1961), 42.

6 The Changing Balance: The Rise of the Small Parties in the 1983 Elections

ROBERT LEONARDI

————The 1983 parliamentary election signaled the opening of a new era for the minor parties, an era characterized by a fundamental restructuring of the party system. In this election Christian Democratic (DC) votes registered their second largest drop (the largest was the 8.4 percent loss experienced in 1953 after the extraordinary showing in the 1948 election); the Communist party (PCI) slipped back for the second consecutive time after thirty years of consistent growth; and the Socialist party (PSI) was only able to make modest gains despite four years of euphoric electoral predictions.[1] The smaller parties, on the other hand, made significant strides forward.

As table 6–1 shows, the small-party vote climbed to 25.8 percent of the total, the largest percentage since the birth of the republic. This election broke the pattern of alternating fortunes among the small parties. The 1983 election results followed significant gains by the small parties in 1979 elections. A similar strong showing for small parties in 1953 had followed on the heels of a less than encouraging result in the 1948 elections.[2] In 1953 the small-party political victory quickly dissipated because the major beneficiaries of that gain —the monarchists and the neo-Fascists—were in no position to exploit it within the existing governmental context. In 1983 the major gains were made by those minor parties of the center—the Republicans (PRI), the Social Democrats (PSDI), and the Liberals (PLI)—that are squarely in the thick of the political battle and members of the governing coalition.

Among the minor parties, only those of the left (Radical and Proletarian Democracy parties) failed to regain all of the votes they captured in 1979, as table 6–2 shows. The other three party tendencies reported in table 6–2 experienced significant growth. The right wing (represented this time exclusively by the neo-Fascist Italian Social Movement, MSI-DN) rebounded to 6.8 percent of the vote; the centrist parties expanded their share of the vote by 3.4

Table 6-1 Distribution of Votes and Seats for
the Mass and Small Parties, 1946–1983

| Election | Mass Parties[a] | | Small Parties[b] | |
	Percent of Vote	Seats in Chamber	Percent of Vote	Seats in Chamber
1946	74.9	76.7[c]	25.1	23.3
1948	79.5	85.0	20.5	15.0
1953	75.4	81.5	24.6	18.5
1958	79.3	83.4	20.7	16.6
1963	77.4	81.4	22.6	18.6
1968	80.0[d]	84.8	20.0	15.2
1972	76.5	80.3	23.5	19.7
1976	82.8	87.0	17.2	13.0
1979	78.5	83.2	21.5	16.8
1983	74.2	78.7	25.8	21.3

a. Mass parties: DC, PCI, PSI.
b. Small parties: PSDI, PRI, PLI, MSI, PDIUM, SVP, UV, and others.
c. In 1946, Constituent Assembly election; in subsequent elections, calculation is based on Chamber of Deputies.
d. Includes the PSDI then in alliance with PSI in PSU.
Source: Calculated by author from data in Celso Ghini, *Il voto delgi italiani* (The vote of the Italians) (Rome: Editori Riuiti, 1975), 42; Robert Leonardi, "The Smaller Parties in the 1976 Italian Elections," in Howard R. Penniman, ed., *Italy at the Polls: The Parliamentary Elections of 1976* (Washington, D.C.: American Enterprise Institute, 1977), 230; and *Corriere della Sera*, June 29, 1983.

percent; and regionalist party sentiment continued to proliferate. For the first time a regionalist party (the Venetian League) appeared in an "ordinary" region—one of the fifteen regions that in 1970 were given regional political institutions.[3] Before this election regionalist parties had been successful only in the five "special" regions (recognized by the republican constitution as necessitating special consideration in formulating their regional institutions because of particular border, ethnic, or autonomy problems).

In 1983 the minor parties were also unusually successful in translating their electoral successes into parliamentary seats. The actual number of votes cast for the small parties differed from the number of seats they gained in the Chamber of Deputies by only 3.5 percent. In other elections the gap has been much greater—for example, −6.1 percent in 1953 and −5.5 percent in 1948.[4] Small-party representation in the new parliament climbed for only the second time to more than 20 percent of the seats. (The first time was in the constituent assembly election of 1946, when small parties translated 25.1 percent of the

Table 6-2 Small-Party Vote by Political Tendency, Chamber
Elections, 1979 and 1983 (percent and percentage points)

Tendency	1979	1983	Change, 1979–83
Right	5.9	6.8	0.9
Center	8.7	12.1	3.4
Left	5.6	3.7	−1.9
Regional	1.0	1.7	0.7

Note: Right = MSI-DN in 1983 and also DN in 1979; Center = PSDI, PRI, PLI; Left = PR, PDUP, and NSU in 1979, and DP in 1983. Regional = SVP, UV, Trieste List, Sardinian Action, Liga Veneta, etc.
Source: Calculated by the author from data in *Corriere della Sera*, June 29, 1983.

votes into 23.3 percent of the seats.) In the ninth parliament 184 deputies and senators were elected to speak for the minor parties (see table 6–3).

The outcome was even more surprising because two parties (the Trieste List and the Pensioners') missed the electoral quotient by relatively small margins. The Trieste List party was only 596 votes short of satisfying the 40,675-vote minimum required to gain a seat in the Trieste electoral district, and the Pensioners' party (PNP) was prevented from gaining a seat in the Rome electoral district when two other pensioner-oriented parties (Union in Defense of Pensioners and Union of Pensioners and Prepensioners of Italy) attracted 22,367 votes, three times the extra number needed by the PNP to qualify for a seat.

The 1983 election result suggests that some fundamental changes have taken place in Italian politics. Three long-term structural transformations of the party system nurtured the minor parties' victory. The first major change was the shift in leadership (presidents and prime ministers) to members of parties other than the Christian Democratic party. The 1978 election of Sandro Pertini as president helped to consolidate the notion that presidents who were not Christian Democrats (Enrico DeNicola, Luigi Einaudi, and Giuseppe Saragat) have ruled much better than their Christian Democratic counterparts (Giovanni Gronchi, Antonio Segni, or Giovanni Leone).[5] A similar idea developed about the prime ministry during the eighteen-month tenure of the Republican Giovanni Spadolini government. The Spadolini cabinet won widespread enthusiasm among the public and the media in part because of Spadolini's established reputation in journalism and in academia. Spadolini demonstrated that someone other than a Christian Democrat could head a government without causing social, economic, or political disaster.

The era of large-party domination ended with the silencing of any further talk of reconstituting the "historic compromise" formula that had brought the DC and the PCI into close cooperation in the 1976–79 period. When Socialist party Secretary Bettino Craxi became a candidate for prime minister in 1979, attention shifted from the existing government to the possibility of a change in government, eroding the DC's image as the dominant governing party.[6] The DC prime ministers, Francesco Cossiga, Arnaldo Forlani, and Amintore Fanfani, headed lame-duck governments marking time and waiting for Craxi's eventual move. Thus the DC was deprived of the historical certainty that it would choose the new prime minister from its ranks. The Socialist leadership clearly intended to hold the prime ministry, and the Republicans also made a convincing argument for the post.

The second cause of political restructuring was the fragmentation of the party system resulting from the deradicalization of the debate on economic and social policies and the narrowing of differences between ideological groups

Table 6-3 Small-Party Votes and Seats, Chamber and Senate Elections, 1979 and 1983

	Chamber, 1979		Chamber, 1983		Senate, 1979		Senate, 1983	
Party	Percent of Vote	Seats	Percent of Vote	Seats	Percent of Vote	Seats	Percent of Vote	Seats
MSI	5.3	31	6.8	42	5.7	13	7.3	18
DN	0.6	0	—	—	0.6	0	—	—
PSDI	3.8	21	4.1	23	4.2	9	3.8	8[a]
PRI	3.0	15	5.1	29	3.4	6	4.7	10[a]
PLI	1.9	9	2.9	16	2.2	2	2.7	6
PLI-PRI-PSDI	—	—	—	—	—	—	0.9	1
PR	3.4	18	2.2	11	1.3	2	1.8	1
PR-NSU	—	—	—	—	1.2	0	—	—
SVP	0.6	4	0.5	3	0.5	3	0.5	3
UV	0.1	1	0.1	1	0.1	1	0.1	1
PDUP	1.4	6	—	—	—	—	—	—
DP	—	—	1.5	7	—	—	1.1	0
Unione di Sinistra	—	—	—	—	—	—	0.1	0
Trieste List	0.2	1	0.2	—	—	—	0.4	0
Venetian League	—	—	0.3	1	—	—	0.3	1
Sardinian Action	—	—	0.2	1	—	—	0.2	1
Pensioners' (PNP)	—	—	1.4	0	—	—	1.2	0
Others	0.4	0	0.5	0	0.6	0	0.4	0
Totals	21.5	106	25.8	134	19.4	36	25.4	50

a. The PSDI total in the Senate is nine because of Giuseppe Saragat's lifetime appointment. The PRI has 12 because of adherence by the senator elected on the combined centrist party slate and Leo Valiani, who was nominated to a lifetime term by President Sandro Pertini.
Sources: Corriere della Sera, June 29, 1983; and *I Deputati e Senatori del Nono Parlamento Repubblicano* (The deputies and senators of the Ninth Republican Parliament) (Rome: La Navicella, 1983).

in the system.[7] Center-minded voters no longer see the Christian Democrats as the only bastion against radical change. The Communist party has undergone considerable change, and large numbers of moderate voters no longer feel the need to continue to "hold their noses" and vote for the Christian Democrats.[8] Now they can vote their true sentiments and opinions. In a sense, the 1983 election signaled the end of the ramifications of the "1948 electoral panic," when minor party support was drained off to buttress the DC.[9] The DC vote in 1983 was only 2.3 percent below its showing in 1946, while the minor parties moved for the first time slightly beyond (+0.7 percent) their 1946 total.

A third important development has been the slow regionalization of the political system. The creation of a nationwide system of regional political institutions in 1970 may have preceded true regional political consciousness.[10] Regional consciousness is developing, however, as exemplified by the emergence of a party like the Venetian League in Veneto, and by the reaffirmation of regionalist parties in the special regions.[11] Parties organizing around local grievances and single issues have been strikingly successful in making inroads into a political system that has been dominated historically by nationally oriented parties.

The elections of 1979 and 1983 demonstrated that the smaller parties have moved to a new level of political power. Their numbers in parliament have increased so that in 1983 they were a necessary consideration for any government coalition, except a grand DC-PCI coalition. Small-party votes not only make possible center-left coalitions, they also provide for the first time the possibility of a parliamentary majority for a lay leftist coalition. This resurgence of small-party fortunes is even more surprising considering that as recently as 1976 political commentators were predicting that the minor parties would quickly disappear from the political scene as the system evolved toward a standard two-party system. The small parties have avoided such a scenario by driving a wedge between the two large parties in the system. They have successfully moved the PCI away from the historic compromise and the DC toward programmatic retrenchment.[12] The small parties seized the political initiative by forcing the DC to return to the center-left, by making their support indispensable for any coalition, and by reducing the hegemonic hold of the DC on government institutions. Up to 1983, the small parties continued to make electoral gains despite the sharp turn toward the right taken by the Socialist party leadership after 1979 to prepare the groundwork for the eventual formation of a five-party, center-left coalition led by Bettino Craxi.

The Lay Center Parties, 1979–1983

By 1979 the economy had already become the major campaign issue because of concerns about Italy's competitive position in Europe and in the Western world. The oil shortage of 1974 had jolted the Italian economy with high rates of inflation, and the recession that followed increased fears that the situation would spin out of control. The drop in production and in productivity, the rise of unemployment, the continuing upward spiral of government deficits, and the steady devaluation of the lira on foreign money markets caused special concern. The Cossiga government's "failure to enact an anticrisis package in 1980 left the Bank of Italy and its tight money policies as the sole defense against an unmanaged devaluation" and against economic decline.[13]

The Republican Party   The Republican party (PRI), the Liberal party (PLI), and the Social Democratic party (PSDI) all made gains in the 1983 elections, but most of the media attention went to the advances of the PRI. In 1983 the Republicans polled their highest vote ever, even surpassing the 4.4 percent reached in the constituent assembly elections in 1946. The party's success in 1983 was no fluke. Most of the preelection polls predicted that the PRI would receive more than 5 percent of the vote, and Giovanni Spadolini, the party secretary and former prime minister, was clearly one of the most popular political personalities during the campaign. The PRI campaign used the image of Spadolini as "the Italian politician that you would like to invite to dinner," but it also emphasized the issues that had bothered Italians during the previous four years—the economy, terrorism, and the morality of public figures. The party's strategy was to impress in the public's mind the steps taken by the Spadolini government (June 1981–November 1982) to resolve these problems.

By June 1981 the country was ready for the change in economic policies advocated by Spadolini when he presented his cabinet to parliament. Spadolini proposed to stop the economic slide by imposing wage and price controls, renegotiating the automatic escalator clauses in workers' contracts, restricting the expansion of the money supply, applying the tax law strictly to cover all professions and all lines of work, requiring a cash-register receipt in all commercial transactions and services, and promoting capital investments and economic restructuring in the private sector through more flexible public fiscal and credit policies.

Spadolini argued that a practical indicator of progress on the economy was whether the inflation rate could be brought below 16 percent. To the surprise of many, his government achieved that goal by the end of 1982. There were also signs that the economy had turned the corner toward recovery in some key industries such as automobiles and chemicals. The actual economic picture was still quite bleak, however. Real growth decreased more in 1982 than in any other postwar year except 1975. The gross national product fell by 0.5 percent, and gross fixed investments fell by 5.3 percent.[14] Unemployment rose above 10 percent, and total employment dropped by 75,000 workers. Despite the critical economic situation, public opinion did not blame Spadolini for the crisis, but instead blamed the DC and the PSI ministers (Beniamino Andriatta and Rino Formica) for the political squabbling that prevented the Spadolini program from being implemented.

The PRI also benefited from the Spadolini track record on terrorism. At the beginning of 1982 the Italian authorities were able for the first time to break a major Red Brigades operation. The liberation of American General James L. Dozier, following on the heels of the capture of Giovanni Senzani and a group of terrorists of *Prima Linea* (First Line), represented a definite turning point in the struggle against left-wing terrorism. At the same time a growing number of repentant terrorist leaders—for example, Patrizio Peci and Antonio Savasta—actively cooperated with the police to dismantle the terrorists' network of safe houses, supporters, and arms caches. By the end of the year the number of terrorist incidents had declined dramatically, and the government was able to say it had won the battle against terrorism. The PRI's stance against terrorism was never compromised by the actions of any of its national leaders. In contrast, DC prime minister Francesco Cossiga and party vice-secretary Carlo Donat Cattin were involved in the furor in 1980 over the escape of Marco Donat Cattin (the vice-secretary's son) from arrest on the charge of being one of the leaders of *Prima Linea*.[15] To the chagrin of the DC and public opinion, it was revealed that Cossiga was the source of the tip.

The PSI had always assumed a "soft" stance on dealing with terrorist demands.[16] After the kidnapping of former prime minister Aldo Moro, the PSI favored meeting Red Brigades demands. The PSI was instrumental in breaking the Cossiga government's united front during the Giovanni D'Urso kidnapping in 1980. Newspapers close to the PSI published Red Brigades documents, and, as part of the deal to release D'Urso, the government agreed to the terrorists' demand to close the Asinara special security prison.

The eighteen months as prime minister did not leave Spadolini or the PRI with a tarnished moral image, either. The public did not perceive Spadolini as being motivated by self-aggrandizement. The public image of Socialist party leader Bettino Craxi did not fare as well when he attempted to use the PSI's control of a few key economic ministries to manipulate the succession crisis at ENI (the state petrochemical company).

PRI electoral fortunes were also aided by the party's decision not to take part in the subsequent Fanfani government because of disagreements with the other parties on the choice of economic policies. Thus the party was able to go into the 1983 campaign as the original standard bearer (the other parties—DC and PSI included—moved toward similar policies) of austerity, rationalization, and reinvestment, which the other government parties had tried to obstruct during the Spadolini prime ministry.

Another issue of major concern in the 1983 campaign was the involvement of elected officials, top bureaucrats, and prominent members of the media in secret societies and underworld organizations. In 1981–82 the national political scene was rocked by the unraveling of the P-2 affair, a small group of individuals around Licio Gelli who had spun a web of collusion that threatened to compromise the political system. Gelli, as the head of the secret Masonic lodge called "Propaganda 2" (or the shortened version P-2), had succeeded in building an informal structure of power and influence that made his personal intervention crucial in many governmental appointments or financial affairs, thereby effectively short-circuiting the formal institutional structure of power in the country.

The scandals involving the corruption of local officials (as in Turin and in Liguria) and the revelations of ties between politicians and the *camorra* (criminal organization) in Naples broke just before the 1983 election. The DC and the PSI were the parties most heavily compromised by these revelations. The PRI remained untouched by the scandals,[17] permitting it to cast itself as "the party that deserves your trust because it is different from others."

The PRI also assumed clear positions on the other campaign issues. It favored a new edition of the center-left government committed to a serious economic program; it supported the 1979 North Atlantic Treaty Organization (NATO) decision to deploy cruise missiles; and it wanted a resumption of European Economic Community (EEC) talks to revive the community after the deadlock that had resulted during the 1983 Athens conference.[18] Party leaders were particularly sensitive to the need for presenting the PRI as a party with a leader and policies that were equal to the challenge posed by Europe. At the end of the campaign expectations were high in the PRI that the party would finally be able to capture more than 5 percent of the vote.

The Liberal Party　Expectations for major gains were also high among the Liberals. The party had become an integral part of the governmental coalition in the four years between elections. It had been excluded from ministerial positions only once, during the second Cossiga government. After 1979 the PLI exchanged representation in the media for representation in the government. The Liberals did not embark on any major political campaign between 1979 and 1983 as they had done in 1978–79, attacking the government of national solidarity and advocating a return to the center-left. After 1979 they relied on the strategy of providing concrete examples of the PLI's ability to manage power correctly.

The PLI hoped that the 1983 election would change its status as the smallest of the small governing parties. When the election results became clear on the evening of June 27, the PLI party secretary, Valerio Zanone, expressed surprise at the slow pace of the PLI resurgence. One of the reasons for this relatively slow growth was that the PLI program was not substantially different from that of the governmental partners. The PLI favored economic austerity, cleaning up corruption, continued adherence to NATO, and deployment of cruise missiles. But the other government parties took the same stand on these issues. Therefore, it was difficult for the PLI to differentiate its programmatic stance from that taken by the other parties in the five-party coalition. The other misfortune of the PLI was that it did not have a charismatic leader who could use personality to strike a different posture. Valerio Zanone saved the party from extinction in 1976, renewed the leadership and party organization, and placed the party on a more centrist ideological footing. He did not, however, plunge personally into the thick of the governing process but instead delegated government responsibility to other PLI leaders such as Renato Altissimo. Zanone preferred the purely political role of party secretary to that of government or parliamentary leader.

The Social Democratic Party   The PSDI leader, Pietro Longo, did not hesitate to take the plunge in 1983 into the governmental arena. He accepted the post of minister of finance in the new Craxi government. Longo, in contrast to Zanone, has reveled in creating controversy, being obstinate, and bucking official policies in order to protect the PSDI's voting base. An example was the PSI's response to a change in the pension law, which the PSDI strongly opposed within the coalition and tried its best to obstruct through the activities of its ministers.

Italian Social Democracy is quite different from its counterparts in other European countries. It has been from the beginning a minor party, with the support of only one-twentieth of the electorate. The PSDI has little internal ideological debate.[19] Most of the PSDI voting base is composed of pensioners, housewives, white-collar workers, and small commercial/industrial interests. After a brief period in 1979 of trying to force local PSDI leaders to abandon coalitions with the PCI, the party assumed a more pragmatic approach to power: It occupies public offices whenever and wherever possible.

Between the elections of 1979 and 1983, the PSDI's position in the national debate concentrated on three essential points: support for the deployment of the cruise missiles and for U.S. foreign policy initiatives in the Middle East and in Central America; support for Craxi's campaign for the prime ministry; and flexibility on budget cuts. The PSDI adopted the position that budget cuts should not be made at the expense of the weaker elements of society. As a consequence, the PSDI did not support cuts in pensions or social services for the handicapped or the elderly. One of the more original aspects of the PSDI economic program was its proposal to reduce the discount rate and to impose a larger tax burden on the wealthy. The 1983 election results demonstrated that the PSDI had maintained its electoral base intact. Though it did not make gains similar to those of the PRI and the PLI, the party did not lose any political ground. It subsequently received a number of important posts in the Craxi government.

The Italian Social Movement   Despite the substantial gains made by the PRI, the MSI-DN remains the largest of the small parties with 6.8 percent of the vote. The party's support increased by 1.5 percentage points in 1983, an increase that was not forecast by any of the preelection polls.[20] MSI-DN gains were predictable, however, because of the demise of National Democracy (DN) after its electoral debacle in the 1979 parliamentary elections, because of the increase in neo-Fascist votes in large metropolitan areas in the South and in the 1980 local government elections, and because of the liquefaction of Radical party support throughout the country. In 1983 Italy celebrated the hundredth anniversary of Benito Mussolini's birth. The anniversaries of important Italian historical figures produce an outpouring of media attention (articles in newspapers and magazines, books, electronic media programs, and special celebrations). The celebration of the Mussolini centennial had the effect of rehabilitating the founder of fascism. It was once again respectable to talk about the former dictator in a positive light outside of MSI-DN circles.

Nevertheless, the calm nature of the neo-Fascist campaign was a surprise to everyone. For the first time since the end of the war the MSI-DN was able to conduct a normal campaign. Local officials did not boycott its meetings. Neither opposition groups nor party members resorted to violence, and the MSI-DN was free to campaign where it wished. Giorgio Almirante, the party secretary, gave speeches in cities where before it would have been difficult for him to walk the streets. Thus the MSI-DN unexpectedly enjoyed the fruits of ideological depolarization. Another reason for this increased sense of ease was the disappearance of the fear that a party like the MSI-DN could come to power through a military coup. The democratization of Portugal, of Greece, and of Spain demonstrated that military regimes did not offer any viable alternative to representative government, social well-being, or economic growth. Authoritarian governments were not respected members of the European community. The effect of depolarization on attitudes toward the MSI-DN would have been even greater if the "missini" had not insisted on using the symbols, phrases, and salutes of the Fascist period in their public demonstrations and party rhetoric.

The nature of its public pronouncements has not, however, prevented the party from opening a new dialogue with the Socialist party. Two examples of the Socialists' growing acceptance of the MSI-DN occurred in July when the prime minister–designate consulted with Almirante on the same basis as he did with the other party secretaries before deciding on the composition of his cabinet. The Italian embassy in Washington extended formal courtesies to

Almirante during his fall 1983 trip to the United States. The political rehabilitation of the MSI-DN probably will not lead to an eventual acceptance of its votes in parliament by the Craxi government, but the party does have a role in the aggressive anti-DC strategy that the PSI is trying to implement. For the neo-Fascists as well as the Socialists, a weakened Christian Democratic party offers a golden opportunity to siphon off voters.

The program illustrated by the MSI-DN to its electorate during the campaign concentrated heavily on denouncing the political status quo for the "partyocracy's" disregard of public opinion, the graft and corruption that was rampant among public officials, and the inability of the governing coalitions to solve the country's major economic and social problems. The solution proposed by the right wing was a restructuring of the institutions that pointed toward a reinforcement of the executive branch and provisions for the direct election of the president, in essence an Italian version of Charles de Gaulle's Fifth French Republic. The MSI-DN also wanted to implement the same model of government at the subnational level.

At the end of the campaign, the MSI-DN leadership fully expected to make a good showing. Public opinion had forgotten the fear of the right wing generated by the 1980 Bologna railroad station bombing. Political violence in the schools and in the streets had been substantially reduced, and the issues uppermost in the minds of the electorate—the economy, scandals, nuclear war—did not call into question the nature of the MSI-DN. Hopes were high that the conservative vote would move to the "true" right-wing party in the system.

The Radical Party and Proletarian Democracy   The area to the left of the PCI was the only minor-party block to poll fewer votes in 1983 than in the previous election. What were the sources of this decline? The arrangement of the party lists changed. PDUP (Democratic Party of Proletarian Unity) decided not to field a separate slate, and instead presented its candidates in the PCI electoral lists. The original reason for a separate PDUP list in 1979 was to wean the PCI away from the historic-compromise strategy and urge it to adopt a "unity of the left" policy. That was accomplished in 1980, so the PDUP had no reason to present a competing list in 1983. DP (Proletarian Democracy) presented itself in 1983 as an autonomous party, no longer aligned with the mixture of small parties and movements that reduced its effectiveness in 1979.

The Radical party maintained until the end an ambiguous stance on the election. Its initial position was that the election was a farce, and that participation in the election would only provide legal cover for the malfeasance of the governing parties. The depolarization of the 1983 political debate deprived the extreme left parties of their traditional ideological justification and political ammunition. The DC leader, Mario Cappanna, was uncommonly subdued and conciliatory in his televised presentations to the voters. Finally, much of the progress since 1979 on social-service legislation and on social issues deprived the left of "postbourgeois" social and civil rights issues. Women's groups, impatient with the male-dominated parties, talked of forming an independent party to deal with women's issues and needs.[21]

The disaffection of women's groups was symptomatic of the general decline of creative energy that had animated the Radicals and other far-left groups in the late 1970s. The PR insisted on snatching defeat from the jaws of victory. An example of this suicidal tendency was its stubbornness in presenting a "free abortion on demand" option in the 1981 referendum on the existing abortion law demanded by the Catholic antiabortion forces. The lay and leftist parties defending abortion found themselves simultaneously attacked from opposite positions by the Catholics and by the Radicals. Despite being caught in the cross fire, the proabortion forces received a solid majority. The Radicals came away with less than 10 percent of the votes. Another example of PR obstinacy occurred when the PCI changed its coalition strategy to support for the leftist alternative (which officially was also the PR position). The Radicals continued to hammer the PCI as if nothing had changed. Even stranger, though, was the transformation of the once libertarian and completely open nature of the party in 1976 and in 1979 to a monolithic structure in 1983. In the earlier years a number of individuals had provided ideas and leadership to the party. In 1983 Marco Pannella reigned as the sole and supreme leader. The Communists took delight in pointing out that democratic centralism was alive and well in the Radical party. A number of the former PR leaders joined the PSI or the DP, or they left politics entirely.

The Radicals did not propose any fundamental change in policy for the 1983 electoral campaign. They talked about the unacceptable nature of the entire political and institutional setting. One innovation that the Radicals did bring to the campaign was to propose the candidacy of Toni Negri, the ideological (and perhaps organizational) leader of Proletarian Autonomy (*autonomia*). In his writings Negri advocated a diffused form of violence that he said expressed the crisis of the capitalist state and the awakening of the working class to its historic role.[22] Negri was arrested in 1979 on the charge of being the mastermind of *autonomia*'s campaign of violence in Padova (where Negri taught) and in other cities. The trial of Negri and the other members of *autonomia* began in 1983. The PR's objective in putting Negri on their list of candidates was to gain his automatic release from jail if he were elected. Through the Negri campaign the PR attempted in one stroke to attract back to the party the former components of Continuous Struggle (*Lotta Continua*), who had left to join the Socialists, and the intellectuals who had protested the length of Negri's detention without trial.

Negri's candidacy was not completely supported by all members of the

PR, however. Some had misgivings about the party's prejudging Negri's inno-cence before the courts had decided. When the new parliament voted to send Negri back to jail as requested by the prosecutor, the Radical party members abstained. Negri fled to France before the authorities could return him to his cell. When it was all over, the Negri affair undermined the credibility of the PR leadership. If the party had really believed that Negri was innocent, it should have backed his fight to remain free. If instead the party felt that he was being properly prosecuted for crimes that he did commit, then his name should not have been presented on the party's list.

The Radicals argued that the whole electoral process was a farce, and that the increased number of voters who did not bother to vote or who cast blank/invalid ballots vindicated the party's point of view. Pannella suggested that these voters agreed with the Radical position and could be considered PR votes. Thus the party proposed to the 1983 voters: do not vote or vote for the Radicals.[23] The Radical party vote fell to 2.2 percent from its high of 3.4 percent four years earlier. In the process the party lost twelve representatives in parliament. The change in parliamentary strength did not matter to the Radicals, however, because they refused to cast their votes on *any* issue during the first months of the new legislative session as part of their continued protest against the system.

Proletarian Democracy held a different position. DP did not shy away from participating in the representative institutions. Since it first gained access to elected public office in 1975, DP has become progressively institutionalized. In contrast to the Radicals, DP sees as its political purpose the defense of the interests of the working class *and* the attempt to prevent the Communist party from drifting rightward to embrace the needs of the bourgeoisie. Proletarian Democracy leaders such as Mario Cappanna are firmly committed to de-veloping a prospective leftist government that can present itself as an alterna-tive to the DC rather than supporting the DC as the left did during the historic-compromise period. As a result, DP's electoral campaign stressed alternatives to government policies, such as nuclear disarmament, withdrawal from NATO, a nuclear-free energy policy, and a complete restructuring of tax and fiscal policies.

The Regionalist and Single-Issue Parties

The election results of 1983 disproved the 1979 prediction that "the tide in favor of local lists has reached its crest and is bound to ebb in the coming years."[24] Instead the local factor has increased in political importance and electoral support. In 1983 it was no longer the Trieste "Watermelon" party that caught the pollsters and political observers by surprise, but the Venetian League (*Liga Veneta*), the Sardinian Action, and the Pensioners' parties.

Local and single-issue lists became attractive because of the increased region-alization of economic and political power after the 1977 regional decrees and the 1980 reform of the national health system; the crisis of the DC; and the growing lack of public confidence in national political leaders.

Today local officials have the political responsibility for allocating a quan-tity of resources that was unheard of ten or fifteen years ago. The local VIPs are no longer the parliamentarians or the national party bosses but the mayor and the regional assessor for agriculture or health. Just as politicians are realizing that moving from local into national politics may not increase their power, citizens are beginning to demand more local control of resources and decision making.[25] The Venetian League, for example, had on top of its list of demands for 1983 housing and employment for Venetians; greater regional autonomy; taxing powers for local government bodies; and opposition to nuclear plants, to the draft, and to the presence of large military bases and heavy industrial plants in Veneto. After the election some DC leaders thought that the shift of votes from the DC to the Venetian League was motivated by the lack of DC leaders in the national government. But a more likely scenario is that regional parties like the Venetian League in 1983 and the Trieste List in 1979 attracted voters who protest the focus on national issues rather than on the issues that are of vital concern to the local populace. This course of events earlier undermined the careers of political leaders such as Luigi Gui, Mario Ferrari-Aggradi, and Mariano Rumor. Now it has affected the entire DC party organization.

Another development that has created additional space for regionalist parties has been the growing secularization of Italian society. Defense of the church and religiosity are no longer reason enough to vote DC. Once the DC shell has been broken, it will be easier for former Christian Democrats to respond to more specific programs that concern local demands and tangible changes in daily life. Defense of universal principles of Western civilization, the church, and the free market, the norm for the past forty years, is no longer tolerable when jobs and housing are scarce, when social services are increas-ingly expensive, and when children are addicted to drugs. Thus in Trieste, when the Trieste List began to lose ground, the Christian Democrats did not benefit at all.

The PNP received 502,841 votes that probably defected from the DC. The PNP directed its message to the approximately two million Italians who live on a pension of $155 a month. These individuals are forced at age sixty-five to seek a job to make ends meet. Pensioners in Italy have been particularly affected by inflation and periodic tax increases. To alleviate the effects of these conditions the PNP advocated a rigorous income tax system that was capable of collecting taxes from the professional and commercial sectors that have evaded paying taxes. The party also proposed increasing payments to those at

Table 6-4 Small-Party Vote in the North,
Center, and South, 1979 and 1983 (percent)

Location	MSI-DN	PLI	PRI	PSDI	PR	DP
1979						
North	3.3	2.6	3.3	4.2	3.9	—
Center	5.6	1.3	3.1	2.9	3.6	—
South	7.9	1.3	2.6	3.9	2.7	—
1983						
North	4.8	3.7	6.4	4.0	2.7	1.8
Center	7.0	2.0	4.5	3.2	2.5	1.3
South	9.6	2.2	3.5	4.8	1.3	1.0

Source: *Rinascita*, July 1, 1983.

the bottom of the pension scale and prohibiting those with adequate pensions from working at all. The suspicions of elderly voters that the DC and the other government parties would not move in this direction was probably heightened by the neocapitalist campaign rhetoric about sacrifices, cutting deficits, and reintroducing incentives into the market place. The loss of confidence in the DC and in national leaders in general was also evident in the PNP's call for an end to parliamentary immunity. Leaders of the Pensioners demanded that severe penalties be instituted for public officials found guilty of corruption. The PNP also recommended cutting the total number of parliamentarians in half. Thus, the flowering of parties like the PNP and the Venetian League expressed the voters' doubts that the existing parties and leaders could provide adequate solutions for specific geographic areas or social groups.

A Geographical Analysis of the 1983 Results

As in 1979, the small-party gains in the 1983 elections were spread fairly evenly throughout the country. Table 6-4 illustrates the uniform distribution of the average increases or decreases in votes experienced by each party. For example, the MSI-DN vote rose by an average 1.5 percent nationwide in 1983. In the North its increase was 1.5 percent, in the center 1.4 percent, and in the South 1.7 percent. The Liberals experienced similar gains. The Radicals' losses were also uniform. The uniformity of the PR losses and of the MSI gains might suggest that the neo-Fascist component of the 1979 PR gains had returned to the parent party. This migration, the return of the former DN, and a few DC votes account for the MSI-DN increase.

Two parties whose votes were not uniformly distributed over the national territory are the PRI and the PSDI. The Republicans almost doubled their votes in the northern part of the country, added 50 percent in the center, but advanced by only one-third in the South. The rise of PRI political fortunes was thus predominantly tied to the fervor of northern industrial, professional, and middle-class interests. This was particularly noticeable in cities like Turin and Milan, where the PRI became the third party in size after the PCI and the DC. The PSDI demonstrated a reverse trend. It lost votes in the North, made slight gains in the center, but advanced strongly in the South. The PSDI probably gained votes from the ranks of white-collar workers in the public sector seeking to support the party that would not do away with all types of protection for people on fixed incomes and in low-paying but steady jobs.

Analysis of the difference in party votes in the nation's provincial capitals (the "center") versus noncapital cities (the "periphery") confirms these trends. Table 6-5 shows that the PRI vote rose twice as fast in the centers, while the MSI-DN, PSDI, PLI, and DP votes rose uniformly in center and in periphery. The Radical party suffered its heaviest losses in the capital cities, where its vote fell 40 percent; in the periphery its total fell only 30 percent. DP's total shows no great geographic variation. The party is slightly stronger in the North and in capital cities, but the differences are not overwhelming. In general, DP was able to pick up the support of sectors of the intelligentsia, students, and teachers. But its entry into parliament depended on the addition of the labor component in the country's largest industrial area (Milan) to meet the electoral quota.

Figure 6-1 illustrates that the small-party vote in Italy's eleven major cities (population of over 300,000) confirms the pattern already witnessed in the provincial capitals. The small-party vote in the major cities increased on the average 0.3 percent in relation to the provincial capitals.[26] The only exception to this pattern was the MSI-DN major-city vote, which was fully 1 percent above the "center" vote. A comparison of the 1983 vote with the 1979 vote shows that all of the parties except the PR had an improvement in fortunes; the most dramatic changes took place in the MSI-DN vote and in the PRI vote.

Table 6-5 Small-Party Vote in Center and Periphery, 1979 and 1983 (percent)

Location	MSI-DN	PLI	PRI	PSDI	PR	DP	PDUP-NSU
1979							
Center	7.0	2.7	4.0	3.8	5.5	—	2.2
Periphery	4.3	1.5	2.5	3.9	2.4	—	2.2
1983							
Center	8.9	3.9	6.8	4.0	3.2	1.7	—
Periphery	5.8	2.4	4.2	4.1	1.7	1.3	—

Note: Center is defined as provincial capitals and periphery as nonprovincial capital cities.
Source: Calculated by author from data provided by the Carlo Cattaneo Institute, Bologna, Italy.

Figure 6-1   Small-Party Vote in Major Cities, 1976–1983 Parliamentary Elections. Note: Major cities are defined as those with populations over 300,000. Eleven cities fall into this category. Source: Calculated from data in *Rinascita*, July 1, 1983.

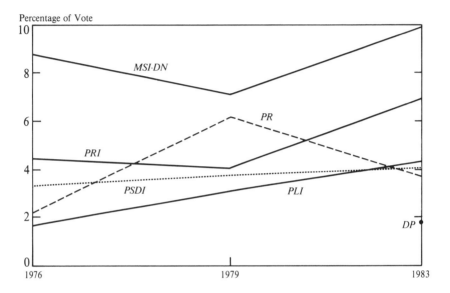

Percentage of Vote

The Lessons of 1983

The 1983 election brought significant changes to the voting base of specific parties, but it did not bring about any fundamental changes in the voting blocs. The election marginally weakened the five-party governing coalition: Its combined vote fell from 57.6 to 56.9 percent. All three major ideological blocs showed similar stability. The four leftist parties dropped to 45 percent, which represented a decline of less than 1 percent from 1979. The four centrist parties received a similar number of total votes, but the centrist-party total was 2 percent less than it had been in 1979. Before the election many commentators and politicians with an eye on the English, the West German, and the American elections thought that the election would strengthen Italy's moderate parties,[27] but the results of the election did not confirm this expectation.

The relative stability of the ideological blocs demonstrates one of the fundamental characteristics of Italian elections: the major exchange of votes occurs *within* rather than *across* ideological blocs. Thus the Christian Democratic losses in 1983 did not swell the vote for the Communist party, and they only minimally fueled the rise of the MSI-DN. Defectors from the DC did, however, help to bring the PRI vote above 5 percent, the Liberal vote almost to

3 percent, the Social Democratic vote once again above 4 percent, and the regional and single-issue parties' vote to an all-time high.

Will the DC decline stop? The administrative-election results of 1985 have shown that though the DC has not been able to recoup all of its 1983 losses, it has significantly slowed down the rate of decline. The party's image and recent political fortunes have benefited substantially from the change in attitude toward the party of the nation's media and opinion makers, the focus by the media on scandals affecting leftist rather than Christian Democratic-led local governments, the remobilization of religiously inclined voters by the church hierarchy, the rise of concern over the political and economic ramifications of the Communist party's role as the relative-majority party in the system, and the compression of the ideological space in the center through the adoption by all of the parties of the five-party coalition of a neocapitalist program. As a consequence, the small-party vote has declined. In 1985 the PSDI and PLI leadership did not realize the expectations generated by the 1983 vote or by the formation of the Craxi government. The increased level of conflict with the PCI over social and economic policies benefited the two larger parties in the coalition, but it did little to enhance the electoral fortunes or political clout of the minor centrist parties within the coalition. Of late, there have been signs of problems in differentiating in the public's mind the positions of the minor parties vis-à-vis those of the two larger parties in the coalition. As had already become evident in the analysis of the 1976 election results, large-party conflicts within the Italian political system are detrimental to small-party electoral fortunes. What the small parties need to do is to break out of the political and ideological bind that was woven for them in the aftermath of the 1983 election.

Notes

1. Robert Leonardi, "The Italian Parliamentary Elections of 1983: The Making and Unmaking of Myths," *West European Politics* 7 (April 1984): 188–91.

2. Celso Ghini, *Il voto degli italiani* (The vote of Italians) (Rome: Editori Riuniti, 1975), 93–127.

3. For a discussion of the history and consequences of the regional reform, see Robert D. Putnam, Robert Leonardi, and Raffaella Y. Nanetti, *La pianta e le radici: Il radicamento dell'istituto regionale nel sistema politico italiano* (The plant and the roots: The grassrooting of the regions in the Italian political system) (Bologna: Il Mulino, 1985).

4. The differences for the minor parties between the percentage of votes received and seats awarded in the Chamber of Deputies has been −5.5 (1948), −6.1 (1953), −4.1 (1958), −4.0 (1963), −4.8 (1968), −3.8 (1972), −4.2 (1976), −4.7 (1979), and −3.5 (1983).

5. DC presidents have been implicated in a series of questionable activities while in office. Giovanni Gronchi reportedly encouraged Giuseppe Tambroni in 1960 to experiment with the ill-fated "opening to the right" that led to a near civil war. Antonio Segni became associated with the *carabiniere* general Giovanni DeLorenzo's efforts to topple the center-left government in 1964. Finally, Giovanni Leone had to resign from office in disgrace because of influence peddling by members of his family.

6   Robert Leonardi, "Whither Craxi?: Socialist Party Relations with the Other Major Parties in the Italian Political System" (Paper presented at the U.S. State Department conference on Prospects for the Craxi Government, Washington, D.C., November 8, 1983).

7   For a discussion of the differences in the patterns of depolarization of attitudes among political elites and the general public, see Robert D. Putnam, Robert Leonardi, and Raffaella Y. Nanetti, "Polarization and Depolarization in Italian Politics, 1968-1981" (Paper presented at the 1981 Annual Meeting of the American Political Science Association, New York City, September 1981).

8   On the changing attitudes of voters toward the PCI, see Giacomo Sani, "Ricambio elettorale, mutamenti sociali e preferenze politiche" (Electoral turnover, social change, and political preferences), in Luigi Graziano and Sidney Tarrow, eds., *La crisi italiana* (The Italian crisis) (Turin: Einuadi, 1979), 303-28.

9   James E. Miller, "Taking Off the Gloves: The United States and the Italian Elections of 1948," *Diplomatic History* 7, no. 1 (Winter 1983): 35-55.

10   Comment made by Augusto Barbera during the debate at ISGRE regional studies conference, University of Trieste, Trieste, Italy, June 18-19, 1982.

11   The strong showing of the Sardinian Action party in 1984 and the new regionalist forces in the 1985 regional elections provide further evidence that this is a long-term trend in Italian politics.

12   The important turning points in this strategy were Enrico Berlinguer's November 1980 call for a government of "democratic solidarity" and shift in PCI support for a leftist governmental alliance, and the defeat of the Zaccagnini-Andreotti forces at the February 1980 DC congress by the center-right "preamble" forces.

13   Lawrence and Roberta Garner, "Italy: Crisis as Routine," *Current History* (May 1981): 27.

14   Ferruccio Marzano, "The General Report on the Country's Economic Situation in 1982," *Mezzogiorno d'Europa* (The South of Europe) 3 (April-June 1983): 165-69. Marzano states that the GNP figures would have been worse had not the steady increase of the service sector offset the substantial decreases in industry and agriculture. The 1983 figures prior to the election showed further drops in GNP (−3.6 percent) and increases in the unemployment rate to 12.1 percent.

15   For a discussion of the Marco Donat Cattin case, see Corrado Stajano, *L'Italia nichilista* (Nihilist Italy) (Milan: Arnaldo Mondadori, 1982).

16   On this issue the Socialist party assumed positions parallel to those advocated by Marco Pannella and the Radical party.

17   The only exception to this lily-white PRI image is the Sicilian leadership—for example, Aristide Gunnella—which is reported to have Mafia ties. In December 1983 the PRI leader of Milazzo (a port city in the province of Messina) was arrested on the charge of being the leader of a local kidnapping ring.

18   At the Athens conference the member countries of the EEC were unable to agree on the community budget, the relative distribution of financial burdens, and basic aspects of the agricultural policy.

19   The party's left wing is led by Pier Luigi Romita, who was party secretary for two years before being ousted by Longo in 1978. Under Romita's leadership the PSDI began to cooperate at the local level with the PCI. Prior to 1976 the PSDI had been rabidly anti-Communist. This may, in part, explain the lack of a working-class base.

20   Most of the polls had the MSI-DN at 5 percent.

21   In 1983 there was a significant decrease in the election of female representatives of parliament. Forty-seven females were elected to the Chamber of Deputies in comparison to fifty-four in 1979. Three-quarters of those elected entered the Chamber through the PCI list. The

most conspicuous drop in female deputies came within the ranks of the Radical party, which in 1983 elected only one female in comparison to five in 1979.

22 Antonio Negri, *Il dominio e il sabotaggio* (Domination and sabotage) (Milan: Feltrinelli, 1978).

23 The percentage of people who did not vote rose from 9.6 in 1979 to 11.0 percent in 1983. Of those casting ballots, blank and damaged ballots represented 5.6 percent of the total. See Gianfranco Pasquino, "La protesta dei senza volto" (The protest of the faceless ones), *Rinascita*, July 1, 1983, 15–16.

24 Robert Leonardi, "The Victors: The Smaller Parties in the 1979 Italian Elections," in Howard R. Penniman, ed., *Italy at the Polls, 1979* (Washington, D.C.: American Enterprise Institute, 1981), 187.

25 See Putnam, Leonardi, and Nanetti, *The Plant and the Roots*, 99–124.

26 The small-party vote in the major cities for 1983 is the following: MSI-DN, 9.9 percent; PRI, 7.1 percent; PLI, 4.3 percent; PSDI, 4.1 percent; PR, 3.8 percent; and DP, 1.9 percent.

27 This line of thinking may have influenced De Mita's decision to accept early elections even though he did not have full control over the party organization.

7 Unions and Politics in Italy

CAROL A. MERSHON

————Soon after the 1983 parliamentary elections the adjunct secretary general of the Italian General Confederation of Workers (CGIL), Ottaviano Del Turco, observed that "the union movement used to take on responsibilities of the political system. It was concerned with everything, from health to schools. It was the party of the Italians. . . . [A] season has ended."[1]

This chapter explores continuity and change in the political role of Italian unions. The first two sections outline the evolution of the Italian labor movement from 1944 to 1979, showing how in the 1970s the movement became a channel of political initiative and a stimulus for politico-economic transformation. The third section investigates the course of Italian unionism since the Communist party (PCI) withdrew from the governmental majority in 1979. The fourth section assesses the results of the 1983 election and the political role of Italian unions.[2]

From Reconstruction to the
Eve of the Hot Autumn

For more than a decade after the post–World War II reconstruction, Italian unions were weak and isolated. The unions gained market strength in the 1960s, but the great social mobilization of 1968–70 turned the union movement into a powerful political actor.

The rebuilding of a democratic Italy after years of Fascist rule began in the spring of 1944 when the Christian Democratic (DC), Socialist (PSI), Communist, and other anti-Fascist parties formed a government under Marshal Pietro Badoglio. Meeting at Rome in June 1944, representatives of the three major parties revived the democratic labor movement. They created a single union confederation, the CGIL, out of the workers' organizations that had participated in the wartime Resistance. Northern unions entered the CGIL in July 1945, soon after the liberation of northern Italy.

In certain respects, the legacy of the Resistance was short-lived. The labor movement's strategies during the Resistance offered little guidance to the various currents of Italian unionism as they faced the tasks of economic and political reconstruction. The *consigli di gestione* (joint management councils) and other work place institutions established during the Resistance provoked controversy within the confederation and among the political parties. The *consigli* had disappeared by the early 1950s, while the *commissioni interne* (internal commissions) stayed in place at the shop floor.[3] The Resistance gave many workers hopes for radical change. To Communist leaders, however, the Fascist experience demonstrated the importance of moderation, of broad social and political alliances, and of collaboration in a democratic system. The PCI's secretary general, Palmiro Togliatti, first enunciated this policy at Salerno in April 1944, and the CGIL also embraced it.

The partisan origins of the CGIL strongly influenced the confederation's organization and action. First, the confederation, like the governing coalition, was the site of both cooperation and competition among various political currents. Second, the CGIL became an instrument of the political parties, especially of the Communist party.[4] The union drew its leaders and cadres from the parties, depended on party structures and party ideology to mobilize union members, and followed party strategies. Third, the CGIL therefore concentrated on action in the political arena. The need for government intervention in the shattered economy and for consolidation of democratic institutions contributed, certainly, to the CGIL's attention to politics. Yet "the Communist goals and the relationship between the party and the CGIL further shifted the focus of the union movement away from the factory and toward the political system and the state."[5] Fourth, centralization marked the CGIL, and the category unions, organized by industrial sector, developed slowly. At the factory level, the *commissioni interne* possessed few rights. National multi-industry agreements, negotiated by confederal union leaders and the employers' peak association, the *Confindustria*, dominated collective bargaining.

The CGIL seemed strong but was fundamentally weak and ineffective. The confederation claimed 1.3 million members in January 1945, more than 4.5 million in 1946, and almost 6 million in 1947.[6] Despite this (probably exaggerated) growth, the CGIL remained weak at the shop floor and was plagued by internal divisions. Unable to reconcile the traditions and the interests of its factions, the CGIL failed to devise a concrete economic program coordinating short-term and long-term policy proposals and exercised little influence on government decisions. Moreover, when the reconstruction period came to a close, the CGIL's difficulties increased.

Table 7-1 Union Membership, 1950–1982

Year	CGIL		CISL	
	Number of Members	Percent of All Workers	Number of Members	Percent of All Worker
1950	4,640,528	45.7	1,189,882	11.7
1955	4,194,235	38.1	1,342,204	12.2
1960	2,584,215	21.6	1,324,398	11.1
1965	2,540,555	20.3	1,467,990	11.7
1968	2,461,297	19.3	1,626,786	12.7
1970	2,943,314	22.2	1,807,586	13.6
1975	4,081,399	28.9	2,593,545	18.4
1980	4,599,050	31.2	3,059,845	20.7
1982	4,570,252	30.9	2,976,800	20.1

Note: Percents show union members as a proportion of all wage earners in all sectors of the econom
Dashes (—) indicate information not available.
Sources: For the CGIL, 1950–1980: E. Biagioni, F. Pantile, and C. Pontacolone, *Cgil anni '80: L'evol
zione delle struture organizzative* (Roma: Editrice Sindacale Italiana, 1981), 36, 37. For the CISL, 195€
1975: G. Romagnoli, ed , *La sindacalizzazione tra ideologia e pratica*, vol. 2 (Roma: Edizioni Lavor
1980), 193. For the UIL, 1968 and 1975: S. Coi, "Sindacati in Italia: Iscritti, apparati, hnanzlamentc
Il Mulino (March–April 1979): 202. For the CISL and UIL, 1980, and for all confederations, 198

With the onset of the cold war in 1947, the Christian Democratic party ousted the Communist and the Socialist parties from the governing coalition. The labor movement, reflecting its links to the parties, soon split as well. The Catholic faction withdrew from the CGIL in 1948 and founded the CISL (Italian Confederation of Workers' Unions) with Christian Democratic support. Social Democrats, Republicans, and Socialists established the UIL (Italian Union of Labor) in 1950. The CGIL became the largest of three confederations, dominated by Communists while retaining some independents and Socialists.

Bolstered by a large plurality in the 1948 elections, the Christian Democratic government pursued strategies that depended on the market weakness of the unions and perpetuated the political isolation of much of the working class. The government restricted its expenditure and credit in an effort to promote private capital accumulation. It treated international rather than domestic demand as the primary stimulus to economic growth. To gain a competitive advantage in foreign markets, the government sought to raise productivity while maintaining low labor costs and flexibility in labor use.[7] Unemployment, artificially reduced by a ban on dismissals in the immediate postwar period, increased sharply in the late 1940s and remained high until the late 1950s. The political strategy of the Christian Democrats centered on clientelism. The government distributed patronage to cultivate alliances with the traditional petite bourgeoisie of the South, the industrial bourgeoisie of the

UIL		Total	
Number of Members	Percent of All Workers	Number of Members	Percent of All Workers
—	—	—	—
—	—	—	—
—	—	—	—
—	—	—	—
648,393	5.1	4,736,476	37.1
—	—	—	—
1,032,605	7.3	7,707,549	54.7
346,900	9.1	9,005,795	61.0
1,358,004	9.2	8,905,136	60.2

3. Romagnoli, "Sindacalizzazione e rappresentanza" (Unionization and representation), in G. Baglioni, M. Camonico, and E. Santi, eds., *Le relazioni sinciacali in Italia: Rapporto 1982–1983* (Roma: Edizioni Lavoro, 1984), 213. For wage and salary workers, 1950 and 1955: ISTAT, *Sommario di statistiche storiche dell'Italia, 1961–1975* (Roma, 1976), 145. (The 1950 figure is interpolated using the average growth rates of the following three years.) For wage and salary workers, 1960–1982: ISTAT, *Annuario di statistiche del lavoro*, various vols. (Roma, various years).

North, and the practicing Catholics among the peasantry and the working class. The Christian Democrats excluded the anticlerical sectors of the working class from this social coalition.[8]

In this changed environment the CGIL retained many of its past policies and practices. During the reconstruction the CGIL had made growth in employment its highest policy priority. In 1949 the CGIL incorporated this emphasis into an economic program, the *Piano del lavoro*, whose underlying postulate was that economic development could occur only through a large expansion of the domestic market. Although the success of the government's liberal economic design soon invalidated that notion, CGIL leaders repeated their warnings of economic failure and did not reexamine their policies for several years. The CGIL's dependence on the Communist party persisted, as did its focus on political action. "The CGIL continued to operate as if only sweeping political change (a victory of the Left) would resolve Italy's economic 'crisis' and to favor action in the political arena (general strikes on political issues, especially international ones) above action in the market arena."[9] The CGIL, like the other confederations, did little to build union structures at the factory level.[10] Union activity and collective bargaining remained centralized.

By the mid-1950s, however, the CGIL faced a number of pressures. It preserved its status as the largest confederation but suffered a sizable drop in membership (see table 7-1). CGIL activists met discrimination and even dismissal at the workplace.[11] At the national and at the firm levels, employers and

Figure 7-1   Trends in Italian Strike Activity, 1950–1981. Note: The indicators are expressed as percentages of the 1950 values. In 1950 the number of strikes was 1,272; the size was 2,779; the working hours lost to strikes were 62, 087,000; and workers participating in strikes were 3,535,000. Source: ISTAT, *Annuario Statistico Italiano* (Rome, various years).

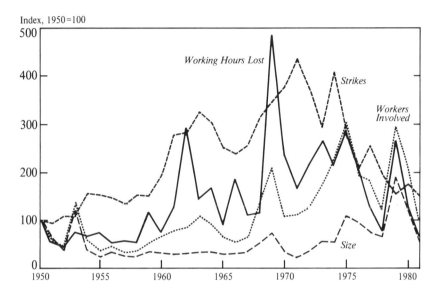

Index, 1950=100

the other unions signed collective-bargaining agreements without the CGIL.[12] Moreover, the CISL emerged as a major challenge to the CGIL. At its inception, the CISL stressed Catholic solidarity and anticommunism. In the mid-1950s these concepts were joined by others: a view of the union as an association of its members rather than as an agent of the entire working class, an insistence on autonomy from political parties, a focus on the factory, and an aggressive wage posture matching claims to the productivity increases of individual firms.[13] These new CISL concepts were not immediately put into practice. Throughout the 1950s the CISL's wage demands lagged behind productivity. The CISL organized its own faction within the DC, and its leaders were elected as Christian Democratic members of parliament.[14] Still, the CISL's distinctive definition of union action helped it to compete organizationally with the CGIL. In contrast to the CGIL, the CISL slightly enlarged its membership during the 1950s. In elections for the *commissioni interne*, the CGIL kept an overall majority of votes, but the CISL registered important gains at the expense of the CGIL. The most consequential victory came in 1955, when the CISL ended the dominance of FIAT's internal commission by the CGIL.[15]

Attempting to address these problems, the CGIL reconsidered both its relationship with the Communist party and its traditional subordination of factory and wage concerns to national and political issues. In 1956 the CGIL and the PCI formally renounced the "transmission belt" doctrine of union-party relations.[16] Although the bonds between the CGIL and the PCI by no means dissolved in subsequent years, the CGIL began to assert some autonomy from the party. It also moved toward an emphasis on plant-level bargaining (officially approved as CISL policy in 1953 and by the CGIL in 1960); and it encouraged the establishment of union sections in the work place (first projected in 1954, just after the CISL launched plans for sections). The CGIL thus sought to reconstruct its support at the base and to link rank-and-file mobilization with advocacy of political and economic reforms at the national level.[17]

Economic and political conditions became more favorable to the labor movement in the early 1960s. The "economic miracle" brought new groups into the work force and gave the unions leverage in the labor market: Unemployment decreased from 5.2 percent in 1959 to 2.5 percent in 1963 and hovered around 3.5 percent in the last half of the decade. As cold war tensions waned, the Christian Democrats expanded their coalition to the non-Communist left and embraced principles of Keynesian demand management. The Socialist party entered government in 1963.

These altered conditions shaped the contract settlements of 1961–62. Workers won substantial wage increases in the first big strike wave since World War II (see figure 7–1). The category unions of the different confederations, especially in the metalworking sector, collaborated during contract negotiations. The loosening of partisan ties helped the unions to identify a common interest in exploiting their newfound market strength. Employers in state-held industries bargained independently of the *Confindustria*, accepting "check-off" payments from wages for union dues, limited time off for union activity in the work place, and plant-level negotiation of piece rates, production bonuses, and job classifications.[18]

The early 1960s thus promised the labor movement a new ability to influence the decisions of government and employers. These hopes were disappointed. The proponents of reform, initially a slim majority within the government, neither enlarged their numbers nor engaged the full support of the unions. The Christian Democratic–Socialist coalition could not reconcile its conflicting aims: It wished to integrate the unions into the political process and at the same time to weaken the PCI, the party that most represented working-class interests; it proposed to restructure the economy yet not disturb the clientele network that kept the DC at the center of power. In 1968 the labor movement appeared to wield little more influence in society than it had in 1960.

Two examples illustrate the obstacles to social reform and to labor integration. First, the government chose a traditional policy instrument—sharp monetary restriction—when threatened by inflation and by balance-of-payments problems in the winter of 1963–64. These problems derived only in part from the recent rise in wages, yet the government's response concentrated on disciplining labor costs and the unions.[19] The ensuing recession lasted longer than expected, through 1966. It reduced the unions' market power, as evidenced in the collective-bargaining round of 1965–66. Second, the government's planning effort largely excluded the unions and yielded few social reforms. In 1963 the government began preparing a five-year plan.[20] It at first tried to include the unions in labor market and economic planning. But the unions soon discovered that their views did not significantly affect the drafting of the plan. The goals of the plan received the cautious endorsement of many CGIL and CISL leaders, but both unions expressed reservations about planning mechanisms.[21] After repeated delays, parliament formally approved a plan in July 1967. The government implemented few of the outlined reforms. Although state intervention in the economy increased during the 1960s, it served neither to remedy structural flaws nor to meet the needs of the industrial working classes. Instead, this intervention expanded and reinforced clientele relationships between the government parties and social groups other than the organized working class.

Despite the frustration of initial promise the years from 1960 to 1968 witnessed a consolidation of changes begun in the 1950s. Decentralization of union organization and collective bargaining progressed. The unions devoted more resources to the task of building factory-level union structures, but they obtained limited results.[22] Over the course of the decade, category unions assumed a more important negotiating role as industry contracts replaced the national interindustry contracts prevalent in the 1950s. Bargaining at the factory level was confined to specified, narrow issues. The debate on planning accelerated the CGIL's move away from revolutionary rhetoric and the CISL's move toward concern for general politico-economic reform. As their strategies converged, the CGIL and CISL cooperated more effectively and grew more independent of political parties. These developments laid the basis for additional future change.

The Hot Autumn and Its Aftermath

The unprecedented level of intensity of industrial conflict in 1968–70 transformed the labor movement, the economy, and the balance of political power in Italy.[23] Figure 7–1 contrasts strike activity before and during these years. An increasingly tight and compartmentalized labor market, dissatisfaction with postrecession wage restraint, and the discontent of recent arrivals to the industrial work force fueled the strike explosion. The initial disputes of spring 1968, led by older skilled workers, surprised many union leaders. In the fol-

Table 7-2 Diffusion of Factory Councils, 1970–1977

Year	Metalworking Sector		All Sectors	
	Factory Councils	Delegates	Factory Councils	Delegates
1970	1,374	22,609	—[a]	—
1971	2,556	30,943	—	—
1972	4,291	42,886	8,101	82,923
1973	—	—	9,813	97,161
1974	—	—	16,000	150,000
1977	—	—	32,021	206,336

a. Dashes (—) indicate data not available.
Sources: I. Regalia, "Rappresentanza operaia e sindacato: mutamento di un sistema di relazioni industriali" (Workers' representation and the union: Change of an industrial relations system), in A. Pizzorno et al., *Lotte operaie e sindacato: ilciclo 1968–1972 in Italia* (Bologna: Il Mulino, 1978), 224; and M. Regini, *I dilemmi del sindacato: conflitto e participazione negli anni settanta e ottanta* (Union dilemmas: Conflict and participation in the 1970s and 1980s) (Bologna: Il Mulino, 1981), 49.

lowing months, and especially during the "Hot Autumn" of 1969 (the most intense period of labor conflict), young, mostly immigrant, semiskilled workers dominated industrial strife. Soon conflict intensified in traditionally strike-prone industries (such as metalworking) and spread to new firms, regions, and groups of workers. Workers put forward new demands for reduction of wage differentials, redefinition of job hierarchies, and influence over the organization of production.

Undertaking major organizational innovations, the unions moved to acquire control over the rapidly evolving work-place mobilization. From 1969 to 1972 the unions fostered a large turnover of activists and rank-and-file leaders. First with unofficial encouragement and then as official policy, the unions supported the establishment of factory councils as the new form of work-place representation (see table 7–2).[24] The factory councils embodied the values of egalitarianism, direct democracy, and union unity expressed so forcefully during the Hot Autumn.[25] The diffusion of factory councils, along with sustained worker mobilization, led to a decentralization of collective bargaining: for the first time, factory-level agreements became important and numerous.[26] The confederations took several steps toward unification. They agreed on an incompatibility rule in 1969: Union officials could no longer hold elective or party offices. In 1970 the CISL abandoned the concept of associational unionism. A year later the three confederations approved plans for a unitary, classicist organization of Italian workers, to promote social and economic reform. By July 1972 the drive for a complete merger had waned, and the Federation of CGIL-CISL-UIL was created. As testimony to the skill with which the union had channeled the energies of the Hot Autumn, membership in the CGIL, CISL, and UIL rose between 1968 and 1972 by 31.8 percent.[27]

Strategic innovations paralleled organizational innovations. Acting in concert, the three confederations attempted to fuse market and political initiatives into a platform for comprehensive politico-economic change. They incorporated into union strategy the new contractual claims of the semiskilled industrial workers and generalized the gains won in the most militant factories and sectors. The unions viewed the party system as an inadequate mediator of the new demands for reform and withdrew further from party tutelage. They often bypassed the parties to negotiate directly with government in a "struggle for reforms" in pensions, housing, health services, education, southern development, transport, and the taxation system.[28] By defining interdependent goals for the market and political arenas, the unions sought to build alliances between the work force and broad sectors of the Italian population, and to coordinate the actions of different levels of union structure.

The Hot Autumn brought dramatic economic consequences. Large wage gains exceeded productivity growth and expanded labor's share of the national income.[29] Italian industries' profit rates diminished just as international competition was growing.[30] Worker mobilization and bargaining over work conditions, procedures, and technology greatly reduced employers' flexibility in the use of labor. Although inflation showed a moderate initial increase (from 1.4 percent in 1968 to 5.7 percent in 1972), the foundations were laid for much higher inflation in the future.[31]

An equally great, but more gradual, evolution in electoral outcomes and governmental action and composition accompanied economic change after the Hot Autumn. Parliament enacted the *Statuto dei Lavoratori* (Workers' Statute) in 1970. The statute ensured union rights at the work place and protected individual workers against dismissals, transfers, and changes of jobs.[32] Thereafter, widening differences between the PSI and the DC hobbled reform attempts.[33] Legislation on pensions, housing, and hospitals in the early 1970s presented no radical departures, but it dangerously raised government budgetary commitments. These concessions to the unions were made "without challenging the interests of the classes tied to the Christian Democratic power structure, and above all without modifying the system of payoffs as a way to find the funds needed to cover the increased spending."[34] Its equilibrium shaken in the wake of the Hot Autumn, the center-left government in 1972 called the first early elections in Italy's postwar history. The Christian Democrats formed a centrist government with the Social Democrats and the Liberals after the elections.

Having failed to obtain significant reform, the unions in 1973 became more defensive on shop-floor issues and began to specify more precise reform proposals. They sought to prevent firings in the work place, to limit layoffs, to control the transfer of workers within and between factories, to protect real wages, and to reduce overtime and work hours in an effort to create more jobs. The unions' most visible achievements regarded wages: The 1973 contractual round provided for high wage increases; and the 1975 agreement between the *Confindustria* and the confederations expanded and equalized the coverage of the *scala mobile* (cost-of-living escalator).[35] As for reforms, the unions stressed economic issues over expansion and reorganization of social services. The unions focused on structural reform of the economy, employment growth, development of the South, reform of state activity in the economy, and workers' control over investments. In contrast to the 1969–72 period, the unions pursued their reform goals primarily through the contractual process.[36] Although consultations between unions and government continued, the political parties came to serve as intermediaries in the negotiations. Both sets of policies, shop floor and societal, tended to recentralize initiative within the union movement.[37]

By officially adopting an austerity policy in January–February 1978, the unions returned the search for reforms to the political arena.[38] The unions offered to exchange wage containment and labor mobility for more efficient government intervention in the economy, a commitment to full employment, and a union role in directing the investment process at the firm, sectoral, and national levels. This policy marked a new approach to the strategic choices that had confronted the unions since the Hot Autumn.[39] Since 1969 the unions had used their newfound power to press simultaneously for short- and long-term ends, for improvements in wages and working conditions, and for politico-economic reforms. The unions now announced the overriding importance of reforms and expressed a willingness to make contractual concessions to obtain them. The exact content of the concessions—and, indeed, the austerity policy itself—provoked a controversy within the labor movement that persisted into the 1980s.[40]

In 1976 the unions had started to turn their attention from the market to the political arena. Three sets of factors contributed to the change in emphasis: economic conditions, internal union developments, and political changes.

Economic crisis encouraged the unions to reconsider political action. Italy took part in a worldwide boom from mid-1972 to mid-1974, which brought increased prices, balance-of-payments deficits, and speculation against the lira. With the steep rise in energy prices because of the oil embargo and the government's sharp monetary restriction, the economy swung into recession in 1975. The brief recovery in the winter of 1975–76 led to a currency crisis and to a new spurt of inflation. The government once again imposed restrictive monetary and credit measures, which reduced investment and slowed economic growth from mid-1976 to mid-1978. Several long-term trends in the labor market accompanied these oscillations in economic activity: a decline in the mobility of the work force; concentration of unemployment in the South and among youth and women; and expansion of the "invisible economy," which escaped the tax and social security systems and employed nonunionized workers. The unions concluded that their attempt to force structural reform through market action was not succeeding. Indeed, their work-place strategy was even helping to sharpen the divisions between employed industrial workers —protected against dismissal by law and contract and insulated from inflation by the *scala mobile*—and the rest of the labor force.[41]

Organizational pressures also prompted the unions' change in strategy. By the late 1970s the unions faced a work force far more heterogeneous than that which had participated in the Hot Autumn. The proportion of wage and salary workers in industry had decreased while service-sector employment had grown. More women and white-collar workers had entered the labor force, and the number of male blue-collar workers had fallen. As these new groups emerged, signs of sectionalism appeared among workers. The memberships of some industry federations pressed for narrow benefits and against societal reforms. Autonomous unions, unaffiliated with the confederations, voiced particularistic demands and attracted more adherents, especially among state and municipal employees. The unions viewed a change in strategy as necessary to transcend this fragmentation of interests.[42]

For union leaders (and many other Italians) the most salient political event of the mid-1970s was the Communist party's bid for governmental power. The leftward shift of the Socialists in the late 1960s had raised doubts about the durability of Socialist–Christian Democratic collaboration. The Communist party in 1972–73 had formulated a program calling for a "historic compromise" between Communists and Catholics. Soon after, electoral returns strengthened the Communists' claim for a role in national government: The Christian Democrats and the church were defeated in the 1974 divorce referendum, and the Communists registered startling electoral advances in the 1975 regional elections and in the 1976 national elections. From mid-1976 to early 1979, the PCI played a key role in supporting minority Christian Democratic governments—by joining abstentions in parliament, by supporting a six-party policy agreement, and finally, after March 1978, by a parliamentary consultation agreement, among the DC, the PRI (Republican party), the PSDI (Italian Social Democratic party), the PSI, and the PCI.[43]

These developments posed two problems for the unions. The first concerned the composition of the government. Because union cooperation entered into calculations about different government coalitions, the unions became more involved in party politics. The unions avoided, however, any open declaration in favor of a particular coalition or party within a coalition, and thus preserved union unity. The second problem concerned the content of government, and union, policy. By late 1976 the PCI was arguing that the unions

Table 7-3 Growth, Inflation, and Unemployment, 1979–1983 (percent)

Indicator	1979	1980	1981	1982	1983
Change in real gross domestic product from previous year	4.9	3.9	−0.2	−0.3	−1.4
Change in consumer prices from previous year	14.8	21.2	19.5[a]	16.7	14.7
Unemployment	7.7	7.6	8.4	9.1	9.9

a. In 1981, ISTAT changed the base year for calculating inflation. The figures for 1979–81 use 1976 as their base; those for 1982 and 1983 use 1980 as a base. On the new base (1980 = 100), the CPI in 1981 showed a rise of 17.8 percent.
Sources: OECD, OECD Economic Outlook, Historical Statistics 1960–1981 (Paris: 1983), 44, 83; International Labor Office (ILO), Yearbook of Labor Statistics 1982 (Geneva, 1982), 372; OECD, OECD Economic Surveys, 1983–1984: Italy (Paris: 1984) 10, 13, 14.

should ease economic demands in exchange for public policies designed to restructure the Italian economy.[44]

This stance produced changes in union policy before 1978. In 1976, the secretary general of the CGIL, Luciano Lama, stressed the incompatibility between a policy of austerity and a policy of substantial wage increases. In 1977 the unions accepted the disengagement of severance payments from cost-of-living adjustments. The containment of factory-level collective bargaining produced a decline in strike activity in 1977 (as measured by three indicators) and again in 1978 (as measured by all four indicators used in figure 7–1). But in early 1978 the union movement most clearly responded to its two problems. With the approval of an austerity policy, the unions officially echoed the position of the PCI and tacitly supported the PCI as a partner in national government.[45]

Union Dilemmas, 1979–1983

A new kind of politicization emerged from the Hot Autumn, one defined not by competing party and ideological identifications but by the united pursuit of influence on government policies. From 1979 to 1983 the union movement continued its attempt to influence public policy. It faced, however, new challenges to its shop-floor and societal power and it experienced increasing internal divisions.

As in the decade following the Hot Autumn, stagnation, spurts of growth, and enduring structural imbalances marked the Italian economy. The economy accelerated in 1979 and 1980, only to return to recession in 1981 (see table 7–3). Productivity rose by 4.4 percent from 1978 to 1982, more than in any other country in the Organization for Economic Cooperation and Develop-

Table 7-4 Unemployment by Age, Sex, and Geographic Area, 1981
(percent of labor force)

Location	Males			Females			Males and Females		
	Under 25	Over 25	Total	Under 25	Over 25	Total	Under 25	Over 25	Total
North and center	17.7	1.6	4.0	25.5	6.8	11.6	21.4	3.3	6.7
South	32.4	3.2	8.1	51.1	11.4	21.5	39.9	5.5	12.2
All Italy	22.9	2.1	5.4	32.9	8.2	14.4	27.4	4.0	8.4

Source: OECD, *OECD Economic Surveys, 1982–1983: Italy* (Paris, 1982), 17.

ment (OECD). Improvements in productivity did little to slow inflation, in part because of the inefficiencies of the service sector and of the state bureaucracy.[46] The unemployment rate, which had ranged between 6 and 7.5 percent of the labor force for much of the 1970s, exceeded 9 percent in 1982 and 1983. These aggregate figures obscured extremely high unemployment among young, female, and southern Italians (see table 7–4). The figures also disregarded the large increase in the use of the *Cassa Integrazione Guadagni* (CIG), the state-financed fund paying salaries to laid-off workers. If workers placed on the CIG had been counted, the 1982 unemployment rate would have been 11 percent.[47]

For the first time since the Hot Autumn, the economic crisis touched traditionally protected categories of the work force. At FIAT a series of bitter industrial disputes ended in October 1980 with the placement of almost 23,000 employees on CIG and a march of 40,000 FIAT employees demanding the right to work. Initially hailed as "the Hot Autumn in reverse," the "FIAT Autumn" in retrospect seems more precisely a symbol of the vulnerability of the unions' core constituency to economic dislocation.[48] After autumn 1980, the steepest rise in the use of the CIG occurred in the most industrialized areas of northern Italy, and employers in Piedmont and Lombardy dismissed large numbers of workers for the first time in decades.[49] In 1982 net real wages in industry fell by 2.3 percentage points.[50]

As the unions encountered new difficulty in their defense of shop-floor gains, they met all-too-familiar disappointment in their search for political change. In adopting an austerity policy, the unions offered wage moderation in return for a governmental commitment to reform the economy. Yet, interparty competition and the complications and contradictions inherent in the PCI's governing role led first to the government's failure to formulate the measures deemed necessary by the unions and then to the Communists' withdrawal from the governmental majority in January 1979. The PCI then incurred sizable electoral losses in the June 1979 parliamentary elections.[51]

Four trends in union-government relations emerged in the early 1980s. First, management of the economic crisis became the central problem addressed in union-government negotiations. The dominant themes of union-government relations were anti-inflation measures, including in particular modification of the *scala mobile*. The governments headed by Giovanni Spadolini, more clearly than preceding governments, sought an anti-inflation pact —belatedly obtained in expanded form in the cost-of-labor agreement of January 1983. The unions brought more specific issues to negotiations with the government (for example, aid to firms and sectors in crisis; plans for the steel, chemical, and other sectors; investment policies for state-held firms; and regulation of strikes in the transport sector). Yet the government, which in the 1970s had solicited union cooperation on specific laws, now emphasized meetings on the overall contours of economic policy and the overriding need to reduce inflation.[52]

Second, the greatest change since the 1970s regarded the deepening divisions within the labor movement. For the first time since 1969, the slow pace of union-government negotiations resulted more from union difficulties in finding a satisfactory middle position than from dissent and indecision among government partners. The PCI's exit from the governmental arena in 1979 exacerbated partisan tensions within the labor movement. Thereafter, the CGIL's positions tended to echo the oppositionist stance of the PCI, while the UIL and the CISL tended to support certain aspects of government policy. The CISL and the UIL favored the moderation of wage claims in exchange for expansionary fiscal, investment, and credit policies to be implemented by the government. The CGIL opposed such an exchange as "ideologically unnatural" and appropriate only in the presence of a "friendly government." Whereas the CISL and the UIL envisioned concessions on the *scala mobile* and real-wage stability, the CGIL emphasized a more rigid defense of the *scala mobile* and the automatic compensation of any slowing of the escalator mechanism with tax reductions for low-income workers, lessened tax progressivity for middle-income workers (to counter fiscal drag), and increases in family allowances.[53]

Third, the unions' discussion of anti-inflation measures with the government—and the economic conditions compelling such a discussion—strained relations between the union leadership and its base. Workers expressed dissatisfaction with union initiatives, and union membership declined.[54] Union leaders, in an attempt to bridge their distance from workers, instituted factory-level voting on policy proposals to be presented to the government. In January 1982 about 30,000 assemblies voted on a ten-point union proposal dealing with such issues as southern development, tax reforms, pensions, and the cost of labor. Although almost 3 million of the 4 million participants approved the policy document, an estimated 2.4 million workers attached requests for amendments to their positive votes. Evaluating this outcome, Giorgio Benvenuto of the UIL described the climate in the factories as "one of distrust toward the government and suspicion toward the union movement."[55] Union leaders sent another document, treating contract renewals, employment, and the cost of labor, to the factories in November 1982. This time workers met not in factory-wide assemblies but in smaller office or department gatherings, which encouraged more detailed and less contentious debate.[56]

Fourth, as in the 1970s, union-government relations showed a low level of institutionalization. No permanent structures provided a site for bargaining over economic policy. The Spadolini governments took a new approach, however, in actively promoting negotiations between employers and unions on anti-inflation measures and outlining general parameters to be respected in the negotiations.[57] This strategy led to another novelty: the direct intervention of the government in the negotiations that produced the cost-of-labor agreement of January 1983.[58] The employers' associations and the union confederations agreed to revise the *scala mobile* on the basis of a protocol prepared by the minister of labor, Vincenzo Scotti. Government policy pledges formed an integral part of the accord: The document combined tax reforms and changes in the regulation of the labor market with reductions in working hours, ceilings on wage settlements, and restrictions on plant-level bargaining.[59]

The electoral campaign of May and June 1983 took place near the end of unusually long and bitter national contract negotiations. First blocked by disagreements over the *scala mobile*, these negotiations were now, the unions charged, being prolonged by the *Confindustria* in hopes that the election would produce a victory for the right and thus weaken the unions' bargaining position. The unions also accused the *Confindustria* of trying to evade the promises it had made regarding working hours in the January cost-of-labor agreement.[60] Departing from past practice, the unions conducted contract strikes during the campaign.

Of the four unrenewed contracts, that for the private-sector metalworkers claimed the most attention of political leaders during the campaign.[61] After an appeal from the unions to Prime Minister Amintore Fanfani, on June 7 Scotti resumed an attempt to reconcile the differences between employers and unions, which had stalled the metalworkers' negotiations. The final stages of the campaign were thus punctuated by sanguine statements that the contract could soon be concluded, then by warnings that the mediation effort might fail, and, finally, by recognition that the contract would not be renewed before the elections. Controversy arose at the same time over the cost-of-labor agreement. The Christian Democratic treasury minister, Giovanni Goria, proposed that the agreement be modified to eliminate the effect of dollar revaluations on the *scala mobile*. His suggestion drew extremely sharp criticism from union leaders, who declared that such a position undermined Scotti's mediation attempt.[62]

The day after the polls closed union leaders argued that party stances on the contract renewals and the cost-of-labor agreement had influenced the elec-

Table 7-5 Relationship between Party Vote, 1953 and 1963, and
Membership in Parties and Unions, 1951, 1961 (correlation coefficients)

| Party Vote | Year of Vote | Membership in Party and Union | | | | Year of Membership |
		DC	CISL	PCI	CGIL	
DC	1953	.32		−.61	−.54	1951
	1963	.50	.31	−.69	−.70	1961
PCI + PSI	1953	−.47		.85	.82	1951
	1963	−.45	−.26	.81	.80	1961
PCI	1953	−.33		.84	.72	1951
	1963	−.31	−.31	.82	.72	1961

Source: G. Galli and A. Prandi, *Patterns of Political Participation in Italy* (New Haven, Conn.: Yale University Press, 1970), 68.

toral results. Luciano Lama of the CGIL asserted that "the party that was most penalized, Christian Democracy, [was] the one which presented itself as the most determined supporter of the *Confindustria*'s positions." According to Benvenuto of the UIL, the Christian Democrats "De Mita and Goria gave the impression of making policy against the union movement. . . . The Goria line [regarding the cost-of-labor agreement] has been decisively defeated by these elections. . . . This is, for us and for the contract renewals, the most important fact." Eraldo Crea of the CISL did not comment on the DC's losses but remarked that "whoever in Confindustria circles had bet on a regressive and conservative change of the political framework lost the wager."[63]

The Unions and the Electoral Outcome

The outcome of the 1983 elections holds a certain irony for the union movement. The irony may be summarized in two observations. First, an analysis of aggregate data reveals that the link between union membership and voting behavior has partially weakened over time. Provincial data from the 1950s and 1960s indicate that CGIL membership influenced voting behavior more strongly than did CISL membership. Only in the case of the CGIL did union membership appear as effective as party membership in orienting the vote. The negative association between CGIL membership and the Christian Democratic vote became stronger from 1953 to 1963, while the link between CGIL membership and the leftist vote remained about the same (see table 7–5).

Regional data for the 1972 and 1983 elections disclose continued stability in the tie between CGIL membership and the leftist vote. The trend regarding the DC vote, however, is reversed: From 1972 to 1983 the negative association between CGIL membership and the DC vote declined (see table 7–6). Further-

Table 7-6 Relationship between Party Vote, 1972 and 1983, and Membership in CGIL, 1971 and 1980, by Region (correlation coefficients)

Party Vote	Year of Vote	Membership in CGIL		Year of Membership
		19 Regions	17 Regions	
DC	1972	−.69	−.54	1971
	1983	−.49	−.23	1980
PCI + PSI	1972	.77	.70	1971
	1983	.75	.71	1980
PCI	1972	.79	.66	1971
	1983	.79	.71	1980

Note: The 19 regions include all but Valle d'Aosta, which uses a plurality electoral system: Piemonte, Lombardia, Trentino-Alfo Adige, Veneto, Fruiti-Venezia Giulia, Liguria, Emilia-Romagna, Toscana, Umbria, Marche, Lazio, Abruzzo, Molise, Campania, Basilicata, Pugliz, Calabria, Sicilia, Sardegna. The 17 regions comprise all regions but Valle d'Aosta, Emilia-Romagna, and Toscana.
Source: Computed by the author from electoral returns published in the press, unpublished 1971 CGIL membership data, and 1980 CGIL membership data published by Biagioni, et al., *Cgil Anni '80.*

more, as suggested by the scattergram in figure 7–2, much of the correlation is due to the difference between the Red Belt, the area of north-central Italy (Emilia-Romagna, Tuscany, Umbria, and Marche) that is traditionally a Communist stronghold, and the rest of Italy. Without Emilia-Romagna and Tuscany, which have extremely high rates of unionization, the negative correlation between union membership and party vote drops from 1972 to 1983 quite sharply.[64]

The Catholic subculture in Italy has fragmented, while the Socialist political tradition has not. Several organizations long part of the Catholic world, including the CISL, have become less reliable and willing channels of electoral support for the DC. Fewer members of these organizations than before now vote for the DC.[65]

This partial decline in partisan identification enabled the Italian labor movement to attain a measure of unity, to channel popular demands for socio-economic reform, and so become a powerful actor in Italian politics. Before the Hot Autumn the politicization of the labor movement resided in each union's dependence on political parties. In the 1970s the political role of the movement consisted in the unions' common pursuit of interrelated objectives: influence on the political system, public control of economic development, and representation of broad sectors of the Italian population as well as representation of union members.[66] While maintaining these general objectives, the unions modified their political strategy in the early 1980s. An increase in party influence, though not of the same dimensions as in the past, slowed union decision making. Economic crisis has threatened the unions' shop-floor power. The unions no longer strive, as in the 1970s, to use market strength to promote political reform. They have attempted instead to use relations with the government to counter market vulnerability.

Second, the evolution in electoral behavior brought the PCI closer to governmental power in the late 1970s and led to the emergence of non-DC prime ministers in the 1980s. The 1983 elections, however, exacerbated rather than eased the union movement's dilemmas. The government of Bettino Craxi, like its predecessors, formulated an austerity program. Unlike its predecessors, the Craxi government showed considerable effectiveness in carrying out that program.

As the first Socialist prime minister in Italy, Craxi enacted measures that are unpopular with many unionists and that have all but undone union unity.[67] No longer, in Del Turco's words, "the party of the Italians," the union movement is now more than ever a partner in economic policy making. The record of the Craxi government suggests that union vulnerability now extends from the market into the political arena.

Figure 7-2 Relationship between 1983 DC Vote and 1980 CGIL Membership, by Region. Source: OECD, *OECD Economic Surveys, 1982–1983: Italy* (Paris, 1982), 17.

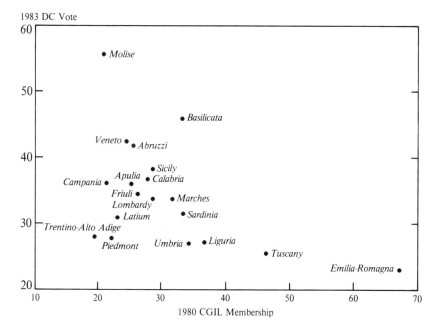

Notes

1   Quoted in T. Fazzolari and S. Gatti, "Ma ci rifaremo cosi: colloquio con Ottaviano Del Turco" (But we will recover this way: Conversation with Ottaviano Del Turco), *L'Espresso*, July 24, 1983, 125.

2   Histories of the Italian union movement include Joseph LaPalombara, *The Italian Labor Movement: Problems and Prospects* (Westport, Conn.: Greenwood Press, 1957); A. Pizzorno, "I sindacati nel sistema politico italiano: aspetti storici" (Unions in the Italian political system: Historical aspects), *Rivista trimestrale di didiritto pubblico* 21, no. 4 (1971): 1510–59; U. Romagnoli and T. Treu, *I sindacati in Italia: storia di una strategia (1945–1976)* (Unions in Italy: History of a strategy [1945–1976]) (Bologna: Il Mulino, 1977); M. Regini, "Labor Unions, Industrial Action, and Politics," *West European Politics* 2 (October 1979): 49–65; P. Lange, G. Ross, and M. Vannicelli, *Unions, Change, and Crisis: French and Italian Union Strategy and the Political Economy, 1945–1980* (London: George Allen and Unwin, 1982).

3   Although the internal commissions survived through the late 1960s, a series of interconfederal accords (in 1947, 1953, and 1966) progressively reduced the commissions' formal contractual responsibilities. Still, the internal commissions—officially neither union bodies nor bargaining agents—in practice performed many union functions and signed collective contracts during the 1950s and afterward. Cf. I. Regalia, "Rappresentanza operaia e sindacato: mutamento di un sistema di relazioni industriali" (Workers' representation and the union: Change of an industrial relations system), in A. Pizzorno et al., *Lotte operaie e sindacato: ilciclo 1968–1972 in Italia* (Bologna: Il Mulino, 1978); Romagnoli and Treu, *I sindacati in Italia*, esp. pp. 117–64.

4   Giuseppe Di Vittorio, a Communist, was the CGIL's secretary general. The Communist current won 57.8 percent of the votes at the CGIL's first congress in 1947, while the Socialist and Christian Democratic currents received, respectively, 22.6 percent and 13.4 percent of the votes. See Joseph LaPalombara, *The Italian Labor Movement*, 107.
     Several factors contributed to Communist predominance within the CGIL: "the prevalence of Marxist attitudes among the rank-and-file workers, the organizational capacity and prestige of the PCI in the Resistance, and the quality of Communist union leadership." D. Blackmer, "Continuity and Change in Postwar Italian Communism," in D. Blackmer and S. Tarrow, eds., *Communism in Italy and France* (Princeton, N.J.: Princeton University Press, 1975), 37.

5   Lange, Ross, and Vannicelli, *Unions, Change, and Crisis*, 103. The authors go on to observe that "until the breakdown of the Resistance coalition, in fact, there were almost no national strikes called by the CGIL despite the severe conditions faced by the workers and the growing social tensions due to the relative failure of government action to alleviate these conditions." (Ibid.)

6   The 1945 count, made before the entry of northern unions into the CGIL, is recorded in D. L. Horowitz, *The Italian Labor Movement* (Cambridge, Mass.: Harvard University Press, 1963), 196. The 1946 and 1947 figures appear in G. Galli and A. Prandi, *Patterns of Political Participation in Italy* (New Haven, Conn.: Yale University Press, 1970), 212. Membership data for the 1944–48 period are not as reliable as those for later years.

7   From 1950 to 1955, real wages in the industrial sector grew by only 6 percent, while profits in that sector increased by 86 percent. From 1948 to 1955, productivity per worker rose by 89 percent. See Lange, Ross, and Vannicelli, *Unions, Change, and Crisis*, 111–12, 193.

8   Sidney Tarrow has termed this a "coalition for patronage." See S. Tarrow, "Italy: Crisis, Crises, or Transition," *West European Politics*, (October 1979): 166–86; and S. Tarrow, "The Italian Party System between Crisis and Transition," *Journal of Political Science* (May

1977): 193–222. See also Guiseppe Di Palma, "Christian Democracy: The End of Hegemony?" in Howard R. Penniman, ed., *Italy at the Polls: The Parliamentary Elections of 1976* (Washington, D.C.: American Enterprise Institute, 1977), esp. 126–31; and M. Salvash, "The Italian Inflation," in L. N. Lindberg and C. S. Maier, eds., *The Politics of Inflation and Economic Stagnation* (Washington, D.C.: The Brookings Institution, 1985).

9   Lange, Ross, and Vannicelli, *Unions, Change, and Crisis*, 112.

10   Relatively few firms had *commissioni interne*. Farneti writes that in 1956 "one-third of the firms in Milan with more than 40 employees had shop committees [or *commissioni interne*]. Trade unions in general had little or no access to firms. The existence of the shop committee was no guarantee of the presence of the trade union within the firm." P. Farneti, "The Troubled Partnership: Trade Unions and Working-Class Parties in Italy, 1948–1978," *Government and Opposition* (Autumn 1978): 424.

11   At its 1956 congress, the CGIL reported that 674 members of *commissioni interne*, 1,128 activists, and thousands of workers had been discharged because of CGIL activity. Horowitz, *The Italian Labor Movement*, 291.

12   In 1954 the *Confindustria* signed an agreement with only the CISL and UIL to consolidate several wage elements. From May 1954 to May 1957, the CGIL signed less than half of the 749 shop-floor agreements concluded in Italy. Ibid., 240–43, 295.

13   These ideas, inspired by the American example, eventually overshadowed the "social Christian" values of the CISL. During the 1950s the UIL did not formulate its own union doctrine. It frequently followed the policies of the CISL. For a discussion of the distinction between "associational" unions (such as the CISL during the 1950s and much of the 1960s) and "classist" unions (such as the CGIL), see A. Pizzorno, "Fra azione di classe e sistem corporative: osservazioni comparate sulle rappresentanze del lavoro nei paesi capitalistici avanzati" (Between classist action and corporative systems: Comparative observations of workers' representation in advanced capitalist countries), in A. Accornero, ed., *Problemi del movimento sindacale in Italia 1943–1973*, vol. 11 of *Annali della Fondazione G. Feltrinelli, 1974–1975* (Milan: Feltrinelli, 1976).

14   The CISL leaders held 8.4 and 11.4 percent of the Christian Democratic seats in the Chamber of Deputies during the second (1953–58) and third (1958–63) legislatures, respectively. While the CGIL never formed factions in the Communist and Socialist parties, it had representatives in parliament. CGIL deputies constituted 15.9 percent of the PCI delegation and 5.9 percent of the PSI delegation during the first (1948–53) legislature; 16.1 percent of the PCI group and 10.7 percent of the PSI group during the second legislature; and 10.7 percent of both PCI and PSI groups in the third. Horowitz, *The Italian Labor Movement*, 241, 305; and F. Cazzola and O. Lanza, "La condizione sindacale in parlamento: il caso della CGIL" (The union condition in Parliament: The CGIL case), *Quaderni di rassegna sindacale* (November–December 1981): 119.

15   The percentage of CGIL votes at FIAT fell from 65.6 in 1953 to 36.8 in 1955, and to 21.2 in 1957. The percentage of CISL votes, meanwhile, went from 23.1 in 1953 to 40.6 in 1955, and to 50.2 in 1957. LaPalombara, *The Italian Labor Movement*, 117.

16   A union fits the Leninist image of a "transmission belt" for a party if "a) [it] needs and follows parties in order to mobilize its own base to reach certain ends (it may need the party structure, the ideology, the 'imprimatur,' etc.); b) leadership positions in the union are given through the parties, which in this sense work as a structure to legitimize the leaders; c) styles of leadership, strategies and appeals are systematically borrowed from political parties." Farneti, "The Troubled Partnership," 417.

17   See Romagnoli and Treu, *I sindacati in Italia*, 152–54; M. A. Golden, *Austerity and Its Opposition: Italian Working Class Politics in the 1970s* (Ph.D. dissertation, Cornell University, 1983), 68–93, 212–29; Lange, Ross, and Vannicelli, *Unions, Change, and Crisis*,

116–17, 238–45; P. Weitz, "The CGIL and the PCI: From Subordination to Independent Political Force," in Blackmer and Tarrow, eds., *Communism in Italy and France.*

18   Following the lead of the state employers, the *Confindustria* granted similar concessions in 1963. See W. Kendall, "Labor Relations," in S. Holland, ed., *The State as Entrepreneur* (White Plains, N.Y.: International Arts and Sciences Press, 1972); and G. Sasso, "Partecipazioni statali e politica del lavoro" (State-held firms and labor policy), in G. Cottino, ed., *Ricerca sulle partecipazioni statali*, vol. 1 (Torino: Einaudi, 1978).

19   Templeman notes the sharp annual increases in housing costs from 1960 to 1963, which prompted the imposition in 1963 of rent controls on postwar housing, and the 1963 "capital flight ($1.5 billion in recorded repatriation of exported Italian banknotes) triggered by political uncertainties in connection with the political 'opening to the Left.' . . . In addition, the introduction of dividend withholding at the source at the end of 1962 had an adverse effect on investor confidence." The overall balance of payments deficit amounted to $1.3 billion in 1963. D. C. Templeman, *The Italian Economy* (New York: Praeger, 1981), 6–7.

20   The Italians use the word *programmazione* (programming) to distinguish their planning process from the East European and Soviet direction of the economy.

21   Both the CGIL and the CISL rejected self-limitation of wage demands and expressed reluctance to participate in the planning process. The UIL rapidly accepted the plan. The CGIL judged that the plan dwelled too much on wage restraint and not enough on policy implementation. In 1967 those Communist and Socialist parliamentarians who belonged to the CGIL abstained from voting to enact the plan, while other PCI parliamentarians voted against the plan. (This was the first time that CGIL parliamentarians did not adhere to the party vote.)
      The CISL eventually agreed to the planning process. Still, the ideas of wage restraint stressed in the plan contradicted the elements of CISL strategy that had emerged in the mid-1950s. Furthermore, the government's failure to achieve many of the projected reforms reinforced those within the CISL who criticized the confederation's ties to and compromises with the DC. See Lange, Ross, and Vannicelli, *Unions, Change, and Crisis,* 120–23, 250–54; Weitz, "The CGIL and the PCI," 552–54; and P. A. Allum, *Italy: Republic Without Government?* (New York: Norton, 1973), 167–72.

22   The number of *commissioni interne* in the metalworking sector peaked at 1,023 in 1965. (Seven years later, there would be 4,291 factory councils in that sector.) Regalia, "Rappresentanza operaia e sindacato," 225.

23   A large literature treats the Hot Autumn. Two good analyses in English are: I. Regalia, M. Regini, and E. Reyneri, "Labor Conflicts and Industrial Relations in Italy"; and A. Pizzorno, "Political Exchange and Collective Identity," in C. Crouch and A. Pizzorno, eds., *The Resurgence of Class Conflict in Western Europe since 1968* (New York: Holmes and Meier, 1978). Salvati compares the limited consequences of industrial conflict in the early 1960s with the large consequences of industrial conflict at the end of the decade in M. Salvati, "Way 1968 and the Hot Autumn of 1969: The Responses of Two Ruling Classes," in S. D. Berger, ed., *Organizing Interests in Western Europe: Pluralism, Corporatism, and the Transformation of Politics* (Cambridge: Cambridge University Press, 1981).

24   The issue of spontaneity versus union sponsorship in the councils' emergence has often been debated. The most careful research argues against the spontaneity thesis: Even where workers appeared to elect delegates "spontaneously," they received aid from a union functionary. See the review of evidence in Regalia, "Rappresentanza operaia e sindacato," 179–84, 195–222; and I. Regalia, "Delegati e consigli di fabbrica nelle ricerche degli anni '70" (Delegates and factory councils in the research of the 1970s), *Annali della Fondazione Luigi Einaudi*, vol. 13, 1979 (Torino: Einaudi, 1980), esp. pp. 388–92.

25   The councils brought the members and local leaders of the three confederations into a single

shop-floor structure. The councils' electorates and the councils themselves include workers not enrolled in the union. Workers meet in departmental assemblies to nominate their colleagues as council delegates and vote immediately thereafter by show of hands. The councils generally lack institutionalized individual leadership. Many large councils elect collective leadership in the form of an executive committee (*esecutivo*) whose membership is rotated among all council delegates. This picture of "common practice" should not obscure wide variation across councils (especially in the South, in small firms, and outside of industry). Cf. P. Negro, "Le ricerche sui Consigli di fabbrica," *Quaderni di Rassegna Sindacale* 21, no. 104 (September–October 1983): 208–21; Regalia, "Delegati e consigli di fabbrica nelle ricerche degli anni '70," esp. pp. 397–400, 404–6; Regalia, "Le rappresentanze sindacali di base," in G. Baglioni, M. Camonico, and E. Santi, eds., *Relazioni sindacali* (Italia: Rapporto 1982–1983, Rome, Edizioni Sadoro, 1984).

26   The number of company contracts in industry rose from 1,124 in 1967 to 6,900 in 1971. L. Albanese, F. Liuzzi, and A. Perrella, *I consigli di fabbrica* (The factory councils) (Rome: Editori Riuniti, 1973), 22.

27   See the sources listed in table 7-1.

28   The *lotta per le riforme* (struggle for reforms) contained "echoes of the [CGIL's] *Piano del lavoro*, and, to a lesser degree, of the more reformist orientation of the CISL's statements on economic development in the 1950s." Three major differences distinguished the reform policy from past strategy: The three confederations acted as a united front to promote the reforms; the reforms did not replace or take precedence over contractual objectives; and the unions tried to use market power to enhance their ability to bargain directly with government. Lange, Ross, and Vannicelli, *Unions, Change, and Crisis*, 137. Cf. G. Giugni, "Stato sindacali, pansindacalismo, supplenza sindacale" (Union state, pansyndicalism, union substitution) (1970), reprinted in *Il sindacato tra contratto enforme* (Bari: De Donato, 1973); A. Accornero, "La Cultura conflittuale del Sindacato" (The conflictual culture of the union), *Giornale di diritto del lavoro e di relazioni industriali* 5, no. 6 (1983): 267; and A. Accornero, "Sindacato e rivoluzione sociale: il caso italiano degli anni '70" (Union and social revolution: The Italian case in the 1970s), *Laboratorio politico* 1, no. 4 (July–August 1981).

29   Total nominal hourly wages of blue-collar workers in industry rose by 23.4 percent from 1965 to 1969 and by 149.9 percent from 1969 to 1974. In 1960 the shares of GNP going to labor and capital were, respectively, 52.7 and 47.3 percent. In 1970 the shares were 59.2 and 40.8 percent, and in 1975, 68.9 and 31.1 percent. T. Treu, "Italy," in B. C. Roberts, ed., *Towards Industrial Democracy: Europe, Japan, and the United States* (Montclair, N.J.: Allenheld, Osmun, 1979), 86; ISCO (Istituto Nazionale per io Studio della Congiuntura), "Quadri della Contabilita Nazionale Italiana," Supplement to *Congiuntura italiana*, June 27, 1981, 23.

30   Profit rates in the Italian economy dropped from 27.8 percent in 1960 to 17.6 percent in 1970, and to 8.7 percent in 1975. Sylos Labini identifies the primary cause as the less-than-proportional transfer of cost variations (most important, wage increases) to prices. P. Sylos Labini, *Sindacati, inflazione e produttivita, 6a edizione* (Unions, inflation, and productivity) (Bari: Laterza, 1977), 163–64.

31   In 1973 inflation moved to 10.8 percent. For the next ten years it remained above 12 percent, usually in the 15 to 20 percent range. Organization for Economic Cooperation and Development (OECD), *OECD Economic Outlook, Historical Statistics 1960–1981* (Paris: 1983), 83.

32   The statute, buttressed by subsequent judicial interpretation, thus joined national contracts in circumscribing employers' decisions about the use of labor.

33   Following setbacks in the 1968 elections, the Socialists severed their alliance with the Social Democrats and became more insistent proponents of reform. The DC moved to the right in an effort to recoup its losses to the neo-Fascist Italian Social Movement (MSI) in the local

elections of 1970 and 1971; DC conservatives began to speak of excluding the PSI from government. See M. Salvati, "Muddling Through: Economics and Politics in Italy 1969–1979," *West European Politics* (October 1979): 34–36; and S. Hellman, "The Longest Campaign: Communist Party Strategy and the Elections of 1976," in Penniman, *Italy at the Polls, 1976*, 160–64.

34   Salvati, "Muddling Through," 36.

35   Wage indexation has existed in Italy since 1945. The 1975 agreement made it much more effective. From 1970 to 1974 the *scala mobile* represented, on average, about 25 percent of the nominal hourly wage increases in manufacturing; from 1975 to 1978 the *scala mobile* represented about 55 percent of such increases. Just as important, with equal increments for all workers the post-1975 *scala mobile* narrowed wage differentials. See Templeman, *The Italian Economy*, 22–27.

36   For example, sectoral contracts in the mid-1970s gave the unions access to information on firms' economic conditions and investment plans. Contracts at FIAT, Montedison, and other companies guaranteed investments in the South. See Lange, Ross, and Vannicelli, *Unions, Change, and Crisis*, 158–60.

37   Ibid., 144–61; Regini, "Labor Unions, Industrial Action, and Politics," 58–61.

38   Many referred to the unions' new proposals as the EUR Accords, after the conference center outside Rome where representatives of the three confederations met.

39   Some continuities with past strategy existed. With the EUR policy, the unions retained the reform goals formulated several years earlier and continued to narrow reform priorities. More fundamentally, however, "the union movement acknowledged that there might be an inverse relationship between their contractual demands and their reform policy." Lange, Ross, and Vannicelli, *Unions, Change, and Crisis*, 167.

40   In the EUR accords the unions accepted self-imposed wage restraint but not an absolute decline in working-class living standards; argued that the "egalitarian" compression of wage differentials could damage productivity and disaffect white-collar and skilled blue-collar workers; accepted in principle, but did not specify, modifications in the *scala mobile* mechanism; in a reversal of previous policy, stated that reducing the work week could not be counted on to expand employment; and declared that they would accept mobility of the work force if employers demonstrated the necessity of transfers and if employers allowed the unions to participate in decisions about mobility and industrial reconversion. Ibid., 165–80; Golden, *Austerity and Its Opposition*, esp. chapters 3 and 11; and K. Robert Nilsson, "The EUR Accords and the Historic Compromise: Italian Labor and Eurocommunism," *Polity* (Fall 1981): 29–50.

41   See Salvati, "Muddling Through"; Lange, Ross, and Vannicelli, *Unions, Change, and Crisis*, 142–52, 176–77; and Templeman, *The Italian Economy*, chapter 2.

42   P. Santi, "All'origine della crisi del sindacato" (The origin of the union's crisis), *Quaderni Piacentini*, no 4 (1982): 50–51; ISCO, "Contabilita Nazionale," 38–39; Lange, Ross, and Vannicelli, *Unions, Change, and Crisis*, 160, 164, 178.

43   For an analysis of the emergence of the "historic compromise" policy and subsequent PCI electoral victories, see Hellman, "The Longest Campaign." A succinct summary of the 1976–79 governmental arrangements is found in Douglas A. Wertman, "Appendix A: Government Formation in Italy," in Howard R. Penniman, ed., *Italy at the Polls, 1979: A Study of the Parliamentary Elections* (Washington, D.C.: American Enterprise Institute, 1981).

44   See Joseph LaPalombara, "Two Steps Forward, One Step Back: The PCI's Struggle for Legitimacy," in Penniman, ed., *Italy at the Polls, 1979*; and Lange, Ross, and Vannicelli, *Unions, Change, and Crisis*, 161–63.

45   See LaPalombara, "The PCI's Struggle for Legitimacy," esp. 114–15; Templeman, *The*

Italian Economy, 322–24; and Golden, *Austerity and Its Opposition*, esp. chapters 2, 3, and 11.

46 The findings about productivity and inflation were reported by the CGIL's research institute in its analysis of data from the Bank of Italy and the OECD. "I sindacati: in Italia cresce la produttivita" (The unions say productivity is growing in Italy), *Corriere della Sera*, June 7, 1983, 1.

47 See OECD, *OECD Economic Surveys, 1982–1983: Italy* (Paris, 1982). From 1976 to 1979, the *Cassa* paid about 200 million work-hours per year. In 1981 it paid 471 million hours, and in 1982, 620 million hours. F. Tonello, "Les syndicats italiens et le recul de la democratie ouvriere" (Italian unions and the ebbing of worker democracy), *Le Monde Diplomatique*, May 1983, 19. The Bank of Italy estimates that by the middle of 1983 the CIG accounted for the equivalent of 485,000 jobs in industry (or about 10 percent of dependent employment), as compared to 300,000 jobs in industry at the end of 1981. Reported in OECD, *OECD Economic Surveys 1983–1984: Italy* (Paris, OECD, 1984).

48 It was also a warning of disaffection among the unions' rank and file and of increasing division within the labor movement. We will discuss these trends in a moment.

49 See OECD, *Italy*, 17; M. Ricci, "Cassa integrazione, livelli record" (Record levels of state-subsidized layoffs), *La Repubblica*, October 18–19, 1981, 30; S. Tropea, "Un piano del sindacato per la crisi-Piemonte" (A union plan for Piedmont's crisis), *La Repubblica*, December 1, 1981, 32; G. Leonardi, "Cassa integrazione e licenziamenti affondano anche l'economia lombarda" (Dismissals and state-subsidized layoffs also sink the Lombard economy), *La Repubblica*, December 1, 1981, 32.

50 See "Cresce la produttivita."

51 See Lange, Ross, and Vannicelli, *Unions, Change, and Crisis*, 280–83; LaPalombara, "The PCI's Struggle for Legitimacy"; and Nilsson, "The EUR Accords." For an overview of the prelude to and the outcome of the 1979 elections, see S. Tarrow, "Three Years of Italian Democracy," and S. H. Barnes, "Elections and Italian Democracy," in Penniman, *Italy at the Polls, 1979*.

52 M. Regini, "Sindacati e governi in Italia: che cosa cambia negli anni ottanta?" (Unions and governments in Italy: What is changing in the 1980s?), *Problemi del socialismo* (May–December 1982): 269–72. Regini suggests that a desire to obtain concrete results for the increasingly disaffected union rank and file motivated the unions' periodic shifts from general to specific negotiations.

53 Partisan differences also existed within confederations, between Communists and Socialists in the CGIL, and between the majority of the CISL and the CISL's extreme left wing, tied to Proletarian Democracy (DP) and headed by Piergiorgio Tiboni of the Milanese metalworker federation.

54 The number of active (nonretired) workers belonging to the CGIL-CISL-UIL Federation decreased from 7,299,821 in 1980 to 6,877,106 in 1982. Romagnoli, "Sindacalizzione e rappresentanza," 213.

55 Quoted in Vittorio Sivo, "L'operaio diffida di noi e del governo" (The worker is diffident toward us and the government), *La Repubblica*, January 26, 1982, 30.

56 G. D'Adda, "Il costo del lavoro concordato dai sindacati discusso nelle fabbriche reparto per reparto" (The cost of labor document agreed on by the unions is discussed in the factories department by department), *Corriere della Sera*, November 2, 1982, 3. Union leaders also suggested but did not approve revisions of factory council procedures as a way of strengthening relations with the base. (Critics added that the modifications would serve as well to further reduce the factory councils' autonomy.) Many of the revisions concerned the mechanisms of election to the factory councils. UIL leaders advocated the use of nominating ballots and of secret voting. Leaders from both the UIL and the CISL suggested that elections be

restricted to union members or that factory councils be named by union leaders in each factory. Del Turco of the CGIL proposed larger electoral constituencies and the election of several delegates in each constituency in an effort to ensure representation of minorities. UIL and CISL leaders advised reduction of the size of assemblies (to 50 or 100 people) so that all present would have the chance to participate in discussion. The CISL spoke of reconstituting separate union sections at the factory level (which had existed in the 1950s and 1960s); this idea drew sharp criticism from the CGIL. Tonello, "Les syndicats italiens"; F. Bugno, "Sindacato grande malato" (Sick man union), *L'Espresso*, November 14, 1982, 267; Fazzolari and Gatti, "Ma ci rifaremo cosi."

57   Regini, "Sindacati e governi," 267, 271.

58   In June 1982 the *Confindustria* had announced that it would unilaterally abandon the *scala mobile* at the end of January 1983 unless a new and less inflationary agreement was reached. The day of the *Confindustria*'s announcement, workers in many parts of Italy staged spontaneous strikes; the day after, the unions declared a four-hour national strike. These protests formed part of a long (and losing) battle to enforce the principle that "la scala mobile non si tocca" (the escalator is untouchable).

59   The accord not only altered the *scala mobile* but also limited factory council autonomy and union control over working conditions and increased employers' flexibility in the use of labor. The main provisions of the accord may be summarized as follows. The unions agreed to changes in the computation of the escalator mechanism, designed to slow the rise in the index and to reduce total payments by 15 percent. The government promised a series of measures, including a modification of the income tax system that would reduce fiscal drag and redistribute the tax burden, new allowances for low-income families, assumption of some of the social security contributions previously paid by employers and workers, relaxation of the employers' obligation to recruit employees from public manpower agencies by qualification and number, and establishment of a maximum period for use of the CIG. The government also pledged to meet with unions to examine pension reform and to encourage the formation of an investment fund, which would be financed by a 0.5 percent deduction from wages. The unions accepted ceilings on wage settlements for 1983 through 1985, an eighteen-month ban on demands and strikes over working conditions at the plant level, more intense plan utilization, and greater flexibility of hours. Management agreed to a gradual reduction in the work week, from an average of thirty-nine hours in 1983 to thirty-eight hours in mid-1985. The text of the accord is published in *Corriere della Sera*, June 23, 1983, 2. Despite the government's role, the agreement is not an example of neocorporatist policy making because the negotiations stood as an exception to—not the rule of—patterns of policy making; the negotiations lacked the conditions associated with neocorporatism (most important, control of government by prolabor parties and highly centralized, unified interest organizations); and the negotiations by no means ended the controversy over the cost of labor. See Regini, "Sindacati e governi," 273–79; Santi, "All'origine della crisi," 58–62. For a definition of neocorporatism and an analysis of corporatist policy making in several countries, see G. Lehmbruch and P. C. Schmitter, eds., *Patterns of Corporatist Policy Making* (Beverly Hills: Sage, 1982).

60   In their contract platforms the unions put forward modest salary demands, emphasizing reductions in working hours as a way of limiting the loss of jobs due to technological innovations. This reversal of the EUR policy on working hours was championed, in particular, by the CISL.

61   Textiles, construction, and food processing were the other three industries without national contracts. The public-sector metalworking contract had been signed in April.

62   See the June 1983 issues of *Corriere della Sera*. The private-sector metalworking contract was signed on September 1, twenty months after its expiration date; it was preceded by 180

hours of strikes. In 1979, by contrast, the metalworking contract was signed after a six-month delay and 120 hours of strikes. "Le date di una vertenze passata attraverso tre crisi di governo" (The dates of the dispute which traversed three government crises), *L'Unità*, September 2, 1983, 2; "I rinnovi contrattuali: documentazione" (Contract renewals: Documentation), *Contrattazione* (March–April 1980): 97.

63   S. Revelli, "Lama: le vertenze hanno avuto un peso; Benvenuto: bocciato il rigore della DC" (Lama: The contract disputes carried weight; Benvenuto: The DC's rigor was rejected), *Corriere della Sera*, June 28, 1983, 1. As we will see in a moment, the defeat of attempts to revise the *scala mobile* has proven less than decisive.

64   I want to thank Eligio Biagioni of the National CGIL Organization Department for giving me access to unpublished 1971 CGIL membership data. The 1980 CGIL membership data are disaggregated by region rather than by province. (In 1978–79 the CGIL, CISL, and UIL began to replace the provincial unit of organization with a somewhat smaller unit, the *comprensorio* (district). Some *comprensori* contain portions of two provinces, so that provincial data cannot be derived from district data.) Regional membership data for the CISL have not been published. Because the correlation coefficients apply to different units of aggregation in table 7–5 and table 7–6, the trends in the coefficients rather than the levels of the coefficients should be compared.

65   See Giacomo Sani, "The Italian Electorate in the Mid-1970s: Beyond Tradition?" in Penniman, *Italy at the Polls, 1976*, esp. 114–22; Giacomo Sani, "Italian Voters, 1976–1979," in Penniman, *Italy at the Polls, 1979*, esp. 56–59; and A. Parisi and G. Pasquino, "Changes in Italian Electoral Behavior: The Relationships between Parties and Voters," *West European Politics* (October 1979): 6–30.

66   See Regini, "Labor Unions, Industrial Actions, and Politics," 60–64; Lange, Ross, and Vannicelli, *Unions, Change, and Crisis*, 178–89, 260–67.

67   The story of the *scala mobile* is instructive. In the fall of 1983 employers threatened that they would not pay the full amount of indexation increases and pressed for general renegotiation of the entire *scala mobile* system. In January 1984 the minister of labor, Gianni de Michelis, opened discussions with employers' associations and unions on the government's 1984 economic parties—which included a proposal for modifications of the escalator mechanism. Legislation on the *scala mobile* in February 1984 (supported by the CISL) earned the opposition of the CGIL and evoked protests from large factory councils against national union leaders. In June 1984 the government issued a decree that cut four points off the indexation scheme. The PCI headed a campaign for a referendum on the matter. The referendum, however, left the law intact.

8　The Mass Media in the Italian Elections of 1983

WILLIAM E. PORTER

On June 24, 1983, Giampaolo Pansa of *La Repubblica* wrote a ruminative piece about the electoral campaign. He finished by recounting some remarkable events of recent weeks; including the story of Armaduk, who had come out for the Socialists. Pansa considered him the most *sympatico* Socialist dog he had ever seen.

Armaduk was indeed a dog. He was part of a funny and yet sad fraud perpetrated by a previously unknown explorer named Fogar, who in early April set out from Resolute Bay in Canada, accompanied by his faithful husky, to make his way alone to the North Pole. The two of them were sponsored by *Corriere della Sera* and some advertisers, the most prominent of which manufactured a brand of dog food called Fido. Fogar used a small radio transmitter to communicate with a *Corriere* reporter in Resolute Bay, who wrote breathless dispatches for what is generally identified as Italy's greatest newspaper. Fogar and *Corriere* eventually announced that the pole had been achieved, but contrary evidence began to turn up immediately. In fact, Fogar and Armaduk had been flown most of the way there, had wandered around for a time without knowing where they were, and then had been picked up by the same airline. Fogar appeared on television a couple of times and then faded from public view.

Armaduk, however, became a Socialist and made appearances in the party's behalf. It was not the only remarkable event of what Italians repeatedly referred to as an electoral campaign *all 'Americana*:

- In Arpi, Cicero's homeland, the head of the ticket of the Italian Socialist Movement made speeches in Latin.
- In Trieste, a female independent Communist candidate removed her clothes and harangued citizens on the beach in the nude.
- In Verona, a candidate made speeches from a hot-air balloon.

–In Rome, the number-one candidate of the National Pensioners' party turned out to be thirty-one years old.[1]

Media attention and the attempts to capture it were more important than ever before. This campaign may have helped begin a major change in the way Italian politics work.

It was not that the mass media had become more prosperous, more conscientious, or more responsive to the needs of the Italian political system in the years between elections. In fact for professional journalism these were years of stagnating style, waning commitment, and economic panic. The reform movement that had invigorated journalism during the election of 1976 and, though much diminished, during the election of 1979 as well, had disappeared. The newspaper business collapsed in the mid-1970s, the old pattern of family ownership and quiet subvention giving way to the rise of media conglomerates that were obviously more interested in money than politics and depended completely on the prospect of substantial government assistance. A young entrepreneur named Angelo Rizzoli had built the largest media empire in Italy's history out of the debris.[2] Then it came apart.

Rizzoli's jewel was the *Corriere della Sera*, the Milan newspaper he had bought in 1974 along with the company's other properties—five weekly magazines, one biweekly, three monthlies, a quarterly, and the *Corriere*'s afternoon sibling, *Corriere d'Informazione*.

There had always been gossip and speculation about the sources of funds used to acquire these and numerous other properties. Rizzoli was generally identified with foreign financiers, particularly the German and Swiss (for Italians, anyone with a lot of money is probably Swiss—in spirit, at least). Whatever the sources, Angelo Rizzoli's company collapsed in the early 1980s, and its bankruptcy, particularly the collapse of *Corriere della Sera* enterprises, was a source of national worry as the election of 1983 loomed.

The collapse occurred partly because of the Propaganda 2 or P2 scandal. Propaganda 2 was a secret Masonic lodge. (Propaganda, a nonpejorative word in Italian, refers simply to the dissemination of an idea.) Freemasonry is not illegal in Italy, but lodges must register their memberships. The lodge was unregistered, but that in itself was not important; most Italians today are not that worried about anti-Catholicism. The publication of the lengthy list of members, however, revealed that many of the country's conservative movers and shakers were secret brothers of the organization, thereby suggesting a conspiracy to wrong everybody else. An American parallel is impossible, but perhaps the effect of the list's publication can be suggested by imagining the exposure of a previously unknown chapter of the Ku Klux Klan with the following membership: the officers of some of the country's major banks, the leaders of the Republican party, the Joint Chiefs of Staff, the governors of several states, and among other media personalities the owner and the editor of the *New York Times* or *Washington Post.*

Angelo Rizzoli, his chief financial operative Bruno Tassan Din, and the newspaper's editor Franco Di Bella were identified early on as members of P2. Then the dominoes began to fall. Di Bella resigned as editor. (No less a personage than the president of the republic, Sandro Pertini, chose the new editor.) Roberto Calvi, another member of P2 and president of the Banco Ambrosiano, ended his career with what was presumably his suicide under a bridge in London; his bank, as it developed, owned 40 percent of *Corriere* enterprises through foreclosing on the collateral and wanted its money back. In a climax to the melodrama, Angelo Rizzoli was arrested in February 1983 as were Tassan Din and Angelo's brother Alberto. All three were charged with bankruptcy fraud. There were $22 million unaccounted for in the Rizzoli books.

By the time of the electoral campaign of 1983, an agency representing the Banco Ambrosiano was attempting to sell *Corriere della Sera*, apart from the other properties, without success. The newspaper was still publishing, sustained in some fashion not entirely understood, but its future was decidedly at risk. It was, after 107 years, one more Italian institution that could no longer be counted on.

Newspapers

As the fall of the brief Fanfani government drew closer, political journalists of most newspapers seemed to have no appetite for their task. Few journalists viewed the new elections as an opportunity to cleanse and revitalize Italian politics. In the campaign of 1976 Fanfani had been savaged by the press.[3] Now the accounts of his final brief speech to the parliament, in response to the Socialists' formal notice of withdrawal from the government, were almost sentimental. *La Stampa* summarized the session in one of the traditional long subheads of Italian papers: "Fanfani careful not to make anyone unhappy — Eulogy by Craxi of the President of the Council [Fanfani] — One of the themes of the electoral campaign will be the reform of institutions."[4] The press reflected an awareness that the political system was not working and that it would be difficult to repair. Several themes dominated the reporting of the first days of this crisis:

- the question of the republic's governability
- the expectation that a new parliament would probably do nothing to solve the country's problems
- the boredom at the idea of an election and the expectation of much lower

participation than usual (by smaller parties and by voters who abstain or cast blank ballots)
– the claim that the Socialist-triggered government collapse had resulted mainly from Bettino Craxi's personal ambitions (spurred on by the successes of Mitterrand in France and Soares in Portugal) to become prime minister.

The themes of boredom and nonparticipation received the most attention in the press. *La Repubblica* speculated shortly before the government fell that some smaller parties would probably not participate at all, specifically the Republicans (PRI) and the leftist Party of Proletarian Unity (PDUP). (The Republicans not only participated but also sharply increased their still-modest number of seats; the PDUP participated by joint-listing with the Communists.)

At this early stage, furthermore, both the Christian Democratic party (DC) and the Italian Communist party (PCI) declared themselves opposed to the election. Marco Pannella announced that the Radicals (PR) would not participate (though his followers eventually forced him to recant). As far as the voters were concerned, the first wave of surveys indicated that as many as 16 percent would either refuse to vote or would cast a blank ballot—making abstainers, as somebody pointed out, the third largest party in the country.

There was almost unanimous agreement in the press that the timing of the election was poor. As late as June 18, eight days before the balloting, a survey by an established polling organization indicated that 62 percent of the electorate felt that the election was "inopportune," and only about 17 percent found it "opportune."[5]

The overwhelming attitude was "who needs it?" President Sandro Pertini therefore tried once more to avoid an election. He charged the president of the Senate, Tomasso Morlino, to survey party leaders again in an effort to build a compromise government. The Italian Socialist party (PSI), under Craxi's leadership, refused to participate, however, and insisted on the election. On May 4 the PCI, involved in consultations but sensing their futility, announced that it no longer opposed the idea and began delicate negotiations—that came to nothing—with the Socialists about a potential future government. On May 5 Morlino reported to Pertini that the mission was lost. The next day Morlino died of a heart attack; though apparently unrelated to his political activity, his death was a bizarre footnote. The campaign was on.

Newspapers had few pleasant things to say about the onset of another election season. Enthusiasm had waned considerably since the previous 1979 campaign.[6] By late April and early May the tone of the press approached hostility. An editorial in *Il Secolo XIX* on April 30 stated the difference between 1979 and the new campaign: "One was called to vote then because a political formula, that of national solidarity, was considered worn out. Today there is no new hypothesis to present to the electorate." A few days later Indro

Montanelli, who in 1979 had advised the reader to "hold your nose and vote DC," produced an editorial that made no recommendations at all but simply said wearily, in effect, "Here we go again." (Montanelli did eventually bring himself, at the close of the campaign, to recommend voting for any one party of the five-party coalition proposed by De Mita.)

On May 3 the respected political writer Alberto Ronchey bitterly attacked politicians, the parties, and parliament itself. Ronchey noted the rise in the number of independent candidates, those who identified themselves with a party on the issues but who neither participate in party functioning nor receive party support. He then pointed out the futility of such a role, even if the candidate wins:

> He counts for nothing in the mob of 952 members of the Italian parliament. . . . He does not find either understanding or a common language with those who for their whole lives have never known a genuine profession but have been only party functionaries, always in long committee meetings, long conferences, constantly trafficking in the corridors, and who often are political hacks more skilled in devising empty argument than interested in the substance of the question.
>
> All told, the aggressiveness required today to play a role in the politics of the capital is not for those who do not have the "pure chemical instinct for power and for their own interests." Acumen, the capacity for good judgment, or foresight are not enough without pathological stubbornness and calculated demagoguery.[7]

The first postdissolution statements by party leaders were slightly apologetic. Bettino Craxi, Socialist party secretary, was in an uncommon position. The media identified him as the person responsible for the election only because of his personal ambition to be prime minister. The PSI always has attracted intellectuals and reformers (more journalists probably identify with the PSI than any other party), and a faint aspect of the hustler about Craxi alienated some of them. Many of his early statements, rather than forecasting the benefits of a Socialist victory, either denied personal motives or justified the calling of an election for political gain. In the Socialist paper *Avanti!* on May 11 Craxi attacked the hypocrisy of his critics, pointing out that in Great Britain, the country known as the "father of parliamentary democracy," the upcoming election had been called on even shorter notice by a party already in power, simply for the purpose of extending its strength.

Giovanni Spadolini, after his Republican party decided to participate, was not as defensive as Craxi, but his first speeches and statements were hardly conventional political oratory. He spoke with obvious feeling about the dangers to Italian democracy of nonvoting and made a curious argument in behalf of his own party: vote Republican instead of submitting a blank ballot.

Eugenio Scalfari, perhaps the most respected editor in Italy, wrote an acid commentary during the first weeks of the campaign, under the heading, "The wretched country is almost in a coma; viva Roma! [i.e., the national political establishment]." He evaluated the rhetoric that was beginning to flow: "One after another, the "Fathers of the Country" are finally disclosing themselves. The parties are beginning to take out of the oven programs that are passably concrete; the leaders are indicating hoped-for alliances, or simply the possible alliances. After much shouting against abstention or the blank ballot, they have understood that these are the only ways to represent the citizens' interest in the electoral competition and to block the cresting of a wave of rejection."[8]

The day before, the political cartoonist Giorgio Forattini,[9] now working at La Stampa, published a front-page drawing of a volcano with frantic politicians—Craxi, De Mita, Spadolini, Berlinguer, and Longo—spewing head over heels from its top and with the caption "Anticipated Eruption."

The campaign proved to be, in effect, an extention of Scalfari's analysis. Reporting dropped its original tone of boredom to become workmanlike and dispassionate (for Italian journalism). Corriere accurately predicted the most common subject in a headline: "Polemics about future alliances at the center of the electoral confrontation."[10] The following weeks were filled with stories about conversations among Craxi, Ciriaco De Mita, Pietro Longo, and Enrico Berlinguer in almost every possible combination. La Repubblica again used the device, sometimes called a "battle page" in U.S. newspapers, of carrying material originated by the parties without comment and with evenhanded display. A standing page in Corriere della Sera headed "Elections '83" carried political news and background stories of essentially neutral character. Il Mesaggero, always devoted to elaborate coverage of party politics, had a daily page labeled "The Nation and the Elections" and, as the voting grew closer, another page in the same format headed "The Elections: The Leaders Speak."[11] Most of the country's dailies had some kind of special labeled space for political coverage.

Unlike the campaign of 1979, when the activities of the Red Brigades dominated the front pages,[12] no major ongoing story pushed politics into the background. The big stories in early May were such as Rome's winning the national football championship for the first time in forty-one years, with the photogenic Sandro Pertini in the thick of the celebration. There was continuing coverage of the attempt to dam and rechannel the lava that regularly flows down the sides of Mount Etna. The effort, which used strategically placed dynamite charges, was under the direction of a Swedish engineer called by the press, in an interesting combination of languages, "Mister Tritolo" (tritolo is the Italian word for TNT).

About a week before the balloting the Communists attempted, mainly through their newspaper *L'Unità*, to make an issue of supposed connections between the Red Brigades, the *camorra*, and the Christian Democrats. The *camorra*, originally a secret criminal organization based in Naples during the Bourbon period, has received much attention in the Italian press, particularly since the Red Brigades have faded away. There have been dramatic encounters between police and *camorristi*, most spectacularly the assassination of General della Chiesa, who had been dispatched to Sicily to subdue them. The *camorra* has flourished in the 1980s; the authorities reported shortly before the election of 1983 that *camorra* killings had been running at a rate of about one a day since the beginning of the year.[13]

If the word *terrorist* is taken primarily to refer to groups with political purposes, the *camorristi* are not terrorists but simply criminals. They have a lively career in what might be called functional politics: they are said to have been active in the 1983 election, but only in electing officials they could control. Since both the Red Brigades and the *camorra* are covert and murderous, and since both make great copy, an attempt to tie them together was not surprising. The PCI daily took this connection a step further during the last week of the campaign by adding the Christian Democrats to the mix.

Diro Cirillo, an *assessore* (member of a municipal council) in a suburb of Naples, was kidnapped by the Red Brigades. Negotiations eventually brought about his release. The critical questions were who did the negotiating and what kind of promises were made? When it broke the story, *L'Unità* contended that the Christian Democrats, working through jailed Neapolitan *camorra* boss Raffaele Cutolo, had obtained Cirillo's release by promising to release Cutolo and other jailed members of his clan and by paying the Red Brigades about $1 million in ransom (with Cutolo and the *camorra* as go-between). The deal for Cutolo's release was reported to have been sent out in a letter signed by a high-ranking Christian Democrat, usually identified as Piccoli, one-time secretary of the party. The Christian Democrats replied that Cirillo's release had come about solely through the efforts of his family, and the party knew nothing about it.

The *L'Unità* initiative was, in a way, more interesting than the disputed circumstances of the case. After a fruitless attempt to work out an arrangement with the Socialists for a postelection government, the PCI had decided to raise the thrust of its campaign to a moral plane. Some weeks earlier the Socialists had been shaken when Socialist officials in Piedmont and Liguria were arrested for fraud. This event may have perhaps contributed to the PCI decision. By mid-week before the balloting, the Communists were contending that the two other major parties were tainted and were lying about the Cirillo case.

Two major papers took the accusations in the Cirillo case seriously enough to report them. *La Repubblica* gave the *L'Unità* charges elaborate attention that, though detached by Italian standards, had a subdued tone of sympathy if not acceptance. Four days before the voting, *La Repubblica* said in its front-page *articolo di fondo*: "To put it directly, this is the way things stand: the voters have the right to know for whom they're voting. By this time they know the programs of the parties, their proposals more or less comprehensible or confused for future alliances, their inclinations to the right, to the left, and to the center; if they want to know something of the involvement of the exponents in imbroglios and crimes, they should also know about those. The elections are the sole moment in which the voter is sovereign, and it is to him that institutions must pay respect."[14]

Most Italian dailies decided not to pick up the issue of a DC-*camorra*-Red Brigades connection, a decision about which *L'Unità* complained bitterly before the voting. *Corriere della Sera*, after a cautious summary that emphasized the confusion surrounding the story, printed a letter from Piccoli denying *L'Unità* accusations. Almost all of the newspapers instead focused on the makeup of the postelection government, assuming some kind of coalition was inevitable. De Mita and the DC proposed a five-party grouping, Craxi and the PSI a three-party arrangement. It was the kind of issue that only a politician could find interesting—precisely the kind of thing about which the press had complained as the campaign began. Nevertheless, the press had decided that it was the biggest news at that point.

Several considerations obviously went into that decision. *L'Unità*'s reputation had been badly hurt about a year before by the exposure of fakery in a curiously similar story. At that time it had published a document supposedly proving that the Christian Democrats had passed about $2 million to the Red Brigades for ransom. The document, planted with a trusting female reporter by her lover, was exposed as a fraud. Considering the blatant timing of the 1983 charge, *L'Unità* obviously suffered from a credibility problem.

During the tense elections of 1976, politics completely dominated the news media. In 1979, thanks largely to the Red Brigades, terrorism dominated, but the newspapers also seemed to try deliberately to find other things to emphasize. Newspapers on election day gave great play to the pope's arrival in Poland for the first time.[15]

Interestingly, the pope was once again in Poland toward the end of the 1983 campaign. Although the coverage was good, it did not compare with the coverage the first time around. It is also interesting to note that by 1983 the Italian press seemed to have accepted the pope as much as any other pope. During the first years of his reign, the pope was invariably referred to as "Papa Woytyla," apparently to emphasize his non-Italian origins. By 1983, however, he was almost always called Giovanni Paolo II, even though it was a bit long for a headline.

Two elements in the coverage, present only in a small way in 1976 and

1979, were highly visible in the campaign news of 1983. First, polling became important. The Italian media abandoned the agreement that prohibited the publishing of election polls during the last week before balloting (unlike the French, who, as of this writing, retain such an agreement). The print media made extensive use of the country's new commercial pollsters. *Il Giornale* used the data of Directa. *La Repubblica* carried elaborate analyses from a service called Makno-Repubblica. The weekly newsmagazine *Panorama* used what is probably the best known of Italian pollsters, Demoskopea.

None of these polls proved to be very accurate. All overestimated the total vote for the Christian Democrats and underestimated that for the PCI. *La Repubblica* predicted that the minimum DC vote would be 36 percent and the maximum 37.6 percent. *Il Giornale* estimated that the DC would receive 38 percent and the PCI 30.8 percent. *La Repubblica* had the Socialist minimum at 12.3 percent and the maximum at 13.4 percent.

The DC actually took 32.9 percent of the vote for the Chamber of Deputies, and the Communists took 29.9 percent. The votes of both parties were reduced from their 1979 results, the DC vote by a resounding 5.6 percent, the Communist vote by just less than 1 percent.

The use of pollsters was not a particularly helpful exercise for Italy's newspapers. Although substantial overestimation of the DC vote probably had little effect on the voters, it must have had a large effect on politicians' thoughts about future governments. An indirect effect from the charges of a DC-*camorra*-Red Brigades link may be indicated by this chronology: *Il Giornale*'s poll was taken on June 20; *L'Unità*'s charges, and *La Repubblica*'s and *Corriere*'s reporting of them, came on June 24–25; voting was on June 26–27. There was a remarkably high number of undecideds in the election (most surveys showed more than 20 percent), and these simply escaped the survey net.

The second new element in election coverage was that television became a major source of newspaper political journalism. In 1979 references in the print media to politics on television had been devoted to comments on television's inadequacy. With both private television and government television (Radiotelevisione Italiana, or RAI) carrying heavy schedules of interviews and debates, however, there was in 1983 greater access to candidates than ever before—without the tedious mechanics of covering public meetings or of catching candidates on the fly. Since most Italian political journalism consists of the journalist's subjective ruminations on a statement or action that has caught his attention, television was an ideal source, and the press made the most of it. Constant usage led to curiosity about what was going on in the television business; additional stories reflected that. The candidates themselves talked a good deal about television, particularly those who, like Marco Pannella, felt that they had been treated badly.

Cesare Merzagore of *Corriere della Sera* wrote a retrospective piece on the campaign which, after an introductory paragraph, was direct: "I want first to underline, simply as a premise, the exceptionally broad role of television, with the new, very important contribution of the private networks that revived voters' interest in political matters, as did advertising with the contending parties in direct confrontation, which was more immediate and vigorous than that generally seen on the national [RAI] networks, devoted to journalists who usually try to be accommodating." [16]

Broadcasting

In 1983 television for the first time played a major role in Italy's national elections. In the 1976 campaign RAI had carefully allotted free time to spokesmen for the various parties. The presentations were generally characterized as dull at best and were reviewed in the print media in tones ranging from jocular to contemptuous. RAI had also provided at least a spark of confrontation through press conferences in which a party spokesman could be challenged by a journalist of a different political line. Apparently the 1976 format created conflicts for the *comitato di vigilanza*, a body made up of members of parliament that sets and monitors the rules for political campaigning on RAI. The format in 1979 still gave time to spokesmen for the parties and provided press conferences, but this time the parties were permitted to choose the questioners, which meant that there were no tough questions. The media, and presumably the public, reacted with derision.

Although the private television industry was by 1979 well developed, it gave almost no news coverage of the campaign. Some stations aired commercial spots, most of them poorly made, but others including the Rusconi five-station chain refused to accept any political advertising at all.[17] Private broadcasting, at that point grimly money-minded, played it safe, peddling mass consumer goods interlaced with old animated cartoons and long-dead U.S. network series. With the arrival of spring in 1983 campaign, however, private broadcasting took on not only new vitality but a whole new political role.

On May 11 the parliamentary watchdog commission announced the formula for each party's RAI network in the upcoming campaign. Between May 26 and June 26 each party would have two hours and fourteen minutes for campaigning. This total was divided into the following segments: a press conference of fifty minutes at 8:30 P.M. on Channel 1; a "flash" (the word used by the committee) of five minutes on Channel 1; two press conferences of fifteen minutes each at 1:30 P.M. on Channel 2; three ten-minute programs, one at 1:30 P.M. and two at 9:00 P.M., originated by the party, also on Channel 2; a final appeal of five minutes at 10:00 P.M. on Channel 1; and six minutes of discussion of the election results at 10:30 P.M. on Channel 2. Americans who think this kind of hairsplitting seems preposterous should remember that every country with a state-operated broadcast system and a government with contending parties goes through some variation of the same ritual niggling. The allotment of television time is no easy process.

Although RAI managed to keep the largest share of the audience—at least as indicated by its own figures—the most exciting campaign television in the judgment of both politicians and media professionals was that produced by private broadcasting. The new medium, which became legal when the Constitutional Court decided that the statutory government monopoly extended only to nationwide broadcasting, had changed greatly since the 1979 campaign. Almost completely unregulated by civil authority, private television had begun to operate according to the principles of the marketplace. Single owners had developed chains and acquired audiences. The number of stations was fewer than in the late 1970s when more than sixty stations were in the Milan area alone, but there still were enough stations to outnumber RAI's three channels several times.

In mid-May 1983, for example, the Milan newspaper *Il Giornale* printed the program schedules for the following stations, in addition to RAI's channels 1, 2, and 3: Channel 51, Telemontepenice, Antenna 3 Lombardia, Top 43, Videomilano, Elefante, Telereporter, TVC Globo, Telecity, T 59 Telenova, Telelombardia, and Channel 5 (TVM 65).

The programming on all of these was somewhat scruffy, to say the least. Most had no news broadcasts at all; some scheduled headlines twice a day. Even the channel with the promising name of Telereporter had on one particular day only thirty minutes of news at 9:30 A.M. and another ten minutes at 12:50 P.M. The rest of the channel's programming was filled with four movies —"To Each His Own Destiny," "Dead Sure," "Adam and Eve" (shown twice), and "The Dead Rose Last Night"—and a clutter of old U.S. network series, including episodes of "Hogan's Heroes," "Harry O," "Longstreet," and "The Jeffersons."

It was easy enough, however, to shuffle these kinds of programs around to make room for both political advertising and confrontation, and the private channels did so. The significance of one broadcast was set forth by a writer for *Corriere della Sera*:

> Almost a quarter of a century has passed since John Kennedy and Hubert Humphrey, in the middle of the West Virginia presidential primary, confronted each other on the television screen in what would later be described as the first television duel in the political history of the United States. It soon became a ritual across the Atlantic, and has had growing success in Europe. More than twenty-five million French watched

on May 10, 1974, the confrontation between Mitterrand and Giscard d'Estaing at the Theâtre Elysée.

The "face to face" between De Mita and Berlinguer that "Retequart-tro" [Network Four] will broadcast tomorrow evening at 10:30 has no precedent in Italy and represents one of the innovations of the electoral campaign for the vote on June 26, which is constantly more dominated by modern means of mass communication and by the concept of politics as show business. The broadcast, recorded Thursday, June 16, in a theater in Rome, above all serves as an opportunity for the two leaders of the major parties to put on the table their own proposals and political positions, without excess verbiage or bickering.[18]

At the beginning of the campaign there were calls for some kind of regulation, or at least a gentleman's agreement, to provide equal time for the parties on private television. Neither happened, but the major private outlets did proclaim their dedication to preserving a reasonable balance. Under this vague standard, private broadcasting carried far more campaigning than did RAI-TV's three channels. The three private chains chiefly involved—Canale 5, Italia 1, and Rete 4—carried a hundred hours of coverage, better than four times the amount RAI carried. All three chains offered free time to party leaders and to the parties themselves for programs of their own devising. Almost all the other private stations participated heavily as well. (The word *chains* is used since *network* may be misleading, even though Italians use both *network* and *rete*, their equivalent, under the court decree that authorizes private broadcasting.)

The leading Italian student of private television, political scientist Gianpiertro Mazzoleni of the University of Milan, has pointed out that the 1983 campaign provided two great opportunities for local television stations. First, the campaign legitimized local television as a means of political communication; second, it brought in badly needed revenue. Most local stations are marginally profitable at best. During the last two weeks of the campaign, Mazzoleni carried out a detailed survey of political broadcasting by private stations in the chief city of twenty-three municipalities. Almost 90 percent of these stations carried paid political advertising, mostly in the form of spots that were carried in great number: around 14,000 were broadcast in the final two-week period, according to Mazzoleni's survey group.[19]

All stations contributed free time as well, though on a modest scale, for confrontations such as the De Mita–Berlinguer broadcast, so-called press conferences, interviews with politicians, and, in a new development, call-in programs in which candidates took questions. All of these are very cheap to produce, of course, and were usually scheduled time slots that could not be sold anyway. The final figures on campaign coverage were impressive. Mazzoleni found, for example, that there were almost two hundred candidate interviews among the stations in the survey group. The three big national chains aside, private television stations provided more than eight hundred hours of paid and unpaid campaign programming.[20]

It would be tempting to invent a new rule regarding the symbiotic relation between the mass media and politicians: the more frequently politicians are seen on television, the more party identification erodes. There seem to be no data to that effect, as far as this writer knows, despite the many studies of declining party identification, but there is persuasive indirect evidence.

Television is a powerful transmitter of personality, for a mechanical reason. The small screen forces most camera work to be "tight," that is, concentrated on faces. The performer who is seen repeatedly can easily seem like an acquaintance, or more, to the viewer. The tons of gifts that pour into networks on the birth of a fictitious baby on a soap opera attest to this phenomenon; so does the attention other media give to the death of a television actor in a popular series, for example. This phenomenon is more complicated than was realized in the early days of television, when both political parties in the United States were frantically concerned about finding people who were telegenic. It is usually expressed, however, as a feeling of acquaintance and friendship.

Long before radio broadcasting, the first mass medium with the sense of real personal contact, many Americans liked to boast, "I vote for the man, not the party"—imperfect as their understanding of the candidate might be. The responsible voter in a parliamentary system would not likely say that; he or she votes *primarily* for the party, the organization that supplies the personnel to be voted for and the personnel to be vested with power if the party wins.

The kind of television represented by paid thirty-second and one-minute spots, however, emphasizes the individual campaigner, displaying his or her most attractive side. In 1983 spots on local stations emphasized candidates from a single constituency more than ever before, and the trend spilled over into newspapers. Many of these were independent candidates who had assumed a party label largely to identify their general orientation. Opposing this trend, Alberto Ronchey, himself an *independent laico* candidate in 1970, wrote the bitter column quoted earlier in this chapter; even so, independent candidacies were very visible this time. In view of television's tendency to shift voter commitment from party to candidate, a change in the way the Italian system works may be well under way.

The greater scattering of the vote shown in the 1983 results seems to support that idea. Both major parties lost votes, though the Communists lost fewer than the Christian Democrats. The Socialists, Republicans, Liberals, and Social Democrats all added to their strength. De Mita had been proposing a five-party coalition before the voting and picked up the cry again as soon as the results were known.

It is difficult to explain such a trend except as a vote for individual personalities. Ideological differences among three of those parties—Republicans, Liberals, and Social Democrats—are slight enough to confuse even students of Italian politics; voters were highly unlikely to shift from, say, the DC to one of them because of a difference in doctrine. Along these lines, we may note that the Radical party made few appearances on television; its leader, Marco Pannella, was at war with RAI about time allotments even before the party was committed to participate and had therefore invested little in private broadcasting. In 1983 the number of Radical seats dropped from eighteen to eleven.

An Italian acquaintance of this author's described the Socialist initiative by saying: "Craxi was everywhere. You'd turn him off on RAI and there he'd be on some private channel." The Socialist vote rose about 2 percent, but their seats in the Chamber rose from fifty-seven to seventy-three, and their energetic leader attained his ambition to be prime minister—albeit as much through DC losses as PSI gains.

Obviously television exposure is not the only reason for this redistribution of the vote over parties other than the big two. The remarkable rise in the Republican vote, which jumped from 3.1 to 5.1 percent while Republican seats in the Chamber more than doubled, undoubtedly had much to do with Giovanni Spadolini. The first non-DC prime minister since World War II, he has seemed to grow in public esteem ever since his prime ministership. Much of this growth, in turn, may be tied to his having become a major media figure—more a senior statesman than a politician.

Summing Up

In a television-saturated society, a category to which Italy now clearly belongs, the broadcast and the print media serve quite different functions. Television and radio have what might be called a first-person character: in speeches, commercials, and even news reporting, the candidates and party leaders present themselves directly to the voters. By contrast, even the most objective kind of print journalism, other than speech texts, is a second-person account and is therefore to some extent commentary. In the case of Italian print journalism, commentary and evaluation are constant major factors; political writers are practically drama critics.

The campaign of 1979 produced print journalism that seemed to reflect a striking new disaffection from party politics. Part of the reason was the running story of terrorism, which received a good deal more space in newspaper column inches than the campaign.[21] No such single theme dominated the 1983 election, though traces were visible in the anti-*camorra* campaign.

Newspaper coverage began by attacking the idea of new elections. When the Socialists proved unmovable, a kind of reluctant coverage began, most of it in the traditional pattern of a detailed, sometimes arcane, description and analysis of proposals for coalitions and of the shuffling within the parties as they worked out positions on their lists of candidates. Two new elements also appeared, however: coverage of the problem of voter abstentions and blank ballots and coverage of candidate activities on television. With the sharp decline in the number of outdoor mass meetings, journalists fell to covering television—the medium that had displaced the meetings.

Many thought the overall campaign coverage was, by Italian standards, oddly pedestrian, going-through-the-motions journalism. *L'Unità*'s attempts to connect the Christian Democrats with criminal and terrorist groups seemed not only strident but old-fashioned. Both newspaper and magazine columnists, including Ronchey, Scalfari, and the highly regarded Georgio Galli of *Panorama*, complained about a dull and listless campaign.[22] In *L'Espresso*'s June 19 issue, Nello Ajello commented glumly, "Not many events would justify, in describing this weary vigil on June 26, the use of a lively phrase such as 'electoral campaign.'"

Only the television professionals found the campaign coverage exciting, and they worked hard at making it exciting for the voters. Their efforts impressed politicians and journalists alike. Yet television professionals may overestimate the effects of their coverage. Most of the evidence is indirect, and measuring the effects of mass communication still remains one of the most difficult chores in social science.

A large quantity of campaign broadcasting may actually have little effect on public interest in elections. The percentage of eligible voters who cast ballots in this national election was the smallest since the end of World War II. In other words, the combined percentage of nonvoters—those who cast blank ballots and invalid votes or who abstained—was the highest in the modern era. It reached 18 percent, up three percentage points since 1979 and up almost eight points since the tense election of 1976.

A trend toward the depoliticization of Italian life and the mass media has been increasingly evident in recent years. It is difficult to say what have been the real effects of the sudden explosion of television, particularly private television, into the world of partisan politics. The vastly increased accessibility to the campaign may indeed have made the decline in voting much less than it otherwise would have been. One thing is certain, however: politics-saturated television was not enough to reverse a trend.

On the cover of its last issue before election day in 1976, the popular weekly newsmagazine *Panorama* carried a caricature of a maniacal-looking Amintore Fanfani in a Fascist uniform with death's-heads on the epaulets. On the cover of its last issue before election day in 1979, *Panorama* carried a photograph of Pope John Paul II superimposed on a shadowy feminine face. The caption referred to a youthful romance between the two; a small tag referred to the upcoming voting.

In 1983 six days before the voting, the cover of *Panorama* showed a young woman wearing a parachute and apparently nothing else; as she drifts down against a blue sky she is saying, "I seek adventure." Above the magazine's name is the line, "Survey: Is it better to live in small towns?"

Perhaps the young woman is seeking adventure in small towns. It is increasingly improbable that she is seeking it with the DC, the PCI, or even the Radicals.

Notes

1   *La Repubblica*, June 24, 1983.
2   For accounts of both the journalists' reform movement and the catastrophic economics of the publishing business, see William E. Porter, in Howard R. Penniman, ed., *Italy at the Polls: The Parliamentary Elections of 1976* (Washington, D.C.: American Enterprise Institute, 1977), ch. 8, and *Italy at the Polls, 1979: A Study of the Parliamentary Elections* (Washington, D.C.: American Enterprise Institute, 1981), ch. 10.
3   Penniman, *Italy at the Polls, 1976*, 283.
4   *La Stampa*, April 30, 1983.
5   *Il Giornale*, June 18, 1983.
6   Penniman, *Italy at the Polls, 1979*, 269ff.
7   *La Stampa*, May 3, 1983.
8   *La Repubblica*, May 15-16, 1983 (weekend edition). For an account of Scalfari and *La Repubblica*'s role in current Italian politics, see Penniman, *Italy at the Polls, 1979*, 264-65.
9   For a description of Forattini's work, see Penniman, *Italy at the Polls, 1979*, 270.
10 *Corriere della Sera*, May 9, 1983.
11 The English word *leader*, which appears in the original, has become standard in Italy for high-ranking political figures, perhaps because it is more precise than the ubiquitous *capo*, which means the head of anything.
12 Penniman, *Italy at the Polls, 1979*, 209ff.
13 *Panorama*, June 20, 1983, 60.
14 *La Repubblica*, June 22, 1983.
15 Penniman, *Italy at the Polls, 1979*, 272-73.
16 *Corriere della Sera*, June 24, 1983.
17 For details about broadcasting in those campaigns, see Penniman, *Italy at the Polls, 1976* and *Italy at the Polls, 1979*.
18 *Corriere della Sera*, June 18, 1983.
19 Admirers of the Italian language will be interested, and possibly saddened, to learn that though television terms were in the beginning either Italian or Italianized English—*canale, rete, cortometraggi* (commercials), or simply *pubblicità, televisione*—they have largely given way to U.S. usage, such as *spot, network*, and even *prime time*.
20 The author thanks Professor Mazzoleni for making available his data before publication in Italy. I have rounded the figures somewhat and, of course, have added my own interpretations.
21 Penniman, *Italy at the Polls, 1979*, ch. 10.
22 *Panorama*, June 20, 1983.

9 Italian Elections: The "Rashomon" Effect

JOSEPH LAPALOMBARA

————Do Italy's 1983 elections show something new that is not evanescent or trivial? Was the sharp loss suffered by the Christian Democratic party (DC) an earthquake, a tremor, or just a temporary tic? Is this event, however fascinating, also a "realigning election" that presages the lockstep decline of both the Christian Democratic and Communist (PCI) parties? Are the smaller, laical parties on a roll so to speak that promises to inflate their already disproportionate influence on the formation and breakup of governmental coalitions? Will close inspection of this particular election uncover long-term trends in Italian politics?

Answers to such questions, Giacomo Sani warns us in chapter 2, are elusive. They remain so even if we use conditional words, the subjunctive mood, or other qualifiers that lend an aura of science to the study of social phenomena. In truth, our answers are conditioned by our viewpoints on the question. In the case at hand, the Italian political process is so varied in texture and so rich in nuance that, at best, our many statements (like those in this volume) inevitably produce a "Rashomon" effect. Luigi Pirandello, that sardonic Sicilian, put this syndrome onstage long before Akira Kurosawa brought it to the screen.

Our dilemma is real. On the one hand, there exists no template of interpretation that everyone can use. On the other hand, we know that no matter how determinedly we struggle for greater objectivity, what we "see" will continue to reflect our individual needs, our wishes and beliefs, our ethical and moral codes, and, where politics is the issue, our ideologies.

A real dilemma by definition cannot be solved, and we must either ignore it or be impaled on one of its two horns. Some people who ignore (or deny) the dilemma will insist that the template is there in the form of some theoretical or conceptual scheme and methodological approach that will render social science value free and probabilistic. Karl Mannheim, for example, tried unsuccessfully to overcome the dilemma by force of rhetoric. Karl Marx tried rhetoric too, but he bolstered it with statistics gleaned from the British Museum. Marx made more converts, and more enduring mischief, but the dilemma survives intact. Max Weber, another German, opportunistically created the illusion of *Wirtfreiheit*, but he himself considered the enterprise essentially a fool's errand.

Some of the conceptual models and methodologies of the social sciences when applied to Italy produce puzzling and more often bizarre and even grotesque results. We may think of Thematic Apperception Tests administered to wily South Italian peasants; Need-Achievement experiments with Sicilian adolescents, who have been found wanting in comparison with their American counterparts; or Rokeach Dogmatism Scales, on which bemused Italians do not score very well either. In Giovanni Sartori's felicitous imagery, the conceptual schemes that underlie such research instruments do not travel very well.[1] If, as we may readily imagine, these methods have doubtful value at home, they quickly seem ludicrous abroad.

Another way of dealing with the dilemma is to accept it and make the best of it. The Rashomon effect, in other words, may not only be taken as a given but may also be welcomed. The implication is that all descriptions and interpretations are in some sense "true" and that each of the "truths," even and perhaps especially those that directly contradict each other, will somehow add to our understanding of that which we would explain.

Some analysts will object that, even in the case of such an eclectic approach, we must try to avoid the superficial and to probe for deeper structure and meaning. Perhaps. The real value in accepting the Rashomon effect as a given, however, lies in the Pirandellan insight that, depending on purpose, circumstances, or pure chance, all or perhaps none of what we describe and interpret will prove to be "real" or "true."

In this essay I discuss the 1983 elections and Italian politics, offering evidence of my own or evidence produced by other writers. This evidence, however, will not make interpretive statements more or less "valid." It will at best deepen, or better, multiply, reports made from different standpoints. One reviewer of an earlier volume in this series lamented the paucity in it of "systematic" analysis. I have hinted here at my reaction to such a criticism. I take such statements to mean that, whereas the authors may be satisfied with what is reported, the reviewer is not—another predictable outcome of the Rashomon effect.

Whether there is anything new and interesting about the 1983 electoral results, then, depends on the observer's particular focus (or emphasis) and on the observer's point of view. The 1983 outcome, for example, is certainly typical of most of the ten postwar national elections in the sense that neither its coalition formation nor its consequences in terms of legislative balance were in the least startling. A Rip Van Winkle who had voted in 1953 and awakened to find a Socialist prime minister in 1983 would certainly be surprised, but the overall array of political parties, and the distribution of votes among them (particularly among their left, center, and right-wing blocs), would not raise an eyebrow. If the early 1960s were the point of departure and basis for comparison, the same old center-left would surely seem to have been governing the country without interruption for more than two decades.

Unexpected Outcomes

Certain aspects of the 1983 results were somewhat startling because they were unanticipated. At the top of this list is the DC's sharp decline. To be sure, the Christian Democratic party had taken an even more remarkable nose dive in 1953, but it did so after the 1948 elections, in which the fear that the left might come to power artificially inflated the DC vote. This time the Christian Democrats were expected to hold their own and perhaps even to improve their electoral showing over that of 1979, whereas the Communists, their major opponents, were expected to continue in a decline that had been registered four years earlier.

Neither expectation was quite fulfilled. Furthermore, there were other surprises in the form of very modest Socialist gains and a truly remarkable performance on the part of the Republican party. We might add to our list of unexpected phenomena the performance of new smaller parties representing special regional or other interests, as noted by Leonardi in chapter 6 of this book.

With the exception of the Christian Democratic losses, the deviations from the past were not so sharp as to justify, in the mind of an outside observer, the degree of shock registered in Italy. The shock might be explained by the fact that everyone, including the academic experts on Italian voting behavior, has long since come to believe that Italy has remarkably few "floating voters," and that therefore very little shift of the electorate from one party to another can be expected. I will return to this issue below, when I address the question of whether 1983 represents a "realigning election" in the strict American sense of that term. A second explanation for the shock is that the electoral polls, which Porter rightly indicates played an unprecedented role in the 1983 electoral campaign, misled everyone as to how the ballots would be cast.[2] In particular the polls failed to register the DC's sharp decline, and this fact alone is worth some additional comment.

The Polls and Politics

The hopes of political parties and their leaders spring eternal, and those of Ciriaco De Mita, who heads the DC, are no exception. De Mita is an intelligent, seasoned, canny politician who reached the top by promising to be tough with the Communists, to force the Socialists to choose in advance between the DC and the PCI, and to "renew" and reform his own party, thereby giving it a second wind. De Mita, as Wertman notes in chapter 3, certainly gave the DC a more aggressive image. He also tried to free it from the tarnish of clientelism and the taint of scandal. An important part of his strategy was to beef up the party's organizational apparatus in the largest cities—places where, as this volume's authors show, the DC has been in steady and dangerous decline. De Mita also reached out to the industrialists and the middle class by shunning the DC's populism of old, attacking the welfare state and demanding more "rigor" in the economic management of the country.

As reported by the mass media, De Mita's approach appeared quite productive. He must surely have thought so; during a nationally televised debate with the PCI's Enrico Berlinguer, De Mita made the remarkable statement that there no longer existed in Italy any prejudice against the Communists' forming a government, if electoral results permitted them to do so, as an alternative to the DC. Indeed, shortly before election day De Mita is known to have confided to some of his collaborators that he would not be surprised to see 40 percent of the vote go to the DC.

On the evening of June 27 a long hiatus interrupted the transmission of electoral results by radio and television. Early returns showed the DC and the PCI very close to each other, then dead even, with the PCI later moving slightly ahead. Throughout the peninsula Italians wondered, in dread or in glee, whether the *sorpasso* (that is, PCI plurality) had occurred—which, by De Mita's own acknowledgment, would have given the Communists the right to form a government. As it turned out, the PCI came astonishingly close, inasmuch as the DC stood at 32.9 percent (down from 38.3 percent in 1979) and the PCI at 29.9 percent, only 0.5 percent off its 1979 showing.[3]

How could a leader of De Mita's acumen be so far from the mark? He is, after all, a hard-boiled *notabile* from Avellino who has had to claw his way to the top of his faction-ridden party. No one would accuse such a man of tendermindedness or wishful thinking. The answer is that, along with so many other people, he was victimized by the polls. There were so many polls, all of them showing that the DC would remain stable or would actually edge upward, that everyone was persuaded to believe them.

The pollsters of course have been wrong before, and like their brethren elsewhere, they are highly skilled at making egregious mistakes appear to be errors of just a few percentage points.[4] Thus, if the predicted DC vote were 38 percent and the actual vote only 33 percent, the pollsters would speak of a 5 percent error when in fact in magnitude the error would be more than 13 percent! Nevertheless, the suspicion is now far more prevalent than in the past that the polls err for political reasons as well as for technical reasons. Not only are Italians much more aware than in the past of the use of polling data by political parties seeking weapons in the electoral campaign; like Americans the Italians also express growing concern about mass media that conduct their own polls and thereby create the "news" that they then report and editorialize.[5]

To be sure, as many analysts have noted, Italy has always been the serious pollster's nightmare.[6] In addition to formidable sampling problems, the proportions of respondents who refuse to reveal their political-party preferences or their past or future voting choices remain unusually high. Projections of electoral outcomes based on polls in which more than one-fifth of the individuals sampled fall into the "don't know," "no answer," or "won't talk" categories are, to say the least, both very difficult to make and highly suspect once made.

In addition, we should not overlook the particular pleasure that Italians sometimes take in confounding the experts. False and misleading responses reflect not just perversity; in a culture dominated by the shadow of Benedetto Croce, methodologies of the social sciences that are readily accepted elsewhere have very tough sledding. Furthermore, Italians guard their private affairs from public scrutiny, and especially from official scrutiny, much more assiduously than many other peoples. Remarkable bookkeeping practices, ingenious tax-evasion schemes, solutions to marital problems that until recently excluded divorce, and even the Italian's so-called addiction to *la bella figura* all suggest that the observer's impression may not even remotely connect with reality. Indeed, why should the situation be otherwise when a pollster arrives to ask questions about a person's past, present, or future voting behavior—in a country where, for better or for worse, essentially every aspect of life is permeated with politics! From this perspective, it seems amazing that the polls' error margins are not greater.

The samples typically made in national surveys in Italy, moreover, are much too small to show the nuances in the fortunes of smaller parties that get 10 percent of the votes or less. Thus the Republican party was generally expected to benefit electorally from the quite successful prime ministership of Giovanni Spadolini. No one could or did foresee from polling data that Spadolini's coattail effect would carry the PRI to its largest percentage vote in postwar history and to almost double its representation in parliament.

The case of the Socialist party is much more complex.[7] First, Bettino Craxi and his closest associates were under considerable pressure to bring the PSI a net gain over its dismal performance of 1979. During the intervening four years, Craxi took firm hold of the party, routed the other factions (particularly the left), renamed his own faction "reformist," and garnered that faction a whopping 70 percent of the vote at the PSI's 1983 congress. The drumbeat of the Craxi campaign was meant to encourage additional voters to fall into line after hearing the promises of governability, more morality in government, the reform of political institutions, and greater decisiveness in policy making.

The mass media as well as the polls sensed that Craxi might, so to speak, be on a roll. His gambler's instinct, his sense of timing, his reputation for having *grinta* (guts), and even his negative charisma seemed to be working in the PSI's favor. The momentum was clearly slowed by public scandals involving local PSI organizations in cities such as Livorno and Turin. Such developments, coupled with Giovanni Spadolini's personal appeal in these cities as well as in Craxi's home town of Milan, clearly brought an untoward change in the PSI's electoral fortunes. Although the party gained a bit, its meager showing led *La Repubblica*'s Eugenio Scalfari to remark, "One does not hold the country breathless for four years in order then to bring in an additional 1 percent of the vote."[8]

Craxi's answer was that, although the PSI had been every other party's favorite target in the campaign, it had managed for the first time in two decades to register gains in a national election. He also considered it a major achievement that his party prevented Ciriaco De Mita from reestablishing Christian Democratic hegemony, recreating the old political center and thereby moving Italy in a right-wing direction.[9] Finally, Bettino Craxi became in August 1983 the first Socialist in Italian history to be named to the prime ministership. The pollsters and newspaper writers may not have accurately predicted the electoral results, but in the Craxi ascendancy they got what many had anticipated and now welcomed.

Were the Communists winners or losers? Again, as Fedele notes in chapter 4 of this book, the answer depends on your viewpoint, on your expectations, and indeed on how you count. The pollsters did not expect the PCI to hold steady at its 1979 level, and it did not. In fact, the PDUP, a tiny party earlier formed by a PCI breakaway group, rejoined the PCI and certainly contributed some votes. In 1979 the two parties running separately got 31.8 percent of the vote; running together in 1983 they reached 29.9 percent, which suggests a further PCI decline.

The PCI's leaders obviously regard the numbers differently. Most of their falloff from 1976 took place in 1979. Having been led by the polls, the newspapers, the experts, and many observers within the PCI itself to believe that the electoral hemorrhage would continue, the PCI leaders would understandably label a loss of 0.5 percent, if not an arithmetic gain, then certainly a symbolic victory.[10]

The pollsters and the mass media have a thirty-year unblemished record of inaccurate prognostications regarding the PCI's electoral performance. Possibly the reasons for such failures go somewhat beyond the acknowledged difficulties encountered in the conduct of surveys. A certain amount of wishful thinking, especially on the part of the PCI's most implacable opponents, must surely blur the picture. Similarly, the idea dies hard that the PCI, unlike other parties, attracts primarily "negative" or "protest" votes that are expected to evaporate, for example, once economic conditions and living standards have improved. Very good academic research during the last two decades has been able to dispel such assumptions only partially.[11]

Another reason for the inaccurate estimates is the assumption that what transpires *inside* the Communist party has a direct influence on its fortunes at the polls. Such an assumption is risky when applied to any political party anywhere in the world, in that it credits people on the street with much more interest in and knowledge about the internal affairs of political parties than they actually have. Communist parties, however, more readily lend themselves to this type of reasoning in part because they tend to represent limiting cases of introspection and autocriticism about the nature of the party, its historical mission, its relationship to the masses, and above all its internal affairs.[12]

In addition, the opponents of Western Communist parties, whether they are other parties, government officials, interests groups, or the mass media, are forever pursuing the minutest evidence that these Communist parties may be lacking in democratic credentials. The PCI's failure to deal internally with the nagging problem of "democratic centralism" may be costing the party elec- torally. Such an effect would necessarily register indirectly, that is, through the attitudes and behavior of party militants and cadres. Still, no evidence of any such cause-and-effect relationship in Italy has come to my attention.

Interpreting the Vote

Speculations such as those voiced above remind us that different aspects of elections both encourage and magnify the Rashomon effect. Not only do ob- servers choose a particular angle of vision, to focus, say, on the individual voters, the candidates, the political parties, or the overall electoral results; they choose as well the level of abstraction at which they will interpret their obser- vations. We might wish, for example, to discuss elections in terms of the in- formation they give us about the electoral or political party system, or about the broader governmental or political system, or indeed about broader general theories of democracy.[13]

Whatever the level of abstraction may be, much electoral commentary is based on presumed but alas only rarely available and reliable knowledge about the forces that motivate the *individual voters* to behave as they do. In the case at hand, for example, all manner of claims have been made to the effect that the DC was "punished" by the voters, that the PCI is still considered to be a menace to Italian democracy, or that some voters cast blank ballots because they are alienated from the Italian political system.[14] All such claims must rest in part on two underlying premises: first, that we have good data about the

cognitive structure, the rank-ordered values and preferences, and the evaluations and opinions of the individual voters, and second, that these particular
factors and not others determine whether voters go to the polls and what they
do once they are there.

For reasons that I have already indicated, Italy is not well furnished with
such information. Not only do the public-opinion surveys leave much to be
desired on this score; postwar Italian scholarship on elections, often very good
in its own right, is heavily skewed toward the ecological analysis of aggregate
data.[15] Even in the hands of the more gifted scholars, inferences from such
data about who voted for, or bolted from, which political party—and for what
reasons!—are a difficult and improbable undertaking. As a result, inferences
in this chapter should be understood as tentative and speculative and not as
implying such precise knowledge.

Life as Politics

Italy is easily misunderstood as a striking example of the imagined causal
relationship between the actions of parties and governments and the reactions
registered by the voters on election day. The country is saturated with politics,
not only because of reports in the mass media but also and more fundamentally because society itself is deeply politicized.[16] Little happens in Italy that is
free of ideological and political overtones. Jobs in the private and public sectors
both are awarded with political considerations in mind. State-owned broadcast
networks are paralyzed for months on end, and major banks remain headless
for a decade or more, because the political parties (including the opposition)
fail to find a formula for the distribution of such patronage. Tenured positions
in the universities are assigned only ostensibly on the basis of comparative
merit; politics is a critical consideration, and anyone can readily identify the
political complexion of most university faculties. Culture and the arts represent yet another arena in which the underlying struggle (but also the accommodation!) among left, center, and right-wing groups continues. If "crisis,"
applied to all aspects of society, is the most overused word in the Italian lexi-
con, it is also universally believed that the root cause of any crisis, real or
imagined, lies in politics. *Piove, governo ladro*! ("It's raining, thief of a government") is an old peasant adage that nicely captures the attitude toward life
itself.

The mass media play a major role, not only in saturating the country with
political information, but also in acting out the life-as-politics dimension of the
country. The straightforward news item, presented without political or ideological embellishment, is largely unknown. The political parties, in or out of
government, are notoriously involved and interfere with market processes that
pertain to the ownership of print and broadcast media. The recently sanc-

tioned and still controversial proliferation of private broadcast networks has brought into this sensitive area major industrial interests, all of them with clear political orientations and ties. The same underlying structure affects the country's leading "independent" newspapers.

In view of this life-as-politics dimension, we might imagine Italians to be not only well informed but also highly discriminating in their appraisals of candidates and political parties on election day. The fact that they are not, or in any case that the evidence for any such assertion is quite weak, demands further explanation.

Politics as Spectacle

For at least thirty years, social scientists of American, Italian, and other nationalities have given us mounds of evidence about Italians that include revelations such as the following:[17]

- By comparison with other Europeans, Italians are ill-informed about politics.
- Very high proportions of Italians express little or no confidence in their political leaders or, indeed, in the so-called *classe politica* as a whole.
- About nine in ten Italians say that they have very little esteem for, even revile, the country's political parties.
- By and large, Italians believe that the country's political institutions work badly—or worse.
- Very few of the country's political leaders are given high marks. Even those who escape with passing grades (President Sandro Pertini excepted) fail to attract the support of more than a fifth of the electorate.
- Measured by the benchmarks of "civic culture," "political participation," and "sense of political efficacy" associated with American and British citizens, Italians do very badly indeed.

These are only a few of the enduring characteristics of the Italian citizenry delineated by one survey after another. It is noteworthy that these characteristics persist despite the monumental changes that Italy has undergone in the past few decades.[18] These changes include: (1) marked improvement in the standard of living beginning in the late 1950s; (2) massive, unprecedented population movements from countryside to city, from South to North, and from Italy to various places abroad; (3) the replacement of a heavily agricultural economy with an advanced industrial one; (4) levels of educational achievement that have all but eradicated the once widespread illiteracy; (5) the secularization of society, with a consequent decline in religious practice and the importance of the organized church in politics and society; (6) a depoliticization of the trade unions, in the sense that they are no longer as tied to the political parties as they were in the past; and (7) a remarkable abatement of narrow, ideological partisanship that once made Italy appear, at least rhetorically, to have one of the world's most conflictful political systems.[19]

I could easily add to this list many changes that are clearly structural and therefore long-standing. We must ask instead why all of these changes, including the considerable attenuation of class warfare, find so little reflection in voting behavior and electoral outcomes. The answer, I believe, is to be found in an unusual separation of political events, particularly events that pertain to the actions of the parties, their leaders, and the government, and the choices the electorate makes on election day. Observers are fond of saying that, in Italy, elections change neither regimes nor governments. One frustrated journalist, in the wake of the 1983 results, lamented (wrongly!) that Italy is the only democracy in which people vote without the foggiest idea as to which *government*, as opposed to political party, each vote is intended to encourage or help prevent.[20]

Historians might well reply that Italians have had a century's experience with this state of affairs. The term *trasformismo* dates from the emergence of Italy as a nation-state. It means in part that, whatever may happen at the polls, the *classe politica* will make its own largely independent decisions regarding actual government and public policies. Political scientists might add that, above all, elections are about subtle changes in coalition formation in a system that has been rightly described as highly "syncretistic."[21]

As valid as such replies may be, we might add another that would appear very natural to a Pirandello or Kurosawa. I have in mind politics as spectacle, which provides another way of understanding the separation and indeed disjunction between what might otherwise be considered cause and effect. If politics is essentially spectacle, it is better to consider citizens (and occasional voters) not as participants but rather as participant-spectators. In this framework the relationship between formal political actors and the general citizenry (call them "state" and "civil society" if these terms are more pleasing) is highly esoteric.[22] A conceptual framework that seems nicely suited to, say, the United States, plainly will not work for Italy at all. Edward Banfield did not fully grasp this point and therefore concluded that certain aspects of Italians' behavior amounted to "amoral familism."

If we regard politics as spectacle, we need to suspend even our fondest assumptions about cause and effect and look for alternative explanations. We should not expect, for example, the way in which the political game is played to cause more than a few of the participant-spectators to change their political-party identities and loyalties. In such a framework, the very worst analytical model we might devise extrapolates from economics, treating elections as markets in which rational actors with their votes "buy" one party or another and one government or another. A better model is that which recognizes that Italians go to the polls to "witness," that is, to register their subcultural political identity.

The same surveys that produce, in aggregate terms, many of the negative opinions noted above also show that voters typically exempt their own parties or leaders from disapprobation or treat them markedly better. Furthermore, all of the survey research information must confront at least one further statistic about public opinion and one arresting question. The statistic is this: When asked which political system they would prefer, the same Italians who otherwise sound so disgusted with and alienated from their parties, leaders, and institutions say that they prefer their own system—overwhelmingly.[23] The arresting question is: How is it that so much disgust, lack of trust, and esteem fails to translate into a shift in the relative electoral support for competing parties?

A quick but all-too-easy answer to the question is that the disaffection is reflected in the growth of the so-called third largest party—arithmetically constructed by summing the number of voters who do not vote or who go to the polls to cast blank or invalid ballots. In 1983 this "party" reached more than 18 percent, which is certainly a postwar high point. Even if we were to take such an interpretation seriously, however, which is not my inclination, we had best proceed cautiously. First, 89 percent of the voters *did* go to the polls, a level of turnout that continues to distinguish Italy from virtually all other democracies and is, I believe, consistent with my argument so far. Where the nonvoters are concerned, the trend line (not a linear one!) has ranged from 7.8 percent in the emotion-ridden, "Christ-or-Communism" electoral confrontation of 1948 to 11 percent in the relatively placid, even boring contest of 1983. The last elections took place for the first time not in the spring but late in June; some of the vacationing spectators and potential voters must have preferred the beaches and mountains to the polling place. No democratic pathology is involved.

As for invalid and blank ballots, the percentages of voters who cast them were 2.2 and 0.6 in 1948, respectively, and 5.6 and 2.3 in 1983. Even if we place all of these voters in a rejection-of-the-system category, we would have to add that the trend lines are not really linear and that, even if they were, they would scarcely support the theory that the actions of parties, their leaders, and the government affect outcomes on election day. Even less would these figures support the idea that Italian democracy itself is somehow endangered by the nonvoting or the casting of blank or invalid ballots. The more fundamental point is that, despite certain shifts and trends in voting patterns, which I will discuss below, the overall behavior of the electorate and electoral outcomes of the last thirty-five years appear remarkably static.

Perhaps Italians not only conceptualize politics as just another form of *spettacolo*; but also in a strict sense actually appreciate—that is, *enjoy*—the spectacle. If so, the criticism of parties, leaders, and institutions, the inflated language of politics, the overinterpretation of problems as "crises," and the never-ending laments about how badly the system is working (but how nevertheless *si tira avanti*, that is, Italy somehow improvises, muddles through, or manages)—all of this may simply be an integral part of the larger drama, in which leaders, voters, and institutions are all a part of the same seamless fabric. We may think of the Elizabethan Globe Theater, its structure and, within it, the relationship between actors and groundlings.

We may be reminded, too, that things are not necessarily as they seem. The verbal responses to interviewers need to be seen and appraised in the Italian context—and not against some seemingly universal model of democracies' actual or proper operations. As for the often self-lacerating comments about politics in which Italians overindulge, apparent self-hate has masked a much more interesting underlying dynamic of fierce pride or narcissism at other times in history and in other places as well. I am convinced, for example, that Italians tend to overstate the parlousness of their condition, and especially their political condition, in part because, consciously or otherwise, they intend to demonstrate virtuoso qualities in overcoming adversity.

Political Subcultures

A separation between the actions of political leaders and the behavior of the voters does not in itself fully explain the remarkable postwar stability in the ten postwar national elections. We might interpret such results, for example, as reflecting unusually strong "party identity" in the Anglo-American sense of that concept. Scholars who express reservations about the use of this term in the European context are no doubt correct, I believe, especially in the case of Italy.[24] "Party ID," as it is called, is intimately associated with two-party systems and with relatively large numbers of "independents," or "floating," voters understood in the American sense as constituting a middle group who, for whatever reasons, are shopping around, electorally speaking. The rest of the electorate is said to display weak to strong "identification" with one or the other party and therefore to be more or less easily persuaded to change or shift its party vote.

It is certainly possible to regard Italians in roughly the same way, although we would have to abandon the idea that many of them are either "floating voters" or voters who make radical shifts in their voting behavior of the kind that occur in two-party systems such as that of the United States. In the cases of the Christian Democratic and Communist parties, for example, the evidence is ample that each has a very significant hard core of members and electoral supporters who would surely qualify as persons with exceedingly strong party ID. In fact, commentators often speak of the electorate as subdivided into two "churches," one Catholic, the other Marxist, with a third group usually defined as "laical." It goes without saying, given Italy's experience with organized Catholicism, with a Fascist dictatorship, and with Marxist movements of the Stalinist-Leninist variety, that many of those who support laical parties such as the Republicans or Liberals do so with equal ferocity.

The point about all such identifications, however, is that they are centered not just on a given political party but rather on a much broader political subculture, of which the political is an important manifestation but certainly not the only one. Ordinary political categories such as "left," "center," and "right" do not fully convey the meaning of political subcultural identity precisely because they tend to reflect a single dimension, such as ideology, or an even more unsatisfactory dimension, introduced by the analyst, that proves to be little more than nominal. What is then missed in the meaning of political subculture is precisely the last word, "subculture," which implies a somewhat distinctive system of values and indeed a somewhat distinctive way of life.

We have for many years known of the existence of such subcultures. We also imagined, however, that the transformations of Italian society earlier described, including the advent of modern systems of communication, would rapidly erode these socio-political-cultural enclaves. We learn instead that, with some regional exceptions (such as the "White," or Catholic, Northeast), these subcultures have remarkable staying power. We err in part by assuming that each subculture depends for its integrity and survival on limited communication across and among subcultures as well as on a very rich variety of organizations that encapsulate the individual in the work place, in his religious or recreational practices, and in his home, neighborhood, and village as well as in his political activities.[25]

A person's subcultural identity proves to be not just a way of life, although this aspect remains most important, but also a state of mind. To maintain such identity requires, for political purposes, less the reinforcing influence of many ancillary organizations than the daily reminders, in which Italy abounds, that politics pervades life. As a result, people not only have occasional opportunities, afforded by elections, to register their identity; they are also compelled to assess that identity as part of their daily routine. Italians who tell pollsters that they are uninterested in politics and/or do not discuss politics with friends may or may not be reporting accurately. These same persons probably do not escape from thinking about politics; nor is their claimed lack of interest in politics, if true, likely to undermine their political subcultural identity. For most persons, that identity probably persists through life, inviting us to wonder why any change at all has occurred in electoral behavior and outcomes.

Electoral Realignment?

How much change we claim to find depends on where we individually stand, on how we count, and on what we count. In terms of the party or coalition that winds up forming the government, there has been remarkably little change. To be sure, five of the six governments from 1981 through 1986 (two under Giovanni Spadolini, three under Bettino Craxi) were not headed by Christian Democrats. In view of its relative electoral strength, however, the DC remains the dominant, even if somewhat less hegemonic, element in national government. Except for a few essentially cosmetic changes, today's coalitions look arrestingly like those that held the seats of power in the 1950s. Whether by intention or otherwise, the voters appear addicted to coalition governments in which the spotlight shines on essentially the same old cast of characteristics.

Italian electoral outcomes appear quite static even when we compare any two consecutive national elections. The average net gains and losses registered by the competing parties prove to be among the lowest in any democracy. In 1983, for example, that particular indicator of change amounted to a scant 1.6 percent.

This last statistic is, of course, an average, or mean, that will often obscure quite dramatic changes in fortune experienced by individual political parties, as in the case of the sharp jump in the PCI vote in 1976 and the equally sharp drop in the DC vote in 1983. The statistic may also obscure longer-term trends and changes. In 1948, for example, the DC received 48.5 percent of the vote. By 1983 the proportion had dropped to 32.9 percent, representing a net loss of about one-third of its earlier electoral appeal. In 1953, on the other hand, the PCI received only 22.6 percent of the vote, but by 1976 the PCI had reached its postwar high point of 34.4 percent, only to decline to 29.9 percent eight years later. Numbers and averages sometimes suggest much more stability than is felt by some party leaders, who must often regard elections as a roller coaster.

We can treat electoral outcomes somewhat differently by asking, for example, how groups of political parties, loosely classified in blocs at the "left," "center," and "right" may have fared. The picture that emerges from this exercise shows two periods of stability separated by a fault line that emerged in 1976. From the late 1950s until 1972, the ratio between the center and left blocs was approximately 5:4. In 1976, and in the two elections that followed, the ratio changed to essentially 1:1, with each of the blocs garnering about 45 percent of the vote. Taking this perspective, therefore, we might wish to argue that there has occurred, gradually since the 1950s or sharply in 1976, a leftward drift in the preferences of the electorate.

Two caveats should be added to the last observation. First, the leftward shift is more apparent than real. That is, the Italian Socialist party, once clearly allied with and in some ways even more radical than the PCI, has under Bettino

Craxi's leadership moved considerably to the right. Second, while the electorate has indeed drifted leftward over the years, the drift of governmental
coalitions has been in the opposite direction. This paradox leads many observers to remark that in Italy elections change very little, except, perhaps, in
some nuances relating to coalitions.

There are yet additional ways in which to gauge electoral change. We
might, for example, count the number of competing political parties in national
elections and display the dispersion over time or the concentration of the vote
among these competitors. In 1983, as Leonardi shows, there emerged a number
of regionally or functionally based parties, and we might well speculate whether
an already large number of smaller parties will become even larger, with rather
obvious implications for Italy's nagging problem of "governability."[26] Even in
a nine-party context, which has been Italy's more or less steady state for
several decades, electoral outcomes provide unusual opportunities for testing
theories of coalition formation. Many of these measures, and more, are discussed in this book, and they have been used by other scholars as well. From
all of this empirical work, it is possible to draw a number of conclusions.

First, regarding those aspects of elections that can be objectively and
statistically measured, the ten postwar elections display *no clear trend.*[27] Looking backward, the two phenomena that approach linearity are the gradual rise
in the PCI proportion of the vote between 1948 and 1976 and the equally
gradual increase in the percentage of voters who cast blank or invalid ballots.
A more important point is this: Despite the statistic that shows Italy to be
remarkably stable in terms of the net gains and losses registered on average in
any two consecutive elections that we choose to compare, it is *not* possible to
show that, over time, subsequent elections are increasingly similar to previous
ones.

Second, the widely held view that, as earlier in West Germany, more and
more of the vote will concentrate in only two parties (the DC and the PCI) is
sustained by the evidence. Even here, it is not possible to detect either a trend
or a cycle. Concentration of the vote appears to occur only in those instances
where conditions of the country, and the electoral campaign itself, succeed in
persuading larger numbers of voters that it is necessary to cast ballots for or
against the two leading postwar political protagonists—the Christian Democrats and the Communists. It is therefore highly probable that, in 1983, Ciriaco
De Mita's public "legitimation" of the PCI helped to create an atmosphere that
"released" voters to cast ballots for other parties, including some newer ones.
We might add that the legitimation of the PCI has not yet reached a point
where, if that party were to appear once more at the threshold of governmental
power, another concentration of the vote in the PCI and DC columns would be
avoided.

Third, the hypothesis that the Italian electorate has become so homogeneous that we might expect the relative appeal of competing parties to be more or less similar throughout the country is highly problematic. This hypothesis won support in part because, in earlier years, the PCI was able to "nationalize" its electoral appeal—specifically by making notable gains in the South where it had been notoriously weak. In recent years, however, this tendency has clearly abated. Furthermore, the 1983 results demonstrate that support continues to be regionally diverse not only for the PCI but essentially for all of the competing parties.[28] An important reason for this pattern is the marked staying power of political subcultures that I discussed earlier. The basic point is worth repeating: The nationalization of systems of communication, the reduction of extremes in living standards, the universalization of social and recreational patterns, and even a certain homogenization in the prevailing system and hierarchy of values are not necessarily reflected at the polls on election day. Any theory that makes political variables dependent on these or other so-called underlying social or economic phenomena must sooner or later come to terms with this reality.

Fourth, where the opinions and, more important, the electoral behavior of individual voters are concerned, there has perhaps always been present in Italy much less stability, or stasis, than was commonly believed. We clearly lack information in this area. Further research may actually show us, for example, that there are more "floating voters" than we suspected and that larger-than-anticipated proportions of the electorate actually change their party vote from one election to another.[29] Even if such were the case, however, we would be forced by extant electoral results to agree with observers who argue that there can be considerable voter mobility without commensurate movement in the relative distribution of the vote among competing parties.[30]

Fifth, the major conclusion to draw from all of the above is this: No stretched-to-cover-Italy formulation of the concept "electoral realignment" (or "critical election") is yet demonstrable.[31] This observation is entirely consistent with the arguments of writers who claim that there are now more votes based on issues and fewer votes based on party identification as in the early postwar era. The notion of issue voting clearly implies that some voters are shopping around. Elections do not, however, constitute supermarkets where consumers are inclined to look for, to say nothing of "buying," the party that comes closest to matching their particular issue tastes. In Italy's world of commerce, supermarkets and department stores have been around for a long time. Nevertheless, even in the largest cities, consumers display a stubborn, and I believe admirable, preference for Ma-and-Pa establishments; the more affluent plainly prefer boutiques. The realm of politics is little different. The shopping around that does occur is restricted to one familiar political neighborhood, located within a broad subculture, that is within one of the left, center, or right-wing blocs that I described above. In Italy a "critical election," or electoral realignment, would require significant numbers of voters to cross these blocs, a quite radical decision and step that has thus far not occurred. An electoral system of proportional representation that both encourages and reinforces a proliferation of political parties will continue to make such an outcome highly unlikely.

Generational Change?

If electoral change of enduring importance is occurring at all, it is glacial and therefore not easily discerned, or explained, solely in terms of the results of several elections. Postwar electoral outcomes, as we have seen, do reveal some shifting, if not strictly speaking in a leftward direction, then certainly away from the Christian Democrats. This latter tendency can be more clearly seen because, unlike some of the parties that we would now include in the left grouping, the DC has been present in all ten of the postwar elections. It is nevertheless difficult to describe the changes as representing a left drift because not only the Socialist party but all of the others that were around in the 1950s have changed as well.[32]

However we may label this direction, the glacial drift, if indeed we are seeing one, is probably to be explained not by changes in the opinions and preferences or party choices of the voters but rather by changes in the composition of the electoral body itself. Giacomo Sani, in his sensitive treatment of aggregate ecological and survey research data, first alerted us to this possibility.[33] His argument takes actuarial statistics as its starting point. Such statistics remind us that by "the electorate" we mean an organic concept whose composition is steadily and forever in the process of changing. Many of the people who voted yesterday are no longer alive; many of those who may vote tomorrow are not yet old enough to qualify as members of the electorate.

The overall size of the electorate may thus vary, depending on the size of the population, on whether the population is, in demographic terms, "young," "old," and growing younger or aging, or whether changes are made in the minimum voting age. Beyond this organic dimension we find the effects on the electorate of turnovers at the upper and lower age extremes. In 1983, for example, the *youngest* Italian voter who could also have gone to the polls in 1948 would be fifty-six years old. A large number of the people who determined the earlier electoral outcome were no longer alive in 1983 or had perhaps left the country. Similarly, in each national election after that of 1948, three or more age cohorts voted for the first time, having reached the minimally required age in the interim between elections. This steady turnover and transformation of the electoral body makes the stability in the vote for competing parties, and in the vote for left, center, and right-wing groups of parties, that so many observers have noted seem even more remarkable.

Sani's contention that changes over time relate largely to the generational factor, rather than to other forces that I have discussed, suggests several concluding observations.[34] The decline of the DC, as well as the apparent leftward drift in the national vote, fundamentally reflects the preferences and electoral choices of the younger voters. These voters, for example, are largely responsible for the recent emergence and growth of the Radical party. Surely these voters will also determine whether an Italian version of the Green party will compete successfully in future elections. They are, in addition, more inclined toward issue voting, more impatient with vacuous political rhetoric, and more open, or less hostile or sectarian, about communication across ideological boundaries.

We should absolutely not conclude, however, that the younger voters are less partisan, really freer of subcultural identities, or less likely to make clear-cut and enduring political party choices. In the Italian setting of life as politics and politics as spectacle, we find that younger Italians are quite clear and even more fiercely clear about who they are and where they stand politically than are their counterparts in most other democracies. In this setting, it would be an even more serious mistake to apply to the voter any version of the so-called senescent theory, according to which, as the voter ages, he or she becomes more conservative in political opinions and choice of party. The burden of this essay supports the contrary hypothesis, namely, that the early life experiences of each age cohort subsequently lead to political-party choices that tend to persist throughout life.

The pattern may not be true everywhere and may not hold to the same degree that it does in Italy. In France, for example, there is very high electoral volatility; party fortunes vary sharply over time; and even the Communist party, once very powerful, risks going out of existence. The hypothesis seems to fit Italy very nicely, however, not only because of the subcultural phenomenon but also because, contrary to some claims, the Italian electorate has not been polarized. Most of the apparent polarization is not real—or if you like, it is more rhetorical than substantive.[35] In any event, so-called polarization has thus far served several useful functions, not least that of discouraging the emergence of a genuinely strong radical left or right. It has also been an integral part of the long-standing symbiotic relationship between the Christian Democrats and the Communists, serving their periodic need to array larger numbers of voters in their respective camps. In short, those enduring political identities, as well as relationships among parties, the conduct of electoral campaigns, and finally the casting of votes and the electoral outcome are integral parts of politics as spectacle.

We should therefore expect the overall results of elections to change slowly and only at the margins. The particular left, center and right configurations that we find at a given point in time will tend to dampen and attenuate the effects of even a radical deviation from such a configuration on the part of new and younger voters. If most political-party preferences remain relatively stable throughout life, the better part of a generation must pass before the effects of new preferences, and a new configuration, will be fully reflected at the polls. This line of reasoning is not inconsistent with the sharp jump in the PCI vote in 1976, the sharp dropoff in electoral support for the DC in 1983, or the DC's equally sharp upturn in the regional elections of 1985. The PCI surge resulted from the one-time-only effect of lowering the minimum voting age from twenty-one to eighteen years. In 1976 seven age cohorts voted for the first time, and these young voters caused a temporary ballooning of the PCI vote. The decline since that date probably represents nothing more than a return to more "normal" changes in the electoral body as well as some abandonment of the PCI by those who sat out the elections of 1983 or who cast blank or invalid ballots. It seems reasonably clear, in any case, that those lost Communist votes are not going to the Socialist party; they are certainly not crossing over into the center or right party groupings.

As for the DC losses, several possibilities come to mind, all of them consistent with Sani's well-argued premise that, in view of the electoral configuration of the 1950s, in which the DC was by far the strongest party, the DC has consequently suffered the most as the actuarial process continues to remove older persons from the electoral body. It may well be, for example, that those voters who died during the years 1979–83 were disproportionately those who had consistently supported the Christian Democrats. It is also possible, as some DC leaders themselves have claimed, that the jump in abstentions and in blank and invalid ballots hurt the DC more than might have been expected. The inference to draw from the first of these possibilities is that the DC decline will probably not continue to be precipitous but will begin to level off. The fact that the party, like the PCI, retains a very hard core of voters who have never voted for any other party will tend to have the same mitigating effect.

Even if the 1983 elections did not constitute an "earthquake," and were even less a critical, long-term realignment of the electorate, the DC under Ciriaco De Mita is running scared. Results of the 1984 elections to the European parliament brought the party some hope that its downward slide had perhaps leveled off. On the other hand, the same elections, for the first time in history and only by a hairline, awarded the PCI the *sorpasso*—a plurality of the total vote. It could not have been entirely comforting to the DC to know that the *sorpasso* was achieved not because of growth in PCI electoral appeal but rather because the DC itself was weaker by comparison.

The upshot of the 1983 and 1984 results is that the DC, with predictable help from its Communist partners in symbiosis, has turned to the older strategy of trying to "polarize" the electorate. Once again the party says the danger that the PCI will form a government is real; voters must not give themselves the luxury of shopping around, and each voter must make a fundamental choice between the PCI and the DC. This scenario has been onstage several times before. If it is to play again as in the past, two necessary conditions must prevail. Within the left bloc, the PCI must prevent, as it has thus far, the so-called Mitterrand effect, that is, a shift of voters from the PCI to the Socialist party. Within the center and center-right blocs, the DC will have to recapture voters who in recent years have sat out elections, have cast blank or invalid ballots, or have voted for smaller parties within these blocs. There remains, in any event, little prospect that short- or medium-term outcomes will differ markedly from the pattern that has prevailed in most of the postwar years.[36]

Notes

1 Giovanni Sartori, "Concept Misinformation in Comparative Politics," *American Political Science Review* 64 (December 1970): 1033-53.

2 See Porter, chapter 8, in this book.

3 Strictly speaking, because the PCI ran with the PDUP in 1983 and separately from it in 1979, its drop was greater. See table 5-1 on electoral results provided by Nilsson in this book.

4 Polling organizations have predicted, for example, that the PSI would get 18 percent of the vote in an election where it actually got only half as much. The problem is long-standing. See, for example, the preface in V. Capecchi et al., *Il comportamento politico in Italia* (Electoral behavior in Italy) (Bologna: Il Mulino, 1968). Cf. A. Spreafico, "Le provisioni elettorali" (Electoral forecasts), in Mattei Dogan and O. M. Petracca, eds., *Partiti politici e strutture sociali in Itali* (Political parties and social structure in Italy) (Milan: Comunita, 1968), 124-64.

5 In 1983 television networks, especially the private ones, were widely accused of introducing too much *personalismo*, that is, of concentrating on personalities as they do in American electoral campaigns. See the information on this aspect of the campaign provided by Porter, chapter 8, in this book.

6 For an interesting examination of the problem, see Samuel H. Barnes, "Secular Trends and Partisan Realignment," in R. J. Dalton and P. H. Beck, eds., *Electoral Change in Advanced Industrial Democracies: Realignment or Dealignment?* (Princeton, N.J.: Princeton University Press, 1985). Cf. Giacomo Sani, "Gli Studi sugli atteggiamenti politici di massa: Bilanci e prospettive" (Studies of mass political attitudes balance sheet and prospects), in A. Arculeo et al., *La scienza politica in Italia: Materiali per un bilancio* (Political science in Italy: Materials for an appraisal) (Milan: Franco Angeli, 1984), 333-50.

7 The interesting and troubled transformation of the PSI under Craxi's leadership calls for careful reading. Some basic references include: Gianfranco Pasquino, "The Italian Socialist Party: An Irreversible Decline?" in Howard R. Penniman, ed., *Italy at the Polls: The Parliamentary Elections of 1976* (Washington, D.C.: American Enterprise Institute, 1977), 183-227; G. Pasquino, "The Italian Socialist Party: Electoral Stagnation and Political Instability," in Howard R. Penniman, ed., *Italy at the Polls, 1979: A Study of the Parliamentary Elections* (Washington, D.C.: American Enterprise Institute, 1981), 141-71; G. Pasquino, "Modernity and Reform: The PSI between Political Entrepreneurs and Political Gamblers" (Paper delivered at the Annual Meeting of the American Political Science Asso-

ciation, Washington, D.C., August 30–September 2, 1984); Joseph LaPalombara, "Socialist Alternatives: The Italian Variant," *Foreign Affairs* 60 (Spring 1982): 924–42.

8   *La Repubblica*, June 29, 1983, 4.

9   See Craxi's comments as reported in *Corriere della Sera*, June 29, 1983, 2.

10   See table 5–1, which provides the vote distribution by party for the nine postwar elections.

11   Far from representing, in Hadley Cantril's infelicitous and inaccurate early postwar phrase, the "politics of protest," the vote for the PCI has always had a powerful positive component.

12   Internal debates within the PCI, as well as intellectuals' and political leaders' or journalists' comments on what transpires inside that party, do not really seem to concern the electorate. Similarly, few voters really care about Bettino Craxi's tight, monarchical control of the Socialists.

13   See Sani's remarks on this point in chapter 2 of this book. Because there are so many different vantage points and viewpoints, the results that the voters have wrought will always appear ambiguous.

14   A reading of the political party comment as well as the independent press comment in the first week or two following each election is quite illuminating on this point.

15   See the telling discussion by P. Corbetta and A. Parisi, "Struttura e tipologia delle elezioni in Italia: 1946–1983," (Structure and typology of elections in Italy, 1946–1983), in Arculeo et al., *La scienza politica*, 217–61. A number of my observations below are based in part on this excellent analysis. The different approaches that scholars have brought to the study of the Italian party system are described in S. Belligni, "Italia: Il puzzle del 'sistema partitico': Cosa dicono i politologi" (Italy: The puzzle of the 'party system': What the political scientists say), in ibid., 155–97.

16   It would be fatuous and tedious to provide documentation. A week's reading of the daily press, or random eavesdropping on conversations anywhere in the country, suffices to make the point.

17   The *Eurobarometer* surveys conducted for the European Economic Community place Italians in a category by themselves when it comes to expressing negative views about institutions or leaders. The same is true of the level of interest Italians express in politics. Cf. Sani, "Gli studi"; Samuel H. Barnes and Max Kasse, *Political Action* (London: Sage, 1979); Giacomo Sani, "The Political Culture of Italy: Continuity and Change," in Gabriel A. Almond and Sidney Verba, eds., *The Civic Culture Revisited* (Boston: Little, Brown, 1980); A. Marradi, "Rassegna dei sondaggi sui valori degli Italiani" (A review of surveys on the values of Italians), in Arculeo et al., *La scienza politica*, 291–332.

18   Some values of course do change, as does the composition of the groups that support each of the political parties. See Giacomo Sani, "The Evolution of the Italian Party System" (Paper delivered at the Annual Meeting of the American Political Science Association, Washington, D.C., August 30–September 2, 1984).

19   On the postwar relations of the trade unions with the political parties, and their effects on the political salience of the former, see Carol Mershon, chapter 7, in this book.

20   See the editorial by G. Piazzesi, *La Stampa*, June 29, 1983, 1. Obviously there are many democratic systems in which people vote without a clear sense as to which government will emerge if their vote winds up on the winning side.

21   Samuel H. Barnes not only underscores the disjunction between electoral outcomes and the formation of coalitions; he believes this to be the cause of incoherence and inefficiency in government. I would add that this unhappy result, if indeed it is one, seems to make little difference. See Barnes's *Representation in Italy: Institutional Tradition and Electoral Choice* (Chicago: University of Chicago Press, 1977). Cf. Giuseppe Di Palma, *Political Syncretism in Italy: Strategies and the Present Crisis* (Berkeley, Calif.: Institute for International Studies, 1978).

22 An alternative explanation is, alas, equally plausible, namely that in Italy there exists no "real" separation between political actors and the citizenry, between the "state" and "civil society."

23 See the survey reported by R. Chiaberge in *Sole-24-ore*, June 15, 1983, 3. He suggests that Italians prefer their own system, despite all the negative views they express about it, because they fear the alternative—a leap in the dark.

24 See I. Budge and D. Fairlie, *Voting and Party Competition* (London: Wiley, 1977).

25 The documentation on the point I am stressing here is vast. Recent changes are brought into better focus by: A. Mastropaolo, *Partiti e famiglie politiche nell'Italia repubblicana* (Parties and political families in Republican Italy) (Torino: n.p., 1983); R. Mannheimer, "Gli studi sul comportamento elettorale in Italia" (Studies on electoral behavior in Italy) in Arculeo et al., *La scienza politica*, 263–89; Giacomo Sani, "The Italian Electorate in the Mid 1970's: Beyond Tradition," in Penniman, *Italy at the Polls, 1976*, 81–122.

26 See Leonardi, chapter 6, in this book.

27 The powerful evidence for this conclusion is provided by Corbetta and Parisi, "Struttura e tipologia."

28 The question of whether, or to what extent, and with what consequences the electorate is becoming more "homogenized" is still an open one. See, for example, G. Brusa, *Geografia elettorale nell'Italia del dopoguerra* (Electoral geography in postwar Italy) (Milan: Unicopli, 1983).

29 It remains difficult to determine the stability of the electorate because of the paucity of survey data (good, bad, or indifferent) from the 1950s and 1960s. Until the late 1970s the idea of a "frozen" electorate was accepted as a given. For the contrary view, see P. Corbetta and H. M. A. Shadee, *Comportamento elettorale: Citta e territorio* (Electoral behavior: City and area) (Bologna: Clueb, 1981); A. Parisi and G. Pasquino, *Continuità e mutamento elettorale in Italia* (Electoral continuity and change in Italy) (Bologna: Il Mulino, 1977). Cf. R. Mannheimer's useful review of this issue in "Gli studi."

30 This important and much overlooked aspect is elaborated by A. Parisi, ed., *Mobilita senza movimento* (Mobility without movement) (Bologna: Il Mulino, 1980). See in particular Parisi's essay, pp. 11–40.

31 This is the conclusion of Corbetta and Parisi, "Struttura e tipologia," and of Barnes, "Secular Trends."

32 Some of the problems involved in the use of the left, center, and right as categories are discussed by A. Martinotti, "Le tendenze dell'elettorato italiano" (Tendencies of the Italian electorate), in A. Martinelli and G. Pasquino, eds., *La politica in Italia che cambia* (Politics in a changing Italy) (Milan: Feltrinelli, 1978), 37–65.

33 See the articles by Sani cited above and in Mannheimer, "Gli studi," 288.

34 An interesting collection of essays on generational changes that affect politics is found in R. G. Niemi et al., *The Politics of Future Citizens* (San Francisco: Jossey-Bass, 1974).

35 Paolo Farneti seems to have understood better than anyone else how a highly charged language of politics can exist side by side with—and can indeed be an integral part of—a process and structure that is highly centripetal. See, for example, his "Partito, stato e mercato: Appunti per un'analisi" (Party, state, and market: Notes for an analysis), in L. Graziano and Sidney Tarrow, eds., *La crisi italiana* (The Italian crisis) (Turin: Einaudi, 1979), 113–75; *Il sistema dei partiti in Italia: 1946–1979* (The party system in Italy, 1946–1979) (Bologna: Il Mulino, 1983).

36 The scenario did indeed play well in the regional elections of 1985. The DC comeback was based on the polarization of the electorate, which brought nine of ten voters to the polls. The results returned the relationship between DC and PCI to its more "normal" postwar pattern.

Appendixes

Appendix A
Government Formation in Italy

DOUGLAS A. WERTMAN

The Process of Forming a Government

It is necessary to form a new government after a parliamentary election or, between elections, when the incumbent government loses a vote of confidence or resigns. The president of the republic consults with the leaders of the political parties as well as with ex-presidents and the presiding officers of both the Chamber of Deputies and the Senate. During these consultations the president gets an indication of the possible parliamentary majority and of the candidates for the prime ministership preferred by the leading party (the Christian Democrats so far) as well as some of the other parties. After these consultations, the president names a prime minister–designate.

This prime minister–designate then begins his own round (or two) of consultations with the leaders of many of the other political parties. His consultations as well as the negotiations among the parties ultimately result either in a government or in the prime minister–designate's going back to the president to report failure. If the consultations succeed, the parties of the new government (or the new majority) reach an agreement on the government program as well as on the distribution of cabinet positions among them. Of course, if there is a one-party government or if the program is not coordinated among the majority and any abstaining parties, there may be a much looser agreement on the program and/or on personnel.

If the prime minister–designate's consultations fail, either the president will tell him to try again or, as happens more often, the president will consult again with party leaders and name a new prime minister–designate. If a new candidate is named, the process of forming a government begins again. The president, of course, also has the option of dissolving the parliament and calling new elections.

The prime minister–designate has succeeded when he (1) has reached solid agreement with enough parties to ensure his government a majority in parliament or (2) at least expects that his government will get enough support in parliament to win a vote of confidence. He then reports this to the president, takes office, and asks for a vote of confidence in each chamber of the parliament. To remain in office the government must obtain at least a majority of those voting in each house separately. A failure on the vote of confidence in either chamber means resignation.

Some Important Terms

Being *in the government* means voting for the government on the vote of confidence as well as having ministers in the cabinet. Being *in the majority* means voting for the government on the vote of confidence to help it exist but having no ministers in the cabinet. The government program might or might not be coordinated among the parties in the majority. A party in the majority, particularly in an uncoordinated majority, may on occasion vote against specific legislative proposals of the government. Thus, a government with a *formal* or *numerical majority* (a majority of the votes cast in the vote of confidence) might or might not have a *working parliamentary majority* (enough support on individual measures to get them through parliament).

Abstaining on the vote of confidence means giving the government indirect support by reducing the majority the government needs on a vote of confidence. This practice reached its extreme with the government of *non-no confidence* formed shortly after the 1976 election (only the Christian Democrats and SVP supported the government on the vote of confidence, while the Communists, Socialists, Social Democrats, Republicans, and Liberals abstained). Abstentions might or might not be coordinated among the parties involved, and abstaining parties might or might not have a say in negotiating the program. A party abstaining on the vote of confidence may on occasion (particularly when its abstention has not been directly agreed on among the parties involved) vote against specific legislative proposals of the government.

Being *in the opposition* simply means voting against the government on the vote of confidence. There is no constitutional "loyal opposition" like that of the largest opposition party in the United Kingdom.

A *monocolore* government is one in which all the members of the cabinet come from only one party. The governments formed in 1976 and 1978 were both *monocolore* DC governments.

The *constitutional arc* refers to the political groupings that participated in the Resistance movement during World War II and helped bring about the restoration of a democratic political system in Italy. It includes six parties today: the Communists (PCI), the Socialists (PSI), the Social Democrats (PSDI), the Christian Democrats (DC), the Republicans (PRI), and the Liberals (PLI).

An *exploratory mandate*, like that given to the Senate president, Tommaso Morlino, during the government crisis in early May 1983 prior to the elections, is a means that has been used by the president of the republic beyond his own consultations in particularly difficult government crises to see if a possible majority for a new government exists. It has been done seven times in postwar Italy—first in 1959 and most recently in 1986. Such an exploratory mandate has always been given to the presiding officer of the Senate or the Chamber of Deputies. Because such a mandate implies an impartial search for a majority, the person given it is excluded in practice from becoming prime minister during the government crisis.

Italian Governments, 1979–1983

Governmental negotiations	Government	Composition of majority	Composition of government
June–August 1979, attempts to form government by Giulio Andreotti Bettino Craxi Filippo Maria Pandolfi Francesco Cossiga	First Cossiga government	DC, PSDI, PLI, SVP, Trieste List (PSI and PRI abstain)	DC, PSDI, PLI, and 2 "technicians" (from PSI area)
March–April 1980	Second Cossiga government	DC, PSI, PRI, SVP, UV, Trieste List	DC, PSI,[a] PRI
September–October 1980	First Forlani government	DC, PSI, PSDI, PRI, SVP, UV, Trieste List (PLI abstains)	DC, PSI, PSDI, PRI[b]
May–June 1981, attempts to form government by Arnaldo Forlani Giovanni Spadolini	First Spadolini government	flff, PSI, PSDI, PRI, PLI, SVP, UV, Trieste List	DC, PSI, PSDI, PRI, PLI[c]
August 1982	Second Spadolini government	DC, PSI, PSDI, PRI, PLI, SVP, UV, Trieste List	DC, PSI, PSDI, PRI, PLI[d]
November–December 1982	Fifth Fanfani government	DC, PSI, PSDI, PLI, SVP, UV, (PRI abstains)	DC, PSI, PSDI, PLI
Fanfani government resigns April 29, 1979; "Exploratory Mandate" to Senate President Tommaso Morlino shows no resolution likely; May 4, 1983, President Pertini dissolves Parliament; June 26–27, 1983, parliamentary elections				
July–August 1983	First Craxi government	DC, PSI, PRI, PSDI, PLI, UV (SVP abstains)	DC, PSI, PRI, PSDI, PLI[e]

a. The PSI returned to the government after four years.
b. Government of "equal dignity" in which the three lay parties together for the first time had the same number of cabinet officers as the DC even though the DC had more than twice as many seats in Parliament as the other three government parties combined.
c. Spadolini was the first non-DC prime minister in thirty-five years.
d. For the first time ever, the previous cabinet members were all reappointed to the same positions (the so-called photocopy government).
e. Craxi was the first Socialist prime minister in Italian history.

Appendix B
Italian Ballots, 1983

Reproduced here are Chamber of Deputies and Senate ballots used in the Italian elections of June 26, 1983. The Chamber ballot shows only party symbols. The voter draws an X across the symbol of the party he has chosen. Then, if he wishes to cast preference votes, he writes the names of the candidates he supports, or their numbers, on the party list, in the spaces provided. (Voters may cast three or four preference votes depending on the size of the district.) The number of ballots cast for the party determines the number of seats it wins, while the preference votes determine which candidates will occupy the seats. The Senate ballot shows the name of each party's leader as well as its symbol. The voter folds both ballots before dropping them into the ballot box.

Figure B.1   Outside View of Senate Ballot before Folding

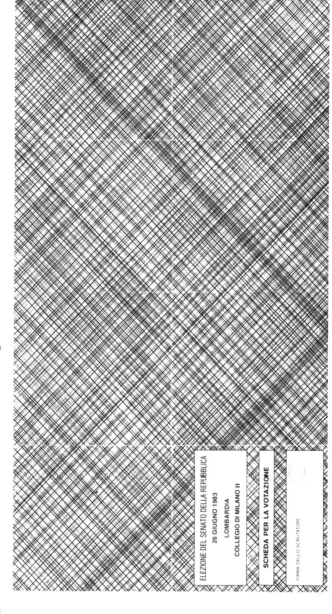

ELEZIONE DEL SENATO DELLA REPUBBLICA

26 GIUGNO 1983

LOMBARDIA

COLLEGIO DI MILANO II

SCHEDA PER LA VOTAZIONE

FIRMA DELLO SCRUTATORE

Figure B.2   Senate Ballot, Unfolded (actual width 15¼ inches)

Figure B.3   Outside View of Chamber of Deputies Ballot before Folding

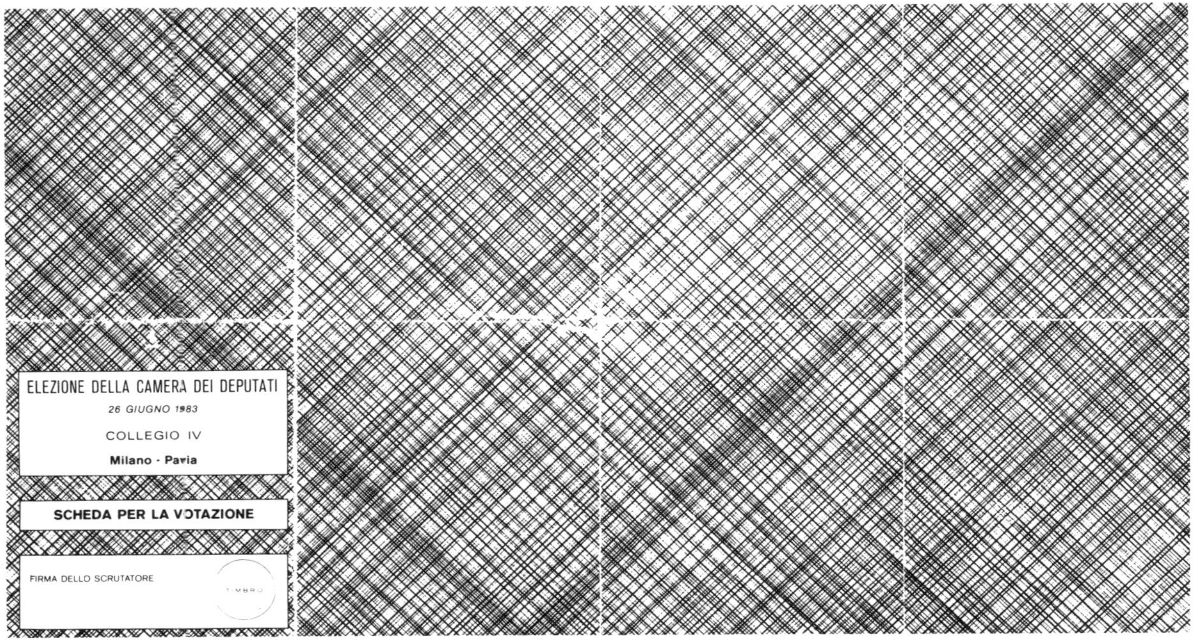

Figure B.4 Chamber of Deputies Ballot, Unfolded (actual width 15¼ inches)

Appendix C
Italian Election Return, 1983
Compiled by RICHARD M. SCAMMON

Table C-1 Chamber of Deputies Election Returns, 1983

Constituency	Total	DC	PCI	PSI
1. Torino-Novara-Vercelli				
Valid vote	2,130,342	516,940	691,972	227,66«
Percent of vote		24.3	32.5	10.
Seats	34	9	12	«
2. Cuneo-Alessandria-Asti				
Valid vote	836,687	301,006	199,775	83,56«
Percent of vote		36.0	23.9	10.«
Seats	11	5	3	
3. Genova-Imperia-LaSpezia-Savona				
Valid vote	1,249,238	341,110	445,280	126,68
Percent of vote		27.3	35.6	10.
Seats	18	6	7	
4. Milano-Pavia				
Valid vote	3,038,842	825,677	945,526	365,53«
Percent of vote		27.2	31.1	12.
Seats	48	14	16	
5. Como-Sondrio-Varese				
Valid vote	1,142,162	419,722	261,256	146,44«
Percent of vote		36.7	22.9	12.
Seats	15	7	4	
6. Brescia-Bergamo				
Valid vote	1,264,679	572,682	285,262	132,02«
Percent of vote		45.3	22.6	10.
Seats	19	10	5	

MSI-DN	PRI	PSDI	PLI	PR	Joint Tickets and Other[a]
118,622	171,380	101,599	126,129	79,106	96,928
5.6	8.0	4.8	5.9	3.7	4.5
2	3	1	2	1	0
35,439	55,653	50,437	70,234	23,218	17,359
4.2	6.7	6.0	8.4	2.8	2.1
0	1	0	1	0	0
65,338	77,245	41,139	59,112	38,348	54,985
5.2	6.2	3.3	4.7	3.1	4.4
1	1	0	1	0	0
173,057	251,774	117,322	123,892	98,023	138,033
5.7	8.3	3.9	4.1	3.2	4.5
2	4	2	2	1	1
60,772	76,813	52,295	46,983	28,885	48,993
5.3	6.7	4.6	4.1	2.5	4.3
1	1	0	0	0	0
59,193	64,366	44,400	40,296	28,627	37,833
4.7	5.1	3.5	3.2	2.3	3.0
1	1	0	0	0	0

Constituency	Total	DC	PCI	PSI
7. Mantova-Cremona				
Valid vote	502,527	168,930	175,593	71,648
Percent of vote		33.6	34.9	14.3
Seats	7	3	3	1
8. Trento-Bolzano				
Valid vote	570,180	157,153	63,182	38,836
Percent of vote		27.6	11.1	6.8
Seats	7	3	1	0
9. Verona-Padova- Vicenza-Rovigo				
Valid vote	1,742,632	804,215	326,433	167,210
Percent of vote		46.1	18.7	9.6
Seats	24	14	5	2
10. Venezia-Treviso				
Valid vote	1,051,291	391,237	257,210	127,003
Percent of vote		37.2	24.5	12.1
Seats	13	7	4	2
11. Udine-Belluno- Gorizia-Pordenone				
Valid vote	802,313	303,828	170,877	98,486
Percent of vote		37.9	21.3	12.3
Seats	10	5	13	1
12. Bologna-Ferrara- Ravenna-Forli				
Valid vote	1,678,486	343,682	808,831	158,809
Percent of vote		20.5	48.2	9.5
Seats	23	5	13	2
13. Parma-Modena- Piacenza-Reggio nell'Emilia				
Valid vote	1,230,661	318,026	572,815	127,699
Percent of vote		25.8	46.5	10.4
Seats	16	5	9	2
14. Firenza-Pistoia				
Valid vote	1,040,077	248,600	514,333	102,797
Percent of vote		23.9	49.5	9.9
Seats	13	4	8	1
15. Pisa-Livorno- Lucca-Massa Carrara				
Valid vote	932,094	254,888	388,677	109,989
Percent of vote		27.3	41.7	11.8
Seats	13	4	7	2

MSI-DN	PRI	PSDI	PLI	PR	Joint Tickets and Other [a]
23,505	19,615	13,267	11,903	9,930	8,136
4.7	3.9	2.6	2.4	2.0	1.6
0	0	0	0	0	0
18,817	27,770	13,874	9,052	13,885	227,611
3.3	4.9	2.4	1.6	2.4	39.9
0	0	0	0	0	3
75,313	87,646	53,339	50,963	43,108	134,405
4.3	5.0	3.1	2.9	2.5	7.7
1	1	0	0	0	1
41,312	55,255	40,417	27,911	26,434	84,512
3.9	5.3	3.8	2.7	2.5	8.0
0	0	0	0	0	0
39,272	43,283	53,779	20,152	19,349	53,287
4.9	5.4	6.7	2.5	2.4	6.6
0	0	1	0	0	0
62,326	135,675	55,034	38,161	31,986	43,982
3.7	8.1	3.3	2.3	1.9	2.6
1	2	0	0	0	0
46,563	49,686	51,389	28,808	20,595	15,080
3.8	4.0	4.2	2.3	1.7	1.2
0	0	0	0	0	0
38,504	48,122	20,447	15,686	21,035	30,553
3.7	4.6	2.0	1.5	2.0	2.9
0	0	0	0	0	0
43,935	45,109	24,946	12,446	16,201	35,903
4.7	4.8	2.7	1.3	1.7	3.9
0	0	0	0	0	0

Constituency	Total	DC	PCI	PSI
16. Siena-Arezzo-Grosseto				
Valid vote	579,379	142,170	282,385	67,487
Percent of vote		24.5	48.7	11.6
Seats	8	2	5	1
17. Ancona-Pesaro-Macerata-Ascoli Piceno				
Valid vote	987,671	329,829	372,205	96,842
Percent of vote		33.4	37.7	9.8
Seats	13	6	6	1
18. Perugia-Terni-Rieti				
Valid vote	676,830	188,503	288,405	84,527
Percent of vote		27.9	42.6	12.5
Seats	9	3	5	1
19. Roma-Viterbo-Latina-Frosinone				
Valid vote	3,221,537	994,889	953,407	318,524
Percent of vote		30.9	29.6	9.9
Seats	50	17	16	5
20. L'Aquila-Pescara-Chieti-Teramo				
Valid vote	812,860	342,719	239,415	78,588
Percent of vote		42.2	29.5	9.7
Seats	12	6	4	1
21. Campobasso-Isernia				
Valid vote	207,717	115,196	40,939	16,457
Percent of vote		55.5	19.7	7.9
Seats	4	3	1	0
22. Napoli-Caserta				
Valid vote	2,149,016	699,831	570,966	255,961
Percent of vote		32.6	26.6	11.9
Seats	40	14	11	5
23. Benevento-Avellino-Salerno				
Valid vote	1,070,375	464,634	209,504	158,995
Percent of vote		43.4	19.6	14.9
Seats	18	9	4	3
24. Bari-Foggia				
Valid vote	1,288,040	443,172	330,567	193,679
Percent of vote		34.4	25.7	15.0
Seats	20	8	6	3

MSI-DN	PRI	PSDI	PLI	PR	Joint Tickets and Other[a]
25,375	19,560	10,712	7,915	7,651	16,124
4.4	3.4	1.8	1.4	1.3	2.8
0	0	0	0	0	0
53,353	46,126	29,142	16,004	15,516	28,654
5.4	4.7	3.0	1.6	1.6	2.9
0	0	0	0	0	0
45,948	21,451	11,527	8,069	9,112	19,288
6.8	3.2	1.7	1.2	1.3	2.8
0	0	0	0	0	0
316,484	152,506	144,479	87,274	116,139	137,835
9.8	4.7	4.5	2.7	3.6	4.3
5	2	2	1	2	0
54,871	20,094	29,086	13,826	12,101	22,160
6.8	2.5	3.6	1.7	1.5	2.7
1	0	0	0	0	0
10,618	6,981	7,532	4,647	2,359	2,988
5.1	3.4	3.6	2.2	1.1	1.4
0	0	0	0	0	0
294,169	69,428	109,356	56,315	40,105	52,885
13.7	3.2	5.1	2.6	1.9	2.5
6	1	2	1	0	0
87,766	30,002	62,946	21,328	10,596	24,604
8.2	2.8	5.9	2.0	1.0	2.3
1	0	1	0	0	0
134,963	39,218	72,930	28,911	16,187	28,413
10.5	3.0	5.7	2.2	1.3	2.2
2	0	1	0	0	0

Constituency	Total	DC	PCI	PSI
25. Lecce-Brindisi-Taranto				
Valid vote	1,068,847	412,542	269,526	144,631
Percent of vote		38.6	25.2	13.5
Seats	17	8	5	2
26. Potenza-Matera				
Valid vote	372,034	171,338	103,767	40,724
Percent of vote		46.1	27.9	10.9
Seats	6	4	2	0
27. Catanzaro-Cosenza-Reggio di Calabria				
Valid vote	1,158,323	425,520	303,535	186,719
Percent of vote		36.7	26.2	16.1
Seats	21	9	6	4
28. Catania-Messina-Siracusa-Ragusa-Enna				
Valid vote	1,498,482	539,919	320,005	198,996
Percent of vote		36.0	21.4	13.3
Seats	25	10	6	3
29. Palermo-Trapani-Agrigento-Caltanissetta				
Valid vote	1,353,797	541,959	295,935	179,137
Percent of vote		40.0	21.9	13.2
Seats	24	11	6	3
30. Cagliari-Sassari-Nuoro-Oristano				
Valid vote	968,426	306,880	279,085	98,162
Percent of vote		31.7	28.8	10.1
Seats	15	6	5	2
31. Valle d'Aosta				
Valid vote	72,247	14,203	16,035	5,266
Percent of vote		19.7	22.2	7.3
Seats	1	0	0	0
32. Trieste				
Valid vote	203,378	47,354	46,652	12,699
Percent of vote		23.3	22.9	6.2
Seats	2	1	1	0

MSI-DN	PRI	PSDI	PLI	PR	Joint Tickets and Other[a]
102,734	36,688	45,011	20,986	10,553	26,176
9.6	3.4	4.2	2.0	1.0	2.4
2	0	0	0	0	0
23,459	4,872	17,306	2,940	3,315	4,313
6.3	1.3	4.7	0.8	0.9	1.2
0	0	0	0	0	0
89,119	42,146	56,917	10,195	9,895	34,277
7.7	3.6	4.9	0.9	0.9	3.0
1	0	1	0	0	0
178,915	74,315	71,610	56,418	17,837	40,467
11.9	5.0	4.8	3.8	1.2	2.7
3	1	1	1	0	0
110,425	63,177	62,554	33,638	19,166	47,806
8.2	4.7	4.6	2.5	1.4	3.5
2	1	1	0	0	0
60,642	29,523	37,254	14,370	15,138	127,372
6.3	3.0	3.8	1.5	1.6	13.2
1	0	0	0	0	1
2,565	—	—	—	—	34,178
3.6	—	—	—	—	47.3
0	0	0	0	0	1
16,398	9,159	5,248	3,991	7,066	54,811
8.1	4.5	2.6	2.0	3.5	27.0
0	0	0	0	0	0

Constituency	Total	DC	PCI	PSI
Total Valid Votes	36,901,170	12,148,354	11,029,355	4,221,785
Percent of vote		32.9	29.9	11.4
Seats	556	218	189	64
National Assignment	74	7	9	9
Total Seats	630	225	198	73

a. "Other" vote includes: *Democrazia Proletaria* 542,476 (7 elected); *Partito Nazionale Pensionati* 504,219; *Partito Popolare Sud Tirolese* 184,971 (3 elected); *Liga Veneta* 125,242 (1 elected); *Partito Sardo d'Azione* 91,809 (1 elected); *Unione Valdostana-Unione Valdostana Progressista-Democratici*

Table C-2 Senate Election Returns, 1983

Region	Total	DC	PCI	PSI
Abruzzi				
Valid vote	687,567	292,939	209,696	75,069
Percent of vote		42.6	30.5	10.9
Seats	7	4	2	1
Basilicata				
Valid vote	304,315	132,169	91,133	35,189
Percent of vote		43.4	29.9	11.6
Seats	7	4	2	1
Calabria				
Valid vote	932,524	322,724	275,129	153,391
Percent of vote		34.6	29.5	16.4
Seats	11	4	4	2
Campania				
Valid vote	2,558,550	837,865	653,225	314,253
Percent of vote		32.7	25.5	12.3
Seats	30	11	9	4
Emilia-Romagna				
Valid vote	2,549,50/	592,686	1,219,906	250,842
Percent of vote		23.2	47.8	9.8
Seats	21	6	12	2
Friuli-Venezia Giulia				
Valid vote	742,660	260,317	168,454	80,740
Percent of vote		35.1	22.7	10.9
Seats	7	4	2	1
Lazio				
Valid vote	2,782,590	848,857	843,680	274,687
Percent of vote		30.5	30.3	9.9
Seats	27	9	9	3

MSI-DN	PRI	PSDI	PLI	PR	Joint Tickets and Other[a]
2,509,772	1,874,638	1,507,294	1,068,555	811,466	1,729,951
6.8	5.1	4.1	2.9	2.2	4.7
33	19	13	9	4	7
9	10	10	7	7	6
42	29	23	16	11	13

Popolari joint ticket 28,086 (1 elected); other lists and joint tickets 253,148.
Source: *Elezioni della Camera dei Deputati e del Senato della Repubblica Giugno* 26, 1983, *Dati Sommari.*

PSDI	PRI	PLI	MSI-DN	PR	Joint Tickets and Other[a]
17,483	19,701	—	49,636	9,364	13,679
2.5	2.9	—	7.2	1.4	2.0
0	0	0	0	0	0
14,498	4,487	2,782	20,184	2,513	1,360
4.8	1.5	0.9	6.6	0.8	0.4
0	0	0	0	0	0
—	—	—	99,620	8,999	72,661
—	—	—	10.7	1.0	7.8
0	0	0	1	0	0
131,849	96,717	62,185	360,251	41,284	60,921
5.2	3.8	2.4	14.1	1.6	2.4
1	1	0	4	0	0
93,841	156,978	57,367	91,685	32,862	53,340
3.7	6.2	2.3	3.6	1.3	2.1
0	1	0	0	0	0
36,786	35,869	17,291	41,291	13,177	88,735
5.0	4.8	2.3	5.6	1.8	11.9
0	0	0	0	0	0
126,001	130,777	86,152	299,852	75,754	96,830
4.5	4.7	3.1	10.8	2.7	3.5
1	1	1	3	0	0

Region	Total	DC	PCI	PSI
Liguria				
Valid vote	1,083,978	311,341	396,637	112,384
Percent of vote		28.7	36.6	10.4
Seats	10	4	5	1
Lombardia				
Valid vote	5,076,325	1,747,002	1,447,823	615,644
Percent of vote		34.4	28.5	12.1
Seats	48	17	15	6
Marche				
Valid vote	852,086	292,894	325,516	83,131
Percent of vote		34.4	38.2	9.8
Seats	8	3	4	1
Molise				
Valid vote	169,713	94,873	—	—
Percent of vote		55.9	—	—
Seats	2	2	0	0
Piemonte				
Valid vote	2,562,235	722,774	788,203	268,594
Percent of vote		28.2	30.8	10.5
Seats	24	7	8	3
Puglia				
Valid vote	1,921,300	642,118	512,861	267,668
Percent of vote		33.4	26.7	13.9
Seats	21	8	6	3
Sardegna				
Valid vote	791,220	261,147	241,571	87,410
Percent of vote		33.0	30.5	11.0
Seats	9	4	3	1
Sicilia				
Valid vote	2,338,456	772,903	531,611	313,699
Percent of vote		33.1	22.7	13.4
Seats	26	10	6	4
Toscana				
Valid vote	2,224,410	587,321	1,044,368	251,171
Percent of vote		26.4	47.0	11.3
Seats	19	6	10	2
Trentino-Alto Adige				
Valid vote	467,781	138,598	54,003	33,626
Percent of vote		29.6	11.5	7.2
Seats	7	3	1	0

PSDI	PRI	PLI	MSI-DN	PR	Joint Tickets and Other[a]
72,298	70,795	—	59,426	27,265	33,832
6.7	6.5	—	5.5	2.5	3.1
0	0	0	0	0	0
192,172	349,351	197,084	255,667	103,697	167,885
3.8	6.9	3.9	5.0	2.0	3.3
2	3	2	2	1	0
25,023	38,185	13,643	43,848	9,715	20,131
2.9	4.5	1.6	5.1	1.1	2.4
0	0	0	0	0	0
7,759	5,537	5,379	12,265	3,642	40,258
4.6	3.3	3.2	7.2	2.1	23.7
0	0	0	0	0	0
137,719	205,564	185,553	130,228	70,992	52,678
5.4	8.0	7.2	5.1	2.8	2.1
1	2	2	1	0	0
107,805	62,766	32,811	236,825	20,348	38,098
5.6	3.3	1.7	12.3	1.1	2.0
1	0	0	3	0	0
—	—	—	57,525	11,822	131,745
—	—	—	7.3	1.5	16.7
0	0	0	0	0	1
127,403	128,791	85,251	281,621	27,482	69,695
5.4	5.5	3.6	12.0	1.2	3.0
1	1	1	3	0	0
48,423	107,803	—	95,732	30,150	59,442
2.2	4.8	—	4.3	1.4	2.7
0	1	0	0	0	0
11,369	22,380	7,642	15,132	9,281	175,750
2.4	4.8	1.6	3.2	2.0	37.6
0	0	0	0	0	3

Region	Total	DC	PCI	PSI
Umbria				
Valid vote	504,027	132,842	229,777	64,095
Percent of vote		26.4	45.6	12.7
Seats	7	2	4	1
Valle d'Aosta				
Valid vote	62,188	11,243	15,116	3,943
Percent of vote		18.1	24.3	6.3
Seats	1	0	0	0
Veneto				
Valid vote	2,477,579	1,074,591	528,362	254,057
Percent of vote		43.4	21.3	10.3
Seats	23	12	5	2
Total				
Valid Vote	31,089,011	10,077,204	9,577,071	3,539,593
Percent of vote		32.4	30.8	11.4
Seats	315	120	107	38

Note: In addition to the 315 elected senators, there are 7 senators appointed for life.

a. "Other" vote includes: *Partito Nazionale Pensionati* 370,756; *Democrazia Proletaria* 327,750; *Partito Popolare Sud-Tirolese* 157,444 (3 elected); *Liga Veneta* 91,171 (1 elected); *Partito Sardo d'Azione* 76,797 (1 elected); *Unione Valdostana-Unione Valdostana Progressista Democratici Popolari* 26,547

PSDI	PRI	PLI	MSI-DN	PR	Joint Tickets and Other[a]
8,085	15,965	5,226	29,285	4,911	13,841
1.6	3.2	1.0	5.8	1.0	2.7
0	0	0	0	0	0
—	—	—	1,999	—	29,887
—	—	—	3.2	—	48.1
0	0	0	0	0	1
98,720	128,117	76,405	101,452	45,041	170,834
4.0	5.2	3.1	4.1	1.8	6.9
1	1	0	1	0	1
,257,234	1,579,783	834,771	2,283,524	548,229	1,391,602
4.0	5.1	2.7	7.3	1.8	4.5
8	11	6	18	1	6

int ticket (1 elected); other lists and joint tickets 341,137.

ource: *Elezioni della Camera dei Deputati e del Senato della Repubblica Guigno* 26, 1983, *Dati ommari.*

Index

Contributors

HOWARD R. PENNIMAN, general editor of the At the Polls series, is adjunct scholar at the American Enterprise Institute. For thirty years he was a professor of government at Yale University and Georgetown University. He is an election consultant to the American Broadcasting Company and the author of several books on U.S. government and politics. Penniman was a member of the official U.S. observer team for the 1982 and 1984 elections in El Salvador and the 1984 constituent assembly elections in Guatemala.

MARCELLO FEDELE is professor of sociology at the University of Rome, where he teaches the history of sociology. His published works include *Teoria e critica della liberaldemocrazia* (Theory and criticism of liberal democracy) and *Classi e partiti negli anni '70* (Classes and parties in the nineteen-seventies). In 1981 he published *La derive del potere* (The Origins of power), a volume devoted to the American political system. He is on the editorial board of *Laboratorio politico*, a social-science quarterly, and contributes to the learned journals of Italy and Europe.

NORMAN KOGAN did his undergraduate and graduate work at the University of Chicago. Since receiving his Ph.D. in 1949 he has taught at the University of Connecticut. He has held both teaching and research positions in Italy under the Fulbright program, the Social Science Research Council, the Rockefeller Foundation, and the Italian Ministry of Foreign Affairs. He is a former president of the Conference Group on Italian Politics and a former executive secretary–treasurer of the Society for Italian Historical Studies. In 1971 he was made a Knight of the Order of Merit of the Italian Republic.

JOSEPH LAPALOMBARA is the Wolfers Professor of Political Science at Yale University. He has written about Italian politics for over thirty years, and his book-length studies include *Italy: The Politics of Planning* and *Interest Groups in Italian Politics*. His political commentary is regularly published in *Corriere della Sera*, Italy's leading daily newspaper.

ROBERT LEONARDI is visiting fellow at Nuffield College, Oxford University, and associate professor of political science at DePaul University. He is coauthor (with Robert Putnam and Raffaella Nanetti) of *La pianta e le radici: Il radicamento dell'istituto regionale nel sistema politico italiano* (The Plant and the roots: The Grassrooting of the regions in the Italian political system) and is currently working on a textbook on Italian politics.

CAROL A. MERSHON is an instructor of political science at Washington University in St. Louis and a Ph.D. candidate at Yale University. The recipient of Fulbright and Social Science Research Council fellowships, she is working on a study of union representation, negotiation, and industrial conflict in Italian factories.

K. ROBERT NILSSON is currently professor of political science and director of international studies at Dickinson College. He was director of that college's Center for International Studies in Bologna, Italy, between 1965 and 1967, 1970 and 1972, and 1980 and 1982. He will return there from 1986 to 1989. He has written on Eurocommunism, the historic compromise, Italian labor unions, and corporatism and has been adjunct senior research scholar in the Institute on Western Europe of Columbia University.

WILLIAM E. PORTER is professor of communication at the University of Michigan. His work has appeared in the two previous volumes of *Italy at the Polls*, and his book *The Italian Journalist* was published in 1983.

GIACOMO SANI is professor of political science at the Ohio State University and the author of books and articles on Italian government and politics that have appeared in Europe and the United States. He is working on a comparative analysis of mass political behavior in Italy, Spain, Portugal, and Greece.

RICHARD M. SCAMMON, coauthor of *This U.S.A.* and *The Real Majority*, is director of the Elections Research Center in Washington, D.C. He has edited the biennial series *America Votes* since 1956.

DOUGLAS A. WERTMAN is currently working for the United States Information Agency in Milan, Italy, on leave from USIA's Office of Research. Before joining USIA he taught political science at a number of universities, including the Bologna Center of the Johns Hopkins School of Advanced International Studies. He has written articles and book chapters on Italian politics, including chapters in the two previous volumes of *Italy at the Polls*.

Library of Congress Cataloging-in-Publication Data
Italy at the polls, 1983.
(At the polls)
"An American Enterprise Institute book."
Bibliography: p.
Includes index.
1. Italy—Elections.   2. Italy—Politics and government
—1976-   .   I. Penniman, Howard Rae, 1916-   .
II. Series.
JN5607.I73   1987   324.945'0928   87-6716
ISBN 0-8223-0755-3
ISBN 0-8223-0787-1 (pbk.)